FDI Qualities Policy Toolkit

OECD
BETTER POLICIES FOR BETTER LIVES

Please cite this publication as:
OECD (2022), *FDI Qualities Policy Toolkit*, OECD Publishing, Paris, https://doi.org/10.1787/7ba74100-en.

ISBN 978-92-64-72453-2 (print)
ISBN 978-92-64-60689-0 (pdf)
ISBN 978-92-64-83647-1 (HTML)
ISBN 978-92-64-38935-9 (epub)

Photo credits: Cover © Apola/Getty Images.

Corrigenda to publications may be found on line at: www.oecd.org/about/publishing/corrigenda.htm.

Preface

The COVID-19 pandemic and its devastating human, social and economic consequences have challenged efforts to achieve the Sustainable Development Goals (SDGs) and the commitments made in the 2016 Paris Agreement. This global crisis has increased the risk of slowing down, or even reversing, progress to make our societies and economies more resilient, inclusive and sustainable. Russia's war against the people of Ukraine has thrown the trajectory of the recovery into doubt, weakened economic prospects and generated further uncertainty. In this context, a key challenge for the international community is to mobilise significant financial resources to accelerate the implementation of the 2030 Agenda for Sustainable Development and ensure that plans for a "decade of action" to advance the SDGs are not side-tracked.

The OECD FDI Qualities Policy Toolkit offers a framework for governments to leverage the catalytic role of foreign direct investment (FDI) in financing the SDGs and supporting an inclusive and sustainable recovery and future growth. FDI is an important source of finance for developed and developing economies. It provides technological and financial resources necessary to improve living standards, boost employment, trigger innovation and deliver green growth. However, FDI does not always go where it is most needed and its impacts on sustainable development are not always positive. To harness investment for inclusive and sustainable economic growth, a comprehensive framework is necessary to guide government actions and more closely align investment policy with sustainability objectives.

Drawing on good practices from different policy areas and country contexts, this Toolkit helps governments to identify policy and institutional reforms that can enhance the positive contribution of FDI to four broad SDG areas: productivity and innovation; job quality and skills; gender equality; and decarbonisation. Together with the OECD FDI Qualities Indicators, launched in 2019, it helps policy makers ask appropriate questions about their economy, institutions and policy settings to measure the sustainable development impacts of FDI and devise whole-of-government approaches to investment policy reform.

The Toolkit is drawn from the long-standing premise underpinning the OECD's approach to investment policy; that open, transparent and non-discriminatory investment policies are the foundation for an investment climate conducive to sustainable development. Strong institutions and effective governance frameworks help maintain a predictable investment environment that can build trust and facilitate investor compliance with societal expectations and the SDGs. The Toolkit also explores the complementary role that targeted and SDG-aligned policy interventions can play alongside these foundational policy principles to modulate the qualities and impacts of investment as well as potential trade-offs among sustainable development outcomes. Aligning domestic and international regulations with sustainable investment goals is crucial. Environmental regulations and labour standards can influence investors' performance and are increasingly being adapted to address the cross-border sustainability footprint of multinational enterprises. A wide range of SDG-aligned business support policies are also warranted to address market failures that may hinder sustainable investment decisions such as environmental externalities, skills mismatches, gender employment and wage gaps.

Policy guidance provided throughout this report complements the OECD's longstanding expertise in shaping investment policies to improve the economic, social and environmental impact of private investment, including through the OECD Policy Framework for Investment and the OECD Guidelines for

Multinational Enterprises. This Toolkit also forms part of the OECD's strategy to help governments turn ambitious climate and sustainability commitments into real action and outcomes by making available the right data, metrics and analytical tools to support policy decisions. This Member-driven initiative draws on the valuable feedback of OECD and partner countries and the active engagement of a wide network of other stakeholders in this international policy community.

With strong support from OECD Members and Partners, we are convinced that the OECD FDI Qualities Policy Toolkit will help to mobilise additional financing in support of the 2030 Agenda for Sustainable Development, inform policy pathways to optimise the strength and quality of the recovery and help deliver global net-zero emissions by 2050.

Mathias Cormann,
Secretary-General, OECD

Manfred Schekulin,
Chair, OECD Investment Committee

Foreword

The FDI Qualities Policy Toolkit reviews policy practices to improve the impacts of foreign direct investment (FDI) on sustainable development. It focuses on four areas of the Sustainable Development Goals (SDGs): productivity and innovation, job quality and skills, gender equality and decarbonisation. Each chapter describes how to assess the impacts of FDI and provides policy recommendations related to governance, domestic and international regulation, financial and technical support, and information and facilitation services.

The Toolkit complements the OECD Policy Framework for Investment, providing more tailored guidance on improving FDI impacts across these four areas of the SDGs. It also draws upon the FDI Qualities Indicators that measure the sustainable development impacts of FDI across host countries. The development of the Toolkit was supported by concrete examples derived from a mapping of FDI Qualities policies and institutions in ten OECD member and partner countries, an initial mapping of FDI-SME policies and institutions in 27 EU countries, and in-depth country assessments of Jordan, Portugal and the Slovak Republic.

This Toolkit builds on an OECD-EU project on FDI and SMEs undertaken by three OECD bodies: the Investment Committee, the Committee on SMEs and Entrepreneurship and the Regional Development Policy Committee. It also includes inputs from the EU-OECD Programme on Investment in the Mediterranean.

The Toolkit incorporates comments received from the OECD Investment Committee and the FDI Qualities Policy Network over 2019-22 and from two public consultation processes in 2021. It also benefits from comments received from directorates across the OECD; international organisations (including the ILO, ITC, UNCTAD, UNIDO, WB and WTO) and OECD stakeholder bodies (BIAC, TUAC and OECD Watch).

Table of contents

FIGURES

TABLES

Acronyms and abbreviations

BCA	Border Carbon Adjustment
BEPS	Base Erosion and Profit Shifting
BIAC	Business at OECD
BIT	Bilateral Investment Treaty
CEDAW	Convention on the Elimination of All Forms of Discrimination against Women
CETA	EU-Canada Comprehensive Economic and Trade Agreement
CIT	Corporate Income Tax
COP26	26th Conference of the Parties
CRM	Customer Relationship Management
CUSBTA	Cambodia – US Bilateral Textile Agreement
EC	European Commission
EIA	Environmental Impact Assessment
ESG	Environmental Social Governance
EU	European Union
EU ETS	European Union's Emissions Trading System
FDI	Foreign Direct Investment
FiT	Feed-in-Tariff
FS	Financial Support
FTA	Free Trade Agreement
GFA	Global Framework Agreements
GHG	Greenhouse Gas
GPEDC	Global Partnership for Effective Development Co-operation
GVC	Global Value Chains
G20	Group of Twenty
ICT	Information and Communication Services
IFS	Information & Facilitation Services
IIA	International Investment Agreement
ILO	International Labour Organization
IPA	Investment Promotion Agency
IPR	Intellectual Property Rights
ISDS	Investor-State Dispute Settlement
JIC	Jordan Investment Commission
KPI	Key Performance Indicators
LCR	Local Content Requirements
M&A	Mergers and Acquisitions
M&E	Monitoring and Evaluation

MNE	Multinational Enterprise
NCP	National Contact Point
NDC	Nationally Determined Contribution
NGO	Non-Governmental Organisation
OECD	Organisation for Economic Co-operation and Development
PFI	Policy Framework for Investment
PPA	Power Purchasing Agreement
PPP	Public-Private Partnerships
RBC	Responsible Business Conduct
R&D	Research and Development
RDB	Rwanda Development Board
RIA	Regulatory Impact Assessment
RTA	Regional Trade Agreement
SDG	Sustainable Development Goal
SEA	Strategic Environmental Assessment
SEZ	Special Economic Zone
SME	Small and Medium-sized Enterprise
SOE	State-Owned Enterprise
SSDS	State-State Dispute Settlement
STEM	Science, Technology, Engineering and Mathematics
STI	Science, Technology and Innovation
TCFD	Taskforce on Climate-related Financial Disclosure
TES	Technology Extension Service
TS	Technical Support
TUAC	Trade Union Advisory Committee
TPP	Trans-Pacific Partnership Agreement
UN	United Nations
UNCTAD	United Nations Conference on Trade and Development
UNFCCC	United Nations Framework Convention on Climate Change
UNIDO	United Nations Industrial Development Organization
USMCA	United States – Mexico – Canada Agreement
VAT	Value Added Tax
VET	Vocational Education and Training
WB	World Bank
WHO	World Health Organization
WTO	World Trade Organisation

Executive summary

Even before the outbreak of COVID-19, it was estimated that achieving the Sustainable Development Goals (SDGs) would require investments of USD 2.5 trillion per year. This gap may since have increased by as much as 70%. Fulfilling the commitments made in the Paris Agreement and curbing climate change will require that investment in renewable energy triple by 2030. Foreign direct investment (FDI) is rapidly shifting out of fossil fuels and into renewables, accounting for 30% of global new investments in renewable energy in 2020, but more investment is needed. FDI is an important source of finance for sustainable development, creating approximately 180 000 jobs every month worldwide. Foreign firms are known to be more productive than domestic firms, pay higher wages and offer women greater opportunities for career advancement. Yet, as the FDI Qualities Indicators reveal, the sustainable development effects of FDI are not always positive, with some countries benefitting more than others and, within countries, some segments of the population being left behind. Impacts can also differ across different areas of the SDGs as some sustainability objectives are mutually reinforcing while others present trade-offs.

The FDI Qualities Policy Toolkit is designed to help governments identify priorities for policy and institutional reforms that can strengthen FDI impacts – or sustainable investment – in four SDG areas: productivity and innovation; job quality and skills; gender equality; and decarbonisation. Each chapter covers one of these area and provides detailed questions to reflect on and assess the policy conditions that influence the impacts of FDI in that area – questions that take into consideration countries' priorities and different levels of development. The Toolkit supports the implementation of the OECD Recommendation on FDI Qualities for Sustainable Development. It complements the OECD Policy Framework for Investment and can be used for self-evaluation and reform design by governments, for country-specific and regional Investment Policy Reviews and for stand-alone FDI Qualities Reviews.

Why the contribution of FDI to sustainable development does not always materialise

FDI can contribute to sustainable development through several channels that need to be carefully examined in order to assess impacts and identify reform priorities. The Toolkit identifies four channels of impacts. The first is the direct operations of foreign firms in host countries, such as deploying new technologies that advance decarbonisation or digitalisation, introducing better gender practices or creating quality jobs and training workers. These operations also have spillover effects arising from three indirect channels: their value chain relationships with domestic firms, whether buyers or suppliers; market interactions through competition and learning effects; and the mobility of workers between foreign and domestic firms. These channels can facilitate knowledge spillovers, and in turn raise productivity and living standards. They can also support the diffusion of better environmental, labour or gender standards.

Positive impacts of FDI on sustainable development do not always materialise if, for instance, foreign firms source their inputs irresponsibly, underpay female employees, or generate significant carbon emissions. Potential adverse effects of FDI also depend on the ability of the host economy to adjust factors of production in response to the arrival of foreign firms. For instance, FDI can crowd out domestic SMEs and worsen income disparities if skills shortages are severe and labour mobility is low. Addressing these challenges and other market failures to maximise the contribution of FDI to sustainable development requires policy interventions – FDI Qualities policies – that act on the different channels of impacts.

What can governments do?

The Toolkit identifies FDI Qualities policies across the four SDG areas covered in the report, and categorises them based on a mapping of policies and institutions in OECD and non-OECD countries. The mapping reveals that FDI Qualities policies involve many policy domains that go beyond those that are conducive to investment in general and, in turn, that policy responses do not fit neatly within any single governmental department or agency. It provides a compendium of good practices and shows that the majority of the identified policies do not explicitly target FDI. However, the way they affect the contributions of foreign and domestic firms to sustainable development can vary, and it is therefore crucial that policy making consider these differentiated impacts. The Toolkit is structured around five principles:

- **Governance.** The institutional setting governing sustainable investment can be highly complex, raising the likelihood of co-ordination failures. Strategies and plans on investment and different SDGs should be coherent and linked to an overarching vision for sustainable development in order to minimise potential trade-offs across policy objectives. More inclusive inter-ministerial co-ordination mechanisms are essential for effective design and implementation of these strategic frameworks. Good governance also requires public consultations, social dialogue and monitoring and evaluation mechanisms to assess existing policies and promote solutions to emerging issues that are driven or amplified by FDI, including digitalisation, climate change and the future of work.
- **Domestic and international regulation.** Open, transparent and non-discriminatory policies provide the foundation for an investment climate conducive to sustainable development but they are not sufficient to tackle the major societal and environmental challenges. A condition for sustainable FDI is that domestic legislation fulfils international standards related to climate action, job quality and gender equality, or sets national standards that are even more ambitious than international ones. Aligning investment and trade agreements with sustainable investment goals is also important to reinforce domestic law and encourage responsible business conduct.
- **Technical and financial support.** Targeted support may be warranted to address market failures that hinder sustainable investment (e.g. R&D costs, environmental externalities, skills mismatches, gender disparities in the workplace) but provision of such forms of support should be transparent and subject to regular review. Governments often use tax incentives or subsidised loans and grants to promote investment in specific activities, sectors and locations. Financial support is sometimes conditional on specific criteria or activities that can help promote sustainable development. Technical support either directly provided or subsidised by governments is an effective means of developing domestic capabilities and enhancing the potential for FDI spillovers.
- **Information and facilitation services.** Insufficient, inaccurate or costly information can create barriers to investment or lead to sub-optimal decisions by economic actors. Investment promotion agencies (IPAs) are key players in bridging information gaps that may otherwise hinder the realisation of foreign investments, and their potential sustainable development impacts. By linking investors to local partners IPAs are essential for the realisation of FDI spillovers. Other information services can include awareness-raising campaigns to help change traditional norms at the root of gender inequality, or information on the carbon emissions embodied in products to raise public understanding of the carbon footprint of their consumption choices. Encouraging corporate disclosure of social and environmental risks through ESG reporting frameworks can help investors assess and communicate their responsible practices and promote due diligence in supply chains.
- **Development co-operation.** Development partners devote a significant portion of their resources to supporting the private sector, by financing initiatives to improve the investment climate, develop

business capacities and build physical infrastructure. Governments and the donor community should work together to identify financial and technical assistance solutions to support policy reforms and implementation, promote alignment with international standards, reduce exposure to social and environmental risks, and support the private sector. Identifying existing donor assistance can help assess alignment with national priorities on investment and sustainable development.

1 Overview and key principles

This chapter provides an overview of the rationale and objectives of the FDI Qualities Policy Toolkit and explains how governments and other stakeholders can use it. It discusses key policy principles on FDI Qualities, drawn from the substantive chapters that provide detailed policy guidance on improving the impacts of FDI on sustainable development, particularly in the area of productivity and innovation, job quality and skills, gender equality, and decarbonisation.

1.1. Rationale and objectives

Achieving the Sustainable Development Goals (SDGs) and fulfilling the commitments made in the Paris Agreement on climate change requires an acceleration in finance and investment. When the SDGs where adopted in 2015, UNCTAD estimated an annual SDG funding gap of USD 2.5 trillion in developing countries (UNCTAD, 2014[1]). According to the OECD Global Outlook on Financing for Sustainable Development 2021, this gap could have increased by 70% due to the COVID-19 pandemic in 2020, including due to a drop in foreign private finance (OECD, 2020[2]). Together with public and other private investments, foreign direct investment (FDI) is an important source of finance for inclusive and sustainable development.

Beyond the quantities of FDI, its qualities also matter, as shown by the OECD FDI Qualities Indicators (OECD, 2019[3]): FDI can play a crucial role in making progress toward all of the SDGs, and in particular to advancing decarbonisation, increasing innovation, creating quality jobs, developing human capital, and promoting gender equality. Yet, the effects of FDI are not always positive, and impacts can differ across areas of sustainable development. Some sustainability objectives are mutually reinforcing while others could present trade-offs. Among countries receiving FDI, some have benefited more than others and, within countries, some segments of the population have been left behind. Efforts to mobilise investment should be aligned with concerns on qualities and impacts of investment, including potential trade-offs, in making progress toward the SDGs. To realise the potential benefits from investment and minimise negative effects and trade-offs, policies and institutional arrangements play a critical role (Figure 1.1).

Figure 1.1. Conceptual framework: FDI Qualities Policy Toolkit

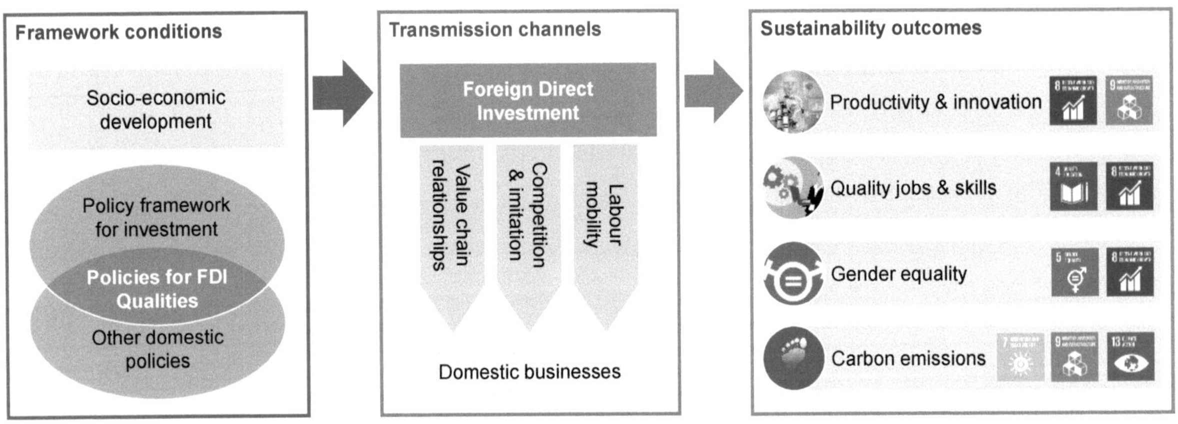

The FDI Qualities Policy Toolkit, together with the Indicators, aims to support governments in enhancing the impacts of FDI on inclusive and sustainable development.[1] It complements the OECD Policy Framework for Investment (PFI) by focusing specifically on international investment and providing governments with detailed guidance on how to influence and improve its qualities, beyond investment climate reform (OECD, 2015[4]). While addressing the investment climate policies covered at length by the PFI, the Policy Toolkit gives more space to the linkages of investment policy with innovation, SME, labour-market, gender and environmental policies that influence the qualities of international investment, as well as trade-offs that may exist across these policy areas (Figure 1.1). It is thus a natural extension of the PFI. Like the PFI, it is not prescriptive, but provides broad policy directions for improving the impact of FDI on sustainable development, thus allowing for a flexible approach according to a country's context and stage of development. In this context, it also recognises that national governments have different priorities, resources and options at their disposal to leverage FDI to advance sustainable development.

The Policy Toolkit targets national governments and their implementing agencies, within and beyond the OECD. It has been further vetted by a number of non-governmental stakeholder groups that are part of the FDI Qualities Policy Network,[2] who may also find it useful. While directed at governments, the Policy Toolkit can generate added value for the private sector and civil society by providing a reference document for good practices on investment policy making. Businesses, supported by investment promotion agencies (IPAs), and civil society can for instance use it for policy advocacy, highlighting potential opportunities of national and international policy communities with regards to FDI and sustainable development.[3] To strengthen the co-operation between governments and the donor community, the Policy Toolkit also includes a guide for development co-operation (OECD, 2022, forthcoming[5]).[4] It addresses development co-operation partners and developing country governments, willing to engage with donors, to enhance the impact of FDI in their economies.

1.2. User guide for the Policy Toolkit

The Policy Toolkit is a practical tool that aims to help governments to:

- assess the impacts of FDI in four areas of sustainable development based on the SDGs (productivity and innovation; job quality and skills; gender equality; and decarbonisation);
- identify opportunities for policy and institutional reforms to enhance such impacts;
- strengthen partnerships with the donor community to support efforts to improve the impacts of FDI in developing countries.

The Policy Toolkit outlines a structured process for reviewing policy and institutional frameworks. It can be used for stand-alone reviews (see Box 1.1 for a description of the pilot FDI Qualities Review of Jordan) or in combination with broader assessments of investment climate reforms (e.g. OECD Investment Policy Reviews). The Policy Toolkit can also be used for self-evaluation and reform design by governments as well as for peer reviews in regional or multilateral discussions.

This overview chapter describes and substantiates a set of core policy principles drawn from the substantive chapters that delve into specific areas of sustainable development. These core principles provide overarching guidance to governments on using diagnostic tools to inform policy action that improves the sustainable development impacts of investment. The users of this Policy Toolkit can refer to the substantive chapters for more concrete guidance on policies for improving the impacts of FDI on specific SDG areas. These chapters tailor the core principles to the specific areas of sustainable development (i.e. productivity and innovation, job quality and skills, gender equality; and decarbonisation) and provide guidance on how to assess the impacts of FDI on them. The chapters provide considerations for policy governance, discuss options for the use of concrete policy instruments and provide good practice examples derived from an initial mapping of FDI Qualities policies and institutions in ten OECD and partner countries (Box 1.2). Beyond the principles, each chapter provides detailed questions and indicators that help policy makers reflect on and evaluate, in a structured way, their policy choices influencing FDI impacts on sustainable development.

Box 1.1. FDI Qualities Review of Jordan: Strengthening sustainable investment – a pilot review

The OECD has been working with the Government of, represented by the Jordan Investment Commission (JIC), on measuring the contribution of FDI to sustainable development and identifying policies to increase the positive impacts of FDI (OECD, 2022[6]). This co-operation between Jordan and the OECD is part of the OECD FDI Qualities Initiative and has contributed to improving the FDI Qualities Policy Toolkit as a hands-on tool for policy analysis and advice. The work has taken place in the context of the EU-OECD Programme on Investment in the Mediterranean, which supports reform efforts to advance sustainable investment in the Middle East and North Africa region.

The assessment provides tailored policy advice to the government on how to strengthen the impact of FDI in each of the four dimensions of sustainable development covered in the FDI Qualities Policy Toolkit. Based on a detailed mapping of policies and institutions, conducted jointly by the OECD and the government, the study examines to what extent public policies support the channels through which FDI affects these sustainability dimensions.

The nine-month process of this pilot review has involved (i) a preparatory phase, including desk research and setting up an inter-ministerial taskforce, (ii) an analytical phase, including the collection of data, fact-finding, consultations, analysis and drafting, and (iii) a policy dialogue phase during which findings and policy recommendations have been discussed in the taskforce and, with peers, in a special session of the FDI Qualities Policy Network (Figure 1.2).

Figure 1.2. Process of the assessment

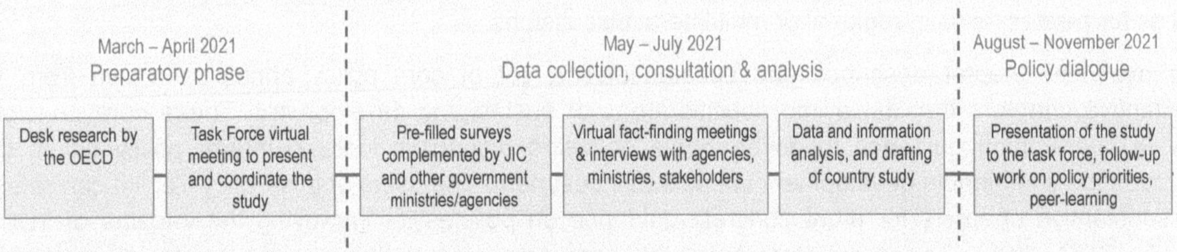

The taskforce has included more than 20 government agencies and international partners in Jordan that work at the intersection of investment and sustainable development. The taskforce has provided strategic guidance and ensured that the information collected by the OECD, and included in the mapping of policies and institutions, is accurate and complete. The taskforce met early in 2021 to discuss the main objectives of the study and in September 2021 to present the results and to get feedback on policy priorities. The Jordan Investment Commission (JIC) and the OECD have jointly co-ordinated this taskforce.

Note: A similar pilot assessment was conducted on Portugal over 2020-22 and the Slovak Republic over 2021-22, focusing particularly on strengthening FDI and SME linkages to enhance productivity and innovation (OECD, 2022[7]; 2022, forthcoming[8])

Box 1.2. An initial FDI Qualities Policy Mapping of ten OECD and partner countries

The Policy Toolkit provides a novel typology to collect information allowing to assess policies and institutions at the intersection of investment and sustainable development. While using this typology to map policies and institutions is a useful tool for self-assessment, a growing database of countries covered in this mapping will allow for cross-country comparison and provides a compendium of good policy practices on investment and sustainable development, which does not exist at the moment. Applying the typology in an initial mapping of ten OECD and partner countries has informed and helped improve this Policy Toolkit. Selected examples on varying institutional arrangements and policies on investment and sustainable development across these countries are illustrated in this report.

The mapping has involved the collection of data on institutional frameworks and co-ordination mechanisms across policy domains related to investment and the four areas of sustainable development covered in this Policy Toolkit (productivity and innovation, job quality and skills, gender equality, decarbonisation). Institutions that were mapped include ministries, government departments and implementing agencies responsible for these policy domains. Data on major national policy initiatives at the intersection of investment and sustainable development, designed or implemented by these institutions, are also collected. Specifically, information on policy targeting, beneficiaries of policy initiatives, policy instrument types and design features has been assembled.

The initial FDI Qualities Policy Mapping includes Jordan, Morocco, Indonesia, Thailand, Rwanda, Senegal, Uzbekistan, Costa Rica, Sweden, and Canada. In addition, as part of an OECD-European Commission project on FDI and SMEs, the mapping has been done for all 27 EU Member States, focusing on policies related to FDI impacts on productivity and innovation (OECD, 2021[9]).

1.3. Key policy principles on FDI Qualities

Provide coherent strategic direction on fostering investment in support of sustainable development, and foster policy continuity and effective implementation of such policies

- Promote investment-related strategies and plans that are coherent with sustainable development objectives.
- Co-ordinate across ministries to support effective policy implementation and continuity of policy priorities in the area of sustainable investment.
- Use public consultations and inclusive decision-making processes involving the private sector and civil society to build consensus on policy reforms on investment and sustainable development.
- Seek to assess the impact of major investment projects on sustainable development and of related policies to identify bottlenecks in policy implementation.

Take steps to ensure that domestic policy, legal, and regulatory frameworks support positive impacts of investment on sustainable development

- Foster an investment climate based on open, transparent and non-discriminatory investment policies, the rule of law and integrity, the prevention of corruption, the promotion of responsible business conduct, and quality regulation, in line with relevant provisions of the PFI.

- Align domestic legal and policy frameworks – including in areas of productivity and innovation, job quality and skills, gender equality, and decarbonisation – with sustainable investment objectives.
- Align international investment and trade agreements with sustainable investment objectives, including by ensuring appropriate domestic policy space and social dialogue to achieve these objectives.

Prioritise sustainable development objectives when providing financial and technical support to stimulate investment

- Consider whether and to what extent financial and technical support can address market failures hampering sustainable development and thereby help attract sustainable investment and improve the capabilities of firms, job quality and skills of workers.
- Take steps to ensure that financial and technical support is transparent and subject to regular reviews.

Facilitate and promote investment for sustainable development opportunities by addressing information failures and administrative barriers

- Raise public and stakeholder awareness on impacts of investment on sustainable development.
- Improve the link between investment promotion and sustainable development objectives, where relevant, including in the areas of quality infrastructure, research, innovation and skills development, and regional development.
- Improve the link between investment facilitation activities and sustainable development objectives, including by taking measures to make procedures for obtaining authorisations and permits transparent and ensure that they are efficiently managed, and by enhancing business linkages between foreign investors and domestic firms.
- Promote responsible business conduct and due diligence in operations, supply chains, and other business relationships – in areas such as corporate governance, consumers, labour standards, the environment, human rights, gender equality and the prevention of corruption – including by taking steps to support enterprises to demonstrate their compliance with international standards on sustainable development.
- In support of sustainable finance and investing, promote the importance of considering comparable sustainability-related factors in FDI decisions and monitoring.

Strengthen the role of development co-operation for mobilising FDI and enhancing its positive impact in developing countries

- Identify ways that financial and technical assistance, such as blended finance, can support the implementation of the above four recommendations to enhance the impact of FDI on sustainable development.
- Promote alignment of donors' assistance with national priorities related to sustainable investment in accordance with relevant international standards, including through the mapping of such assistance, and the identification of potential support gaps or opportunities to replicate or scale-up existing assistance.
- Increase engagement with the private sector, trade unions and civil society, and promote effective multi-stakeholder partnerships aimed at enhancing the impacts of investment on sustainable development, including increased opportunities for women and youth in particular in relation to equal treatment and skills.

1.3.1. Provide coherent strategic direction on fostering investment in support of sustainable development

Ensure policy coherence and co-ordination on investment and sustainable development

National strategies and plans on investment, growth, innovation, jobs, skills development, gender equality, decarbonisation and regional development should be as coherent as possible. Just like for investment climate reforms under the PFI, policy coherence to enhance the impacts of FDI requires a whole-of-government approach. It requires policy responses that do not fit neatly within any single governmental department or agency. Policies and institutions cannot be considered in silos but rather require an adequate and coherent policy mix – including not just investment policies but a variety of policy areas. Cross-ministerial co-ordination mechanisms, including national and sub-national levels of government, can help guarantee and monitor effective implementation of strategic frameworks and ensure continuity of policy priorities in the area of investment and sustainable development. Weak co-ordination can increase the risk of duplication, inefficient spending, low-quality service, and contradictory objectives and targets, all of which can undermine investor confidence and, weaken the potential contribution of investment to sustainable development.

The institutional framework that governs policy formulation and implementation differs from country to country. The approach that governments pursue to organise the institutional framework reflects the priority they give to the role of investment for sustainable development. Different governance structures are feasible as long as appropriate reporting mechanisms and communication channels are in place to ensure policy alignment among different institutions and across national and subnational authorities. The more institutions are involved at the intersection of investment and sustainable development policies, the more complex their governance systems become. Complex systems also involve higher risks of information asymmetry, rising transaction costs, trade-offs and inefficiency. The need for policy co-ordination and coherence is thus even greater in countries with more complex governance structures, requiring a strong governing body that brings together all policy areas at the intersection of investment and sustainable development. Such a body could be an existing committee, such as one that is governing investment policy and promotion more broadly (OECD, 2022[6]).

Engage in public consultations and inclusive decision-making processes involving the private sector and civil society to build consensus on policy reforms on investment and sustainable development

Public-private consultations and social dialogue can promote collective and innovative solutions to emerging issues that are, at least partly, driven by FDI. These may include digitalisation, automation, artificial intelligence and the future of work. Stakeholder consultations also allow for feedback and build legitimacy and consensus around policy reforms and programmes at the intersection of investment and sustainable development. More open and inclusive policy making processes help to ensure that policies will better match the needs and expectations of citizens, businesses and sub-national regions. Greater participation of stakeholders in policy design and implementation leads to better targeted and more effective policies.

Multinational enterprises (MNEs) can, for example, provide useful insights and information on emerging global trends and give directions on what type of policy approaches would be required in the medium- and long-term. For example, in the area of skills, collecting information on foreign firms' skills needs will help governments develop adequate policies, such as training programmes, that can prevent skills mismatches and shortages as well as reducing retraining costs. Many countries have put in place systems and tools for assessing and anticipating skills needs, but limited co-ordination between stakeholders is often a barrier preventing the information from being used further in policy making (Chapter 3).

Assess the impacts of FDI on sustainable development

FDI can have a variety of effects on sustainable development in host countries. These effects are influenced, among other factors, by the characteristics of FDI. They depend for instance on whether the investment involves a new establishment (e.g. new project or a subsidiary) or the acquisition of an existing company, the motivations for the investment (e.g. efficiency-seeking or market-seeking), in which sector and location (metropolitan areas or less developed regions) it takes place, what type of foreign firms are involved (large or SMEs), and what corporate culture and management practices – often determined by policies on responsible business conduct in origin countries – the investment brings with it.

The impacts of FDI involve several transmission channels. Foreign firms directly affect sustainable development through their own operations. The 2022 update of the FDI Qualities Indicators shows, for instance, that foreign firms are more likely to offer formal training opportunities, invest in R&D, and incorporate environmental issues in their strategic objectives (Figure 1.3). Foreign firms' operations also have spillover effects on domestic businesses arising from value chain relationships between foreign and domestic firms, market interactions through competition and imitation effects, and labour mobility of workers (Figure 1.1, orange box). The premise underlying the existence of FDI spillovers is that foreign firms are often more productive, technologically superior and more skill-intensive and, in turn, benefits might spill over to domestic firms. The direction and magnitude of the combined direct and spillover effects of FDI may vary not only among countries, but also across sustainability outcomes. Framework conditions – such as economic structure and development, domestic firms' characteristics and skills of the domestic labour force – also determine the extent to which direct and spillover impacts take place.

Governments should routinely examine the characteristics of foreign direct investment and its impact on sustainable development, both through the activities of foreign affiliates and through spillovers on domestic firms. Understanding the impacts of FDI across economic activities and locations is a pre-condition for identifying weaknesses and strengths of the governance and policy framework. Regularly assessing such impacts should therefore inform policy efforts in that respect. The substantive chapters provide a more detailed overview on how FDI relates to different outcomes and comprise a list of questions and indicators that can guide policy makers in their efforts to better understand FDI impacts and transmission channels. OECD tools, including primarily the FDI Qualities Indicators, and other data tools are described and can be used to address those questions.

The availability of data to assess the impacts of FDI, or specific aspects of these impacts, is not always guaranteed. Therefore, the timely collection of internationally comparable data on investment and business characteristics and practices related to firm size, location, innovation, employment, skills, gender, and the environment can assist governments in assessing the impact of investment on sustainable development. In this context, international and inter-ministerial collaboration can help improve data collection efforts.

Figure 1.3. Sustainable development performance of foreign and domestic businesses

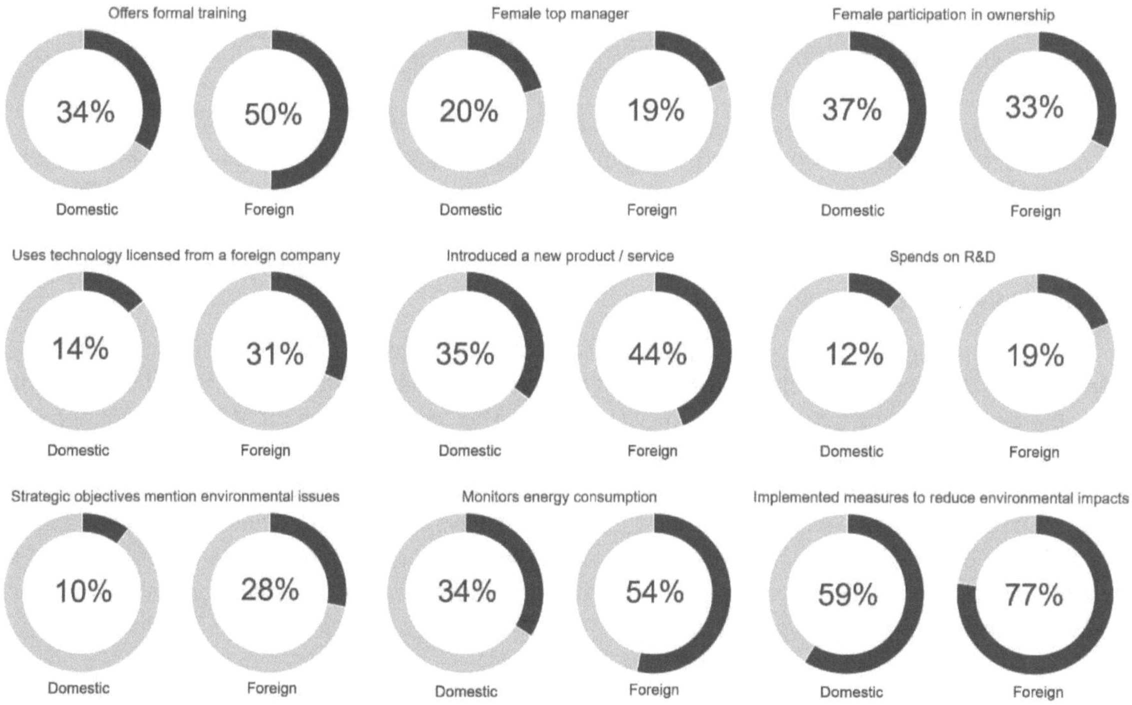

Source: OECD (2022[10]), *FDI Qualities Indicators: 2022*

Develop monitoring and evaluation frameworks to improve the effectiveness of policies influencing the impacts of FDI

Comprehensive monitoring and evaluation (M&E) frameworks are important to improve the effectiveness of government efforts to promote sustainable investment through FDI. M&E has received increasing attention as a result of a growing focus on the performance and efficiency of government institutions. The purpose of M&E is to ensure that a policy action progresses according to schedule and achieves planned milestones, and to evaluate the performance of the action against policy objectives. A comprehensive M&E framework for policies related to the impact of FDI is crucial to identify potential bottlenecks in policy design and implementation, and take corrective action when their performance is not in line with expectations. Although many different approaches to M&E exist, some practices are widely adopted, such as the setting up of a dedicated evaluation unit, the use of key performance indicators (KPIs) and qualitative evaluation methodologies (e.g. surveys, benchmarking, consultations), and the establishment of data tracking tools and feedback processes to ensure that relevant and reliable data are available. A comprehensive M&E framework may involve both ex ante and ex post evaluations of policies, including social and environmental impact assessments.

A recent OECD survey finds that three-quarters of Investment Promotion Agencies (IPAs) view M&E as a key factor that influences their prioritisation strategy. Most IPAs use sustainability-related KPIs such as on productivity and innovation or jobs and about half of the IPAs use metrics related to export and decarbonisation. KPIs such as on job quality or gender equality are rarely used. Yet, KPIs used by IPAs for prioritisation and those for M&E do not always match. For example, no IPA has reported using indicators related to decarbonisation for their M&E although nearly half of IPAs use such indicators to prioritise their activities (OECD, 2021[11]).

1.3.2. Take steps to ensure that domestic policy, legal, and regulatory frameworks support positive impacts of investment on sustainable development

Guarantee open, transparent and non-discriminatory investment policies, the rule of law and integrity, and quality regulation

Open, transparent and non-discriminatory investment policies are key for attracting investment and provide the foundation for an investment climate that is conducive to sustainable development (Box 1.3). The PFI provides guidance in 12 policy areas for investment climate reforms that range from the domestic and international legal framework for investment, competition and taxation to green growth and responsible business conduct (OECD, 2015[4]).

The PFI also highlights the role of strong institutions and good public governance for effective implementation of investment policies, which also applies to policies at the intersection of investment and sustainable development discussed in this Policy Toolkit. The pre-requisites for strong institutions include respect for the rule of law, quality regulation, transparency and non-discrimination and integrity. Effective action across these dimensions will encourage investment and reduce the costs of doing business. Strong institutions help to maintain a predictable and transparent environment for investors, domestic firms and workers. Policy continuity and effective implementation are further facilitated by an environment of trust. High levels of trust can facilitate compliance with laws and regulations, strengthen confidence of investors and workers and reduce risks aversion.

Box 1.3. Openness to FDI can support sustainable development

Openness to FDI not only involves higher investment stocks (Mistura and Roulet, 2019[12]), it is also associated with higher productivity in industries that access new markets as well as in downstream sectors that benefit from potentially better access to high quality inputs and services domestically (Chapter 2). Recent OECD research shows that liberalising FDI in services is positively associated with productivity in downstream manufacturing industries, where SMEs are particularly likely to benefit (Figure 1.4.).

More open FDI regimes also affect the labour market, skills and gender equality. Opening sectors to FDI that are skill-intensive is associated with more demand for skills, although, in the short term, opening may also crowd out domestic firms as their skilled workers move to better paid jobs in foreign affiliates, increasing skill-based inequalities. Increased competitive pressure from FDI also affects the need for domestic firms to invest in innovation and skills development to pay higher wages and retain workers, which leads to an overall increase in the supply of skills in the longer term (Chapter 3). Reducing FDI restrictions in sectors that employ relatively more women could, due to increased demand, increase labour market participation of women and their wages. FDI restrictions tend to be highest in services, which often have a relatively high proportion of women (Chapter 4).

Discriminatory restrictions on the establishment and operations of foreign investors can also diminish the potential of FDI on decarbonisation (Chapter 5). Some sectors that present significant opportunities for decarbonisation efforts remain partly off-limits to foreign investors in many countries – notably, transport, electricity generation and distribution, and construction. Many services, typically associated with lower carbon emissions and in some cases crucial for energy-saving technologies (e.g. digital services), are also more frequently restricted to foreign participation (Gaukrodger and Gordon, 2012[13]).

Figure 1.4. FDI openness in services and productivity in downstream manufacturing sectors

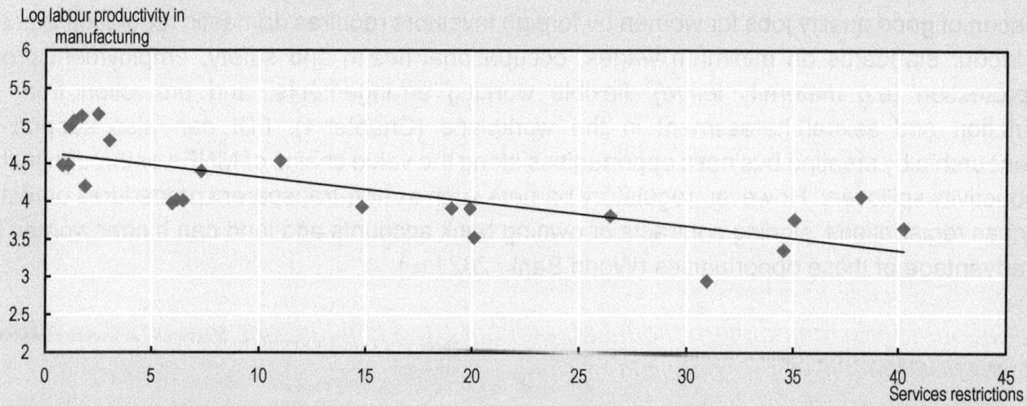

Note: Analysis is based on firm-level data from 23 OECD and developing countries; see methodology in OECD (2019). Services restrictions are based on the OECD FDI Regulatory Restrictiveness Index.
Source: OECD (2019[14]), OECD Investment Policy Reviews: Southeast Asia, https://www.oecd.org/daf/inv/investment-policy/Southeast-Asia-Investment-Policy-Review-2019.pdf.

Ensure that domestic regulations reinforce possible benefits of FDI on sustainable development

Open and competitive markets are not sufficient to tackle the major societal and environmental challenges that, if not addressed, may jeopardise a prosperous and healthy future for people and the planet. Improving impacts of FDI on sustainable development requires more tailored policy considerations and more focus on policies beyond the PFI, including regulatory frameworks on innovation, skills, the labour market, gender equality and the environment. Aligning these frameworks with objectives related to investment as a tool to support sustainable development is key in this context.

Environmental regulations and reporting requirements are, for example, increasingly being adopted to address the cross-border environmental footprint of multinational enterprises (Chapter 5). The EU Taxonomy Regulation, which entered into law in 2020, for instance, places a reporting obligation on certain companies to disclose how much of their global investment is aligned with environmentally sustainable activities. Starting from 2022, large investors (with over 500 employees) with operations in the EU must disclose which proportion of their turnover, capital expenditure and operating expenditure is associated with environmentally sustainable economic activities.

In the area of job quality, stringent employment protection legislation can increase firms' labour adjustment costs but also improves job security. Greater flexibility of the host country's labour market matters for the location choice of foreign investors and affects FDI volumes – and thus potential job creation – as well as their knowledge intensity (Javorcik and Spatareanu, 2005[15]). But job security also protects workers from being fired in response to small fluctuations, which can encourage them to invest in long-term training. Moreover, stricter employment protection can deter or delay labour mobility from domestic to foreign firms while it is typically via this channel that FDI enhances wages in host countries (Hijzen et al., 2013[16]). But it may also protect vulnerable workers that otherwise would have been displaced to lower wage jobs or that would have experienced long-term unemployment. When local production capacities are sufficiently high, more flexible labour markets can host FDI without necessarily reducing employment or increasing wage disparities between foreign and domestic firms (Becker et al., 2020[17]). Labour market policy is most effective when negotiated with trade unions and workers' representatives (Chapter 3).

The creation of good quality jobs for women by foreign investors requires domestic regulation that ensures decent labour standards on minimum wages, occupational health and safety, employment protection, social protection (e.g. maternity leave), flexible working arrangements, and protection from gender discrimination and sexual harassment in the workplace (Chapter 4). FDI can also support female entrepreneurship by creating business opportunities along the value chains of MNEs or through technology and productivity spillovers. However, regulatory barriers such as non-transparent procedures or restrictions on business registrations, signing contracts or owning bank accounts and land can hinder women's ability to take advantage of these opportunities (World Bank, 2021[18]).

Endeavour to join major international agreements and conventions that promote sustainable development and foster responsible business conduct

A fundamental condition for FDI to positively influencing sustainable development is that domestic legislation fulfils international standards and principles on sustainability objectives, such as on climate action, job quality and gender equality, or sets national standards that are even more ambitious than the international ones. Endeavouring to join major international agreements and conventions promoting sustainable development is thus important.

In the area of climate action, the Paris Agreement (2015) is the central international effort to combat climate change aiming to limit global mean temperature change to 1.5°C. Progressively more ambitious climate mitigation commitments are expected from all states party to the treaty over the coming decades. As of January 2021, 187 states and the EU, representing about 80% of global greenhouse gas emissions, had ratified or acceded to the Paris Agreement. Carbon emissions have global effects, regardless of where they were released, meaning that the impact of one country's climate policies is dependent on the climate policies of other countries. The Paris Agreement gives governments, as well as industry and the general public, reassurance of commensurate action from their trade partners (Chapter 5).

International labour standards are essential for ensuring that the global economy, including FDI, provides benefits to all (Chapter 3). The ILO Declaration on Fundamental Principles and Rights at Work (1998) represents the most widely accepted effort to define a set of core labour standards, related to eliminating all forms of forced or compulsory labour, effectively abolishing child labour, eliminating discrimination in respect of employment and occupation, and ensuring the freedom of association and the right to collective bargaining. The Declaration covers eight fundamental conventions and the majority of countries has formally subscribed to some or all them, which has strongly influenced changes in national labour laws. Indeed, many developing countries where poor labour practices in the operations of foreign firms have been a concern tend to have reasonable *de jure* labour standards, in some cases comparable to those in developed countries. But poor labour practices in the operations of foreign firms, and businesses more generally, reflect weak public enforcement of national and international labour provisions. Non-compliance with international labour provisions by foreign firms and their suppliers continues to be a pressing concern in many countries with weak rule of law (see *Principle 2*).

Gender equality and non-discrimination based on sex are fundamental rights enshrined in numerous international human rights instruments (Chapter 4). The UN Charter of 1945 is the first international instrument to establish the principle of equality between men and women. Since then, numerous international human rights instruments have promoted women's rights and contributed to the inclusion of gender equality principles in national legislation, including the UN Convention on the Elimination of All Forms of Discrimination against Women (1979), the Beijing Declaration and Platform for Action (1995), and a number of ILO conventions dealing with gender-specific issues such as the Equal Remuneration Convention, the Discrimination (Employment and Occupation) Convention, the Convention on Workers with Family Responsibilities and the Maternity Protection Convention.

Multilateral initiatives such as the OECD Guidelines for Multinational Enterprises and the ILO Tripartite Declaration of Principles Concerning Multinational Enterprises and Social Policy can help raise awareness about responsible business conduct (RBC), including on labour practices, gender equality and climate action (OECD, 2011[19]). They are non-binding recommendations by adhering governments, supported by employer and worker organisations, which are directly addressed to MNEs. They recommend MNEs, for example, to observe standards of employment no worse than those observed by employers in the host country, or to mitigate the climate impacts of their operations, within the framework of laws, regulations and administrative practices in the countries in which they operate, and in consideration of relevant international agreements, principles, objectives, and standards. They also recommend MNEs to carry out due diligence through their value chain relationships to address existing or potential adverse risks on sustainable development (OECD, 2011[19]).

Align international investment and trade agreements with sustainable development standards and principles

Many countries have concluded investment treaties over the past half century as part of their efforts to foster international investment and, in turn, advance economic development in home and host countries. These treaties take various forms: Since 1959, when the first modern bilateral investment treaty (BIT) was signed, well over 3 000 BITs have been negotiated, of which more than 2 200 are in force today. An ever increasing number of bilateral or multilateral free trade agreements (FTAs) containing provisions on investment cover hundreds of additional bilateral relationships. The focus of these treaties has traditionally been on investment protection. Governments have sought to use investment treaties as instruments to improve legal certainty and reduce unwarranted risk for foreign investors wishing to locate long-term investments abroad. An overarching goal of this approach has been to foster more investment from abroad than may otherwise have been possible in the absence of a treaty, although existing research finds mixed evidence of the impacts of treaties on investment flows (Pohl, 2018[20]).

Only recently have governments begun to consider investment treaties as instruments to influence not only the quantities but also the qualities of international investment in terms of its impacts on sustainable development. While relatively little is known today about the ways that investment treaties influence the impacts of FDI, this is likely to depend crucially on the nature, design, context and interpretation of treaty provisions used for claims and on dispute settlement arrangements. Indeed, the scope of absolute protections and government action with regard to their interpretation are key factors affecting policy space for non-discriminatory regulation. Some recent treaties provide for state-state dispute settlement (SSDS) rather than investor-state dispute settlement (ISDS) for investment protection claims.

Express language addressing social and environmental priorities is also increasingly used in investment agreements, although concrete impact has been difficult to demonstrate. So far, no attempt has been made to assess whether and how investment treaties in general or certain design elements and features in particular influence the qualities of international investment and very little empirical evidence is available that would allow any quantitative statements in this regard. Further research will need to reflect through which mechanisms investment treaties influence the qualities of FDI, which specific treaty provisions are observed in treaties that are tuned towards the qualities of FDI, and what effects these clauses have.

Provisions in these international agreements can be designed to allow treaty parties to make commitments to strengthen domestic law regulation and enforcement in several key areas relating to the qualities of FDI. This could take place for example through provisions that buttress domestic law or its enforcement by including commitments to adopt and enforce key international conventions on labour, the environment or human rights. In addition, provisions could also directly address business conduct by, for example, encouraging observance of RBC standards, requiring compliance with domestic laws or establishing conditions for access to investment treaty benefits (Gaukrodger, 2020[21]).

International investment and trade agreements that are aligned with climate objectives, international labour standards and principles on gender equality and encourage co-operation and monitoring of commitments will thus provide support to government efforts to enhance the positive impact of investment on sustainable development. Yet, these treaties remain a single policy tool among many for governments seeking to improve the sustainability impacts of international investment. Such treaties should not be seen as a substitute for other international and domestic policies designed for long-term improvements in the investment climate and for advancing sustainable development.

1.3.3. Prioritise sustainable development objectives when providing financial and technical support to stimulate investment

Consider financial and technical support to help build domestic capabilities of firms, entrepreneurs and workers that enhance the impact of FDI on sustainable development

Governments can use financial and technical support measures, as well as information and facilitation services (as discussed in the next section) to foster decarbonisation, productivity and innovation, as well as job quality, skills and gender equality. Depending on the priorities for sustainable development, policy attention and types of policy instruments may vary across areas of the SDGs (Figure 1.5).

Figure 1.5. Mix of financial and technical support, and information and facilitation services by area of sustainable development

Area reflects total number of policies by policy instrument and objective. Policy instruments include: financial support (FS); technical support (TS); and information and facilitation services (IFS).

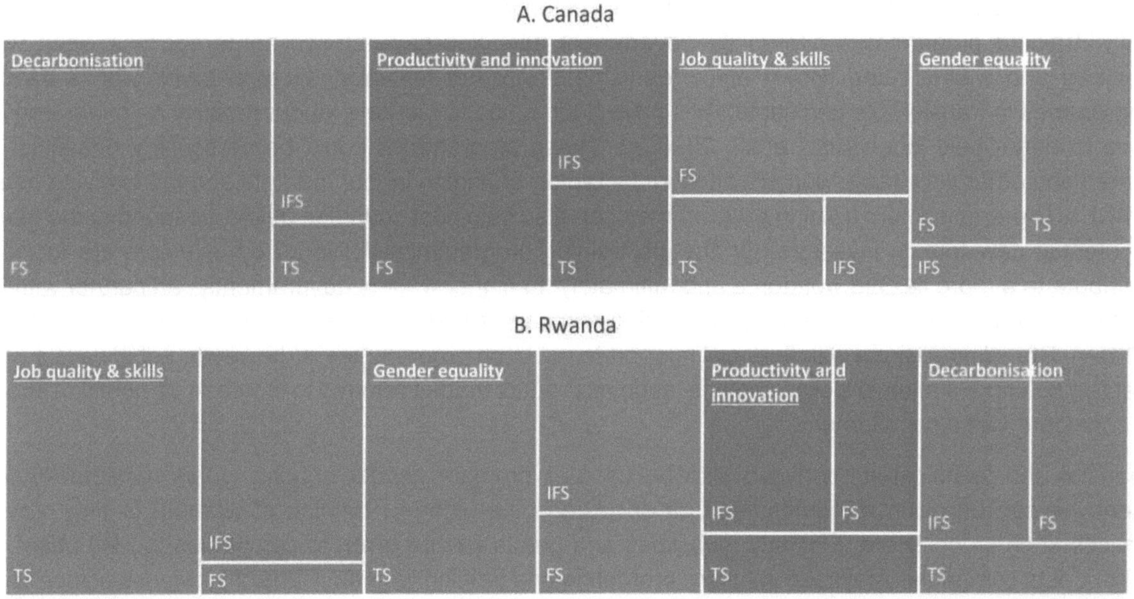

Note: The areas reflect the volume of policy initiatives but do not provide any indication of the relative scope and scale of initiatives (e.g. in terms of budget or number of beneficiaries).
Source: OECD (2022[22]), FDI Qualities mapping: A survey of policies and institutions that can strengthen sustainable investment.

Private investors do not internalise the positive spillovers of low-carbon investments and are likely to under-invest in related technologies and skills compared to socially optimal levels. Targeted financial and technical support by the government is therefore warranted. A wide range of support measures are available to stimulate low-carbon investments and build low-carbon capabilities, and studies have shown the success and cost-effectiveness of the support policy depends crucially on the country context rather than on the specific tool used (Chapter 5). In general, government support for specific low-carbon technologies should decrease over time as related sectors (e.g. renewable energy generation) mature and the costs of the technologies decline. Minimum investment size thresholds for securing financial support can discourage investment by smaller foreign and domestic enterprises, despite their high innovation potential and may be counterproductive. Providing investment incentives to both green and non-green substitutes (e.g. renewable and non-renewable energy) also limits the overall effectiveness measures to stimulate low-carbon investments and reduce the environmental footprint of FDI (OECD, 2021[23]).

Financial support may be used to strengthen production capacities of local firms, particularly small and medium-sized enterprises (SMEs) that enhance the impact of FDI on sustainable development (Chapter 2). Direct lending and grants can be provided to SMEs to help them invest in R&D, acquire new technology, adopt digital and low-carbon solutions, and engage in innovation and internationalisation activities. Various tax relief measures can also be granted to support subgroups of the SME population such as innovative firms and start-ups to expand their business and join global value chains. Supplier development programmes are increasingly part of government support to improve the production capacity of local SMEs and help them become partners and suppliers of foreign firms. These programmes usually assess the need for upgrading SME capabilities in various aspects of their performance and provide coaching and training in quality control, management strategy, financial planning, as well as product certification and foreign market standards. Government agencies may also organise seminars and courses for SMEs, and provide a range of business diagnostic tools to help them assess their innovation and technological capabilities.

Training and skills development programmes raise the skills level of workers and help reduce skills mismatches and shortages that can be amplified by FDI entry or expansion (Chapter 3). Skills upgrading can further enable domestic firms to benefit from potential FDI spillovers (Becker et al., 2020[17]). Albeit costly, training programmes offered by government agencies have shown some success when well-designed and well-targeted (Bown and Freund, 2019[24]). For instance, sectoral training or re-training programmes in transferable certifiable skills have been found to facilitate labour mobility and help workers move to better-paid jobs (Autor et al., 2020[25]). These programmes could be particularly beneficial for women and other vulnerable workers affected by rapidly changing labour markets and the evolving needs of MNEs. Pre-employment training programmes can also help host countries quickly respond to the needs of potential new foreign investors. On-the-job training programmes delivered by investors are found to contribute to a more flexible workforce and, ultimately, to higher wages; governments can partner with the private sector in skill development by supporting companies that train their workers. (Almeida and Faria, 2014[26]). Providing all firms with financial support to run such programmes is, however, not always a cost-effective solution, and other policy aspects, such as product market reforms to increase competition should be considered as a complement.

Financial and technical support can also be used to promote gender equality goals (Chapter 4). Tax incentives can be given to companies that encourage the hiring or training of women, or that provide services such as childcare. Similarly, subsidies and grants can be given to companies to help offset the higher costs companies may face in hiring, promoting and training women. Currently, the use of incentives to promote gender inclusive practices in the workplace remains limited (Kronfol, Nichols and ThuTran, 2019[27]). Due to various economic, social and cultural barriers, female entrepreneurs tend to have fewer entrepreneurial and managerial skills and have more difficulty accessing formal credit than male entrepreneurs (Union, 2019[28]). The 2013 OECD Council Recommendation on Gender Equality in Education, Employment and Entrepreneurship encourages countries to design policy instruments to help female entrepreneurs overcome barriers related to lack of skills and credit. Financial support can take the form of soft loans or microcredit, or tax benefits (OECD, 2017[29]). Technical support can help women entrepreneurs strengthen their skills and grow their business, including to internationalise their operations. This can include training programmes to develop skills in business, management and digitisation, professional advice on legal and tax issues and other business development services.

Ensure that financial support to stimulate investment addresses market failures and is transparent and subject to regular reviews

Governments often use financial support, such as investment tax incentives or subsidised loans and grants, to attract investors and promote investment in specific activities, sectors and locations. Financial support for investors is sometimes conditional on specific criteria related to sustainable development and has thus the potential to advance sustainable development. A new OECD Investment Tax Incentives Database, currently covering 36 developing countries, shows that about a quarter of all tax incentive schemes promote at least one area of sustainable development and 28 of the 36 countries use such tax incentives (Celani, Dressler and Wermelinger, 2022[30]). About half of the countries use tax incentives to promote exports; a third of the countries use tax incentives with specific eligibility conditions and design features to create employment and improve job quality. Other areas – including those associated with skills development, improving environmental outcomes, local supply linkages, and gender equality – are less frequently observed.

The net benefits of these policies are not well understood (Dayan et al., 2021[31]). Further analysis is needed to evaluate the effectiveness of financial support to advance sustainable development. Costs, including impacts on tax revenue for example and the potential to spur rent-seeking behaviour, may outweigh their gains. Transparency about the benefits available to investors is often incomplete; this complicates the assessment of whether the policies in place address market failures, achieve their goals, and at what costs.

The benefits of transparency are recognised among tax and investment policy communities. Under the *OECD Declaration on International Investment and Multinational Enterprises*, adhering countries agree to "endeavour to make such measures [investment incentives] as transparent as possible, so that their importance and purpose can be ascertained and that information on them can be readily available" (OECD, 2011[32]). The OECD's Task Force on Tax and Development has also identified the need for a more effective global transparency framework for tax incentives for investment (OECD, 2013[33]), and transparency is listed as an essential element of good governance in the IMF-OECD-UN-World Bank report to the G-20 Development Working Group on improving use of tax incentives in low income countries (IMF-OECD-UN-World Bank, 2015[34]). Fostering transparency of investment incentives is also an important objective for many countries in ongoing negotiations on investment facilitation at the WTO.

Improving transparency of investment incentives is a first step to better understanding their effectiveness and efficiency. This is particularly important in the context of the COVID-19 recovery, where many governments consider implementing new incentives to attract investors or reducing existing ones due to growing fiscal constraints. In addition to supporting policy evaluation, increasing transparency and awareness of available benefits, eligibility criteria, and awarding processes could also help countries attract untapped investment sources. For example, small and medium enterprises (SMEs) have fewer resources to navigate the often complex legal framework governing incentives (and less power to negotiate agreements directly with governments). But all investors would benefit from access to clear and regularly updated information to assess new investment opportunities. Combined with good governance, greater transparency around investment incentives can support co-ordination across different agencies involved in granting incentives, and strengthen confidence that incentives are granted in a fair and not overly discretionary manner. Greater transparency on investment incentives could also help foster trust and co-operation across countries. This is timely in light of the recent global minimum tax agreement by 137 countries and jurisdictions in the context of the OECD/G20 Inclusive Framework on Base Erosion and Profit Shifting (BEPS), which may affect how governments use investment incentives in the future.

In addition to the need for transparency, financial and technical support should be time-limited and subject to regular review. Net benefits of support programmes are context-specific and may change over time. Monitoring and re-evaluation of financial and other support is often neglected. Government authorities should regularly prepare tax expenditure reports to measure and monitor the costs of tax incentives (OECD, 2015[4]; IMF-OECD-UN-World Bank, 2015[34]). The government should also periodically carry out audits to ensure that financial and technical support measures are not abused. Financial and technical support measures should be reviewed periodically to assess their effectiveness in helping meet desired goals.

Sunset clauses provide opportunities for periodic evaluation, for example to improve efficiency of the incentive, alignment with the intended policy objective and help in identifying and winding down incentives that are no longer needed. Sunset clauses are provisions in a law or regulation stating that sections of it cease to have effect after a specific date, unless further legislative action is taken to extend them. Well-designed and implemented sunset clauses create a natural break that strengthens a firm's incentive to accelerate investment immediately and avoids extensive revenue losses to the government. On the other hand, sunset clauses also introduce an element of uncertainty to investors and increase the complexity of the legal system.

1.3.4. Facilitate and promote investment for sustainable development opportunities by addressing information failures and administrative barriers

Raise stakeholder awareness on impacts of FDI on sustainable development

Assessing investor performance and impacts on sustainable development is not only essential for governments to identify possible policy responses but also to raise awareness among stakeholders and the general public about the impacts of their consumption and investment choices. Governments can use assessments on the impacts of FDI to inform the general public and engage with stakeholders, resulting in a better informed and more inclusive policy debate.

Concerns about access to information on the carbon footprint of consumption and investment choices have led many governments to introduce measures to raise public awareness and understanding of carbon performance, including platforms for dialogue and information sharing, information campaigns, and product labelling schemes. For instance, many governments long ago introduced mandatory energy labelling schemes for appliances, which have been key in helping consumers choose more energy-efficient products. While there are still no regulatory requirements on carbon labelling, some investor-driven initiatives are emerging to cater to customers that are responsive to climate credentials (Chapter 5).

Social and cultural norms in FDI recipient countries can also shape the extent to which countries can leverage FDI for sustainable development. For example, in the area of gender equality, women in host countries may not be able to benefit from the job opportunities generated by foreign investors due to various social and cultural barriers (Chapter 4). Gender stereotypes are at the root of patterns of gender inequality in the labour market, e.g. the fact that women tend to be concentrated in low-value-added sectors and in part-time jobs. Public information and awareness-raising campaigns can help change traditional norms that harm investment impacts on sustainable development.

Link investment promotion and aftercare activities to sustainable development objectives

IPAs are key players in bridging information gaps that may otherwise hinder the realisation of foreign investments, and their potential sustainable development impacts. Their primary role is to create awareness of existing investment opportunities, attract investors, and facilitate their establishment and expansion in the economy, including by linking them to potential local partners. The tools used by IPAs vary widely, ranging from intelligence gathering (e.g. market studies) and sector specific events (inward and outward missions) to pro-active investor engagement (one-to-one meetings, email/ phone campaigns, enquiry handling).

Most IPAs prioritise certain types of investments over others, by selecting priority sectors, countries or investment projects, and allocating resources accordingly (OECD, 2018[35]). The approaches and tools adopted by IPAs increasingly aim to attract investment that supports national sustainable development priorities. A recent OECD survey shows that sustainable development considerations are important for IPAs when setting their prioritisation strategy (OECD, 2021[11]): 90% of IPAs in the OECD use productivity and innovation performance indicators to prioritise investment attraction, and 87% use indicators linked to job creation and skills. About half use low-carbon transition-related indicators.

IPAs also play an important role in keeping their economies attractive and competitive, notably through their policy advocacy role. Working at the intersection of business and public service, IPAs are in a unique position to channel the feedback received from investors to policy makers and advocate for open, transparent and well-regulated markets. With the continued policy uncertainty following the COVID-19 pandemic, IPA's policy advocacy role has become ever more important and is likely to be reinforced in the future.

While IPAs prioritise and attract new investments to fulfil their sustainability goals, they are also providing aftercare services to existing investors to support their operations and facilitate their expansions or reinvestments. Many IPAs provide matchmaking services and organise business-to-business meetings where representatives of foreign and domestic firms are introduced to each other. Many IPAs also organise demonstration and networking events that include knowledge exchange and information sharing. The policy goal is to bring down information barriers and allow foreign firms to identify local suppliers for future collaboration (Chapter 2). Some of these matchmaking programmes specifically target women entrepreneurs to help them connect with foreign investors (Chapter 4). Through these aftercare activities, IPAs should also consider promoting responsible business conduct and encouraging them to more systematically comply with laws, such as those on the respect for human rights, environmental protection, labour relations and financial accountability, as well as to embrace sustainable practices in their business operations.

Streamline procedures for obtaining permits needed for investors to engage in business activities that foster sustainable development

Regulatory burdens and complicated procedures for obtaining permits can dissuade foreign firms from investing when faced with more welcoming environments elsewhere. They can hamper the growth of smaller businesses and their move towards high value added, knowledge-based and low carbon production, which would allow them to establish business linkages with foreign investors too. It is therefore important that regulatory procedures (such as to start a business and to deal with construction permits, environmental licensing, getting electricity, paying taxes, and enforcing contracts) are streamlined, easily accessible and consistent with investment licensing procedures. Having a single window portal for all administrative procedures can help reduce transaction costs for investors, as long as it does not create additional duplication and complexity in the company establishment process.

Less regulation is not always better, however, and may ignore the potential economic, social and environmental benefits of regulation (Thomsen, 2019[36]). An investment and business climate is a complex organism and requires a holistic approach to reform, such as that provided by the PFI. Regulatory reforms should therefore be informed by regulatory impact assessments, including environmental and social impact assessments.

Promote corporate disclosure and fostering interoperability, comparability, and quality of core ESG metrics in reporting frameworks, ratings, and investment practices

Sustainable finance is generally referred to as the process of considering environmental, social and governance (ESG) factors when making investment decisions, leading to increased longer-term investments into sustainable economic activities and projects (Boffo and Patalano, 2020[37]). ESG disclosure is gaining in acceptance because it can provide a useful tool for corporate investors to assess and communicate their socially responsible practices, and for financial investors that seek to assess the potential for social returns in a consistent manner across companies and over time.

Despite substantial efforts to improve ESG disclosure frameworks in recent years, the reporting of ESG factors still suffers from considerable shortcomings with respect to consistency, comparability and quality that undermine its usefulness to investors. Some industry participants have noted that a lack of consistent disclosure frameworks at the international level hinders comparability. While progress is being made by framework developers and providers, there is still no universally accepted global set of principles and guidelines for consistent and meaningful ESG reporting (Boffo and Patalano, 2020[37]).

Better corporate disclosure of climate-related risks will also help aligning the environmental pillar of ESG investment ratings with a low-carbon transition (Chapter 5). Inconsistencies in the construction of ESG ratings across providers, the multitude of different metrics, and insufficient quality of forward looking metrics prevent agencies from supplying consistent and comparable information on transition risks and opportunities across firms and jurisdictions. Notably, rating providers appear to place less weight on negative environmental impacts while placing greater weight on the disclosure of climate-related corporate policies and targets, with limited assessment as to the quality or impact of such strategies. Such limitations could mislead investors with an aim to align portfolios with the low-carbon transition. Greater transparency and precision of climate-related corporate risks along the Task Force on Climate-Related Financial Disclosures (TCFD) recommendations, for example, would facilitate investments into lower carbon assets (OECD, 2021[38]).

1.3.5. Strengthen the role of development co-operation for mobilising FDI and enhancing its positive impact in developing countries

Strengthen co-operation between governments and the donor community to enhance the impact of FDI on sustainable development

Donors devote a significant portion of their resources to supporting the private sector, including to support improvements to the investment climate, enhance productive capacities and develop physical infrastructure. Over the period 2013-19, total private-related support through official development finance reached USD 755 billion in disbursements, representing 45% of total official development finance (OECD, 2021[23]). While donors have traditionally focused on incentivising FDI in developing countries, further consideration to the qualitative dimensions of investment can make donors' interventions more effective and foster greater impact of investment on the SDGs.

Greater co-operation between governments and the donor community can help more systematically integrate the qualitative aspects of investment into donors' activities, and support governments' efforts to enhance the positive impact of investment on sustainable development. Governments and the donor community should work together to identify financial and technical assistance solutions to support policy reforms and implementation, promote alignment with international standards, reduce exposure to financial and sustainability risks, and provide support to the private sector through financial and other instruments, as well as support for business strategies. The forthcoming *FDI Qualities Guide for Development Co-operation* explores different modalities for leveraging development co-operation to enhance the sustainability impact of FDI, and can serve as a framework for donors and developing country governments willing to co-operate in this agenda.

Ensure alignment of donors' interventions with national priorities

In order to ensure the effectiveness of donors' interventions, it is essential to ensure alignment of such interventions with national priorities on investment and sustainable development in recipient countries. Various international instruments aiming to strengthen aid effectiveness, including the Paris Declaration on Aid Effectiveness (2005), Nairobi Outcome Document (2016), and Kampala Principles on Effective Private Sector Engagement in Development Co-operation (2019) reflect a growing recognition that development efforts need to be led by the countries receiving development support (OECD, 2019[39]).

Development co-operation actors and partner countries may consider various modalities to mobilise and enhance the positive effects of FDI, including through support to governments to improve the investment climate, or direct engagement with the private sector to influence the behaviour of foreign investors. The nature and type of relevant interventions may vary depending on the areas of sustainability covered by the FDI Qualities Policy Toolkit that donors and partner countries wish to target.

Identifying and mapping existing donors' interventions can help assess alignment with national priorities on investment and sustainable development, and inform development co-operation strategies. Such a mapping can also help identify potential gaps in the breadth of modalities used and areas of the SDGs targeted, support greater co-ordination of donors interventions, and help identify opportunities to replicate or scale-up relevant interventions.

Engage with the private sector and civil society

The private sector and civil society are key actors and stakeholders of development co-operation efforts to promote investment and sustainable development. Engaging with both the private sector and civil society is therefore essential to inform, implement and monitor development co-operation programmes and projects aimed at mobilising FDI and enhancing its impacts on sustainable development.

Results from a review of 919 private sector engagement projects carried out by the Global Partnership for Effective Development Co-operation (GPEDC) found that only 9% of reviewed projects listed civil society as partners, and even fewer listed business associations (5%) or trade unions (0%). The Kampala Principles on Effective Private Sector Engagement in Development Co-operation, developed by the GPEDC, emphasise the importance of establishing more inclusive partnerships to foster trust through inclusive dialogue and consultation in projects that aim to engage the private sector for development results (GPEDC, 2019[40]).

Donors and governments in developing countries have an opportunity to involve the private sector and promote multi-stakeholder partnerships through interventions directly targeting businesses. Such interventions may include financial participation in sustainable private investment projects, support for responsible business conduct standards (e.g. the OECD Guidelines for Multinational Enterprises and associated due diligence guidance) and multi-stakeholder partnerships that include voluntary, collaborative arrangements between various actors with the aim to work towards a sustainability goal. More broadly, across and throughout interventions targeting the investment climate and spill-over effects, donors and recipient country governments can make development co-operation efforts more effective by consulting and involving various actors and stakeholders, including policy makers, the private sector, civil society and trade unions at all stages of programmes and project cycles.

References

Almeida, R. and M. Faria (2014), "The wage returns to on-the-job training: evidence from matched employer-employee data", *IZA Journal of Labor & Development*, Vol. 3(1), 1-33. [26]

Autor, D. et al. (2020), "The fall of the labor share and the rise of superstar firms", *The Quarterly Journal of Economics*, Vol. 135(2), 645-709. [25]

Becker, B. et al. (2020), "FDI in hot labour markets: The implications of the war for talent", *Journal of International Business Policy*, Vol. 3, 107-133. [17]

Boffo, R. and R. Patalano (2020), *ESG Investing: Practices, Progress and Challenges*, OECD Publishing, https://www.oecd.org/finance/ESG-Investing-Practices-Progress-Challenges.pdf. [37]

Bown, C. and C. Freund (2019), "Active labor market policies: lessons from other countries for the United States", *Peterson Institute for International Economics Working Paper*, Vol. (19-2). [24]

Celani, A., L. Dressler and M. Wermelinger (2022), *Building an investment tax incentives database: Methodology and initial findings for 36 developing countries*, OECD Publishing. [30]

Dayan, S. et al. (2021), *Improving transparency of investment incentives: Draft discussion note*. [31]

Gaukrodger, D. (2020), *Business Responsibilities and Investment Treaties, public consultation paper by the OECD Secretariat*, https://www.oecd.org/daf/inv/investment-policy/Consultation-Paper-on-business-responsibilities-and-investment-treaties.pdf. [21]

Gaukrodger, D. and K. Gordon (2012), *Investor-State Dispute Settlement: A Scoping Paper for the Investment Policy Community*, OECD Publishing, Paris, https://doi.org/10.1787/5k46b1r85j6f-en. [13]

GPEDC (2019), *Kampala Principles on Effective Private Sector Engagement in Development Co-operation.* [40]

Hijzen, A. et al. (2013), "Foreign-owned firms around the world: A comparative analysis of wages and employment at the micro-level", *European Economic Review*, Vol. 60, 170-188, https://doi.org/10.1016/j.euroecorev.2013.02.001 [16]

IMF-OECD-UN-World Bank (2015), *Options for Low Income Countries' Effective and Efficient Use of Tax Incentives for Investment, A report prepared for the G-20 Development Working Group by the IMF, OECD, UN and World Bank*, https://www.oecd.org/tax/options-for-low-income-countries-effective-and-efficient-use-of-tax-incentives-for-investment.htm. [34]

Javorcik, B. and M. Spatareanu (2005), "Do foreign investors care about labor market regulations?", *Review of World Economics*, Vol. 141(3), 375-403. [15]

Kronfol, H., A. Nichols and T. ThuTran (2019), "Women at Work. How Can Investment Incentives Be Used to Enhance Economic Opportunities for Women?", *Policy Research Working Paper 8935, The World Bank Group.* [27]

Mistura, F. and C. Roulet (2019), *The Determinants of Foreign Direct Investment: Do Statutory Restrictions Matter?*, OECD Publishing, Paris, https://doi.org/10.1787/641507ce-en. [12]

OECD (2022), *FDI Qualities Indicators: 2022.* [10]

OECD (2022), *FDI Qualities mapping: A survey of policies and institutions that can strengthen sustainable investment.* [22]

OECD (2022), *FDI Qualities Review of Jordan: Strengthening sustainable investment,*, OECD Publishing, Paris, https://doi.org/10.1787/736c77d2-en. [6]

OECD (2022), *Strengthening FDI and SME linkages in Portugal*, OECD Publishing, Paris, https://doi.org/10.1787/d718823d-en. [7]

OECD (2021), *Council Report on the Implementation of the OECD Recommnedation on the Policy Framework for Investment, Note by the Secretary-General.* [41]

OECD (2021), *Enabling FDI diffusion channels to boost SME productivity and innovation in EU countries and regions: Towards a Policy Toolkit.* [9]

OECD (2021), *ESG Investing and Climate Transition: Market Practices, Issues and Policy Considerations*, https://www.oecd.org/finance/ESG-investing-and-climate-transition-market-practices-issues-and-policy-considerations.pdf. [38]

OECD (2021), *OECD Investment Policy Reviews: Thailand*, OECD Investment Policy Reviews, OECD Publishing, Paris, https://doi.org/10.1787/c4eeee1c-en. [23]

OECD (2021), *Together or separate: Investment Promotion Agencies' prioritisation and monitoring and evaluation for sustainable investment promotion across the OECD countries.* [11]

OECD (2020), *Global Outlook on Financing for Sustainable Development 2021: A New Way to Invest for People and Planet*, OECD Publishing, Paris, https://doi.org/10.1787/e3c30a9a-en. [2]

OECD (2019), *FDI Qualities Indicators: Measuring the sustainable development impacts of investment*, http://www.oecd.org/fr/investissement/fdi-qualities-indicators.htm. [3]

OECD (2019), *Making Development Co-operation More Effective. 2019 Progress Report.*, OECD, https://doi.org/10.1787/26f2638f-en. [39]

OECD (2019), *OECD Investment Policy Reviews: Southeast Asia*, https://www.oecd.org/daf/inv/investment-policy/Southeast-Asia-Investment-Policy-Review-2019.pdf. [14]

OECD (2018), *Mapping of Investment Promotion Agencies in OECD Countries*, https://www.oecd.org/investment/investment-policy/mapping-of-investment-promotion-agencies-in-OECD-countries.pdf. [35]

OECD (2017), *2013 OECD Recommendation of the Council on Gender Equality in Education, Employment and Entrepreneurship*, https://doi.org/10.1787/9789264279391-en. [29]

OECD (2015), *Policy Framework for Investment, 2015 Edition*, OECD Publishing, Paris, https://doi.org/10.1787/9789264208667-en. [4]

OECD (2013), *Principles to Enhance the Transparency and Governance of Tax Incentives for Investment in Developing Countries*, OECD, Paris, https://www.oecd.org/tax/tax-global/transparency-and-governance-principles.pdf. [33]

OECD (2011), *Declaration on International Investment and Multinational Enterprises, 2011 Edition,*, OECD, Paris, https://legalinstruments.oecd.org/en/instruments/OECD-LEGAL-0144. [32]

OECD (2011), *OECD Guidelines for Multinational Enterprises, 2011 Edition*, OECD Publishing, Paris, https://doi.org/10.1787/9789264115415-en. [19]

OECD (2022, forthcoming), *Draft FDI Qualities Guide for Development Co-operation.* [5]

OECD (2022, forthcoming), *Strengthening FDI and SME linkages in the Slovak Republic*, OECD Publishing, Paris. [8]

Pohl, J. (2018), *Societal benefits and costs of International Investment Agreements: A critical review of aspects and available empirical evidence*, OECD Publishing, Paris, https://doi.org/10.1787/e5f85c3d-en. [20]

Thomsen, S. (2019), *How much difference do the Doing Business indicators make?*, https://oecdonthelevel.com/2019/01/15/how-much-difference-do-the-doing-business-indicators-make/. [36]

UNCTAD (2014), *World Investment Report 2014*, UNCTAD, https://unctad.org/system/files/official-document/wir2014_en.pdf. [1]

Union, O. (2019), *The Missing Entrepreneurs 2019: Policies for Inclusive Entrepreneurship*, https://doi.org/10.1787/3ed84801-en. [28]

World Bank (2021), *Women, Business and the Law*, https://wbl.worldbank.org/en/wbl. [18]

Notes

[1] The OECD Council invited the Investment Committee (IC) to "develop and promote the FDI Qualities Policy Toolkit, which could possibly be welcomed by Ministers at the 2022 Ministerial Council Meeting as a tool to complement and support the use of the PFI, thereby further aligning the PFI with the SDG Agenda" (OECD, 2021[41]).

[2] The OECD has established a dedicated multi-stakeholder policy network to support and provide guidance to the FDI Qualities initiative, through policy dialogue and technical discussions on project activities. The network includes government officials from OECD and partner countries; development co-operation practitioners; private sector and civil society; international organisations and academia; and experts from policy communities across the OECD.

[3] The Policy Toolkit does not have dedicated recommendations to businesses, but it calls extensively on governments to adhere to, and implement, the OECD Guidelines on Multinational Enterprises (OECD, 2011[19]). The Guidelines provide recommendations, agreed by adhering governments, on responsible business conduct, i.e. how businesses can avoid harm to people and the planet and improve positive contributions to society. Under the FDI Qualities initiative, the role of businesses, including the identification of good business practices, could be further developed.

[4] The OECD Council further invited the IC to "reinforce co-operation and alignment with development partners, particularly in the development of the FDI Qualities Policy Toolkit" (OECD, 2021[41]).

2 Policies for improving FDI impacts on productivity and innovation

This chapter presents a Policy Toolkit to help governments channel foreign direct investment (FDI) into productivity-enhancing activities and promote productivity and innovation spillovers on small and medium-sized enterprises (SMEs). The chapter describes the various transmission channels through which FDI affects productivity and innovation as well as contextual factors determining the magnitude and direction of such impacts. It also provides a thorough overview of policies and institutions at the intersection of investment and other complementary policies that can enhance the impacts of FDI on productivity and innovation.

Main policy principles

1. Provide strategic direction and ensure policy co-ordination and coherence on investment, innovation and SME development

- Ensure that national development strategies and economic plans provide coherent and strategic directions on investment promotion, innovation and SME development objectives, and foster a whole-of-government approach to supporting productivity growth.
- Mainstream investment considerations into industrial, innovation and SME policy strategies (and vice versa), and systematically consider the role that FDI can play in enhancing the productivity and competitiveness of the economy when adopting economic reform programmes.
- Strengthen policy co-ordination at strategic and implementing levels by establishing inter-ministerial councils, task forces and working groups; encouraging collaboration between implementing agencies; setting up effective multi-level governance systems and involving subnational governments in whole-of-government policy-setting processes.
- Periodically assess the impact of FDI and relevant policies on the productivity and innovation of the domestic economy and promote policy dialogue with foreign investors, local SMEs and other actors of the domestic research and innovation ecosystem to enhance the effectiveness of policy interventions.

2. Ensure that domestic and international regulations create a conducive business environment for FDI-driven productivity growth and innovation

- Develop laws and regulations that support FDI-driven productivity growth by ensuring an open, transparent and non-discriminatory regulatory environment for investment in productive and knowledge-intensive activities, fostering competition and a level playing field, and providing strong protection of intellectual property rights (IPRs).
- Simplify overly burdensome regulations that may undermine business capacity and incentives to engage in innovation and technology development while at the same time ensuring that efforts to reduce the regulatory burden on business do not lead to a "race to the bottom" in terms of social and environmental standards.
- Ensure that labour market laws enable domestic firms, in particular SMEs, to retain and attract highly skilled workers through regulatory exemptions, incentives for job training of their employees, and measures to address labour shortages in FDI-intensive sectors.
- Ensure that financial market laws and regulations facilitate access to finance for innovative and technology-intensive activities undertaken by foreign and domestic firms, by addressing financial stability risks, setting conducive framework conditions for the development of equity markets, and increasing the availability of alternative financing instruments.
- Integrate innovation and SME policy considerations into international investment agreements (IIAs) to promote international co-operation and dialogue on technology transfer issues, while at the same time ensuring that IIAs reduce regulatory barriers to knowledge-intensive investment, foster competitive markets and strengthen domestic legal frameworks for intellectual property rights protection.

3. Stimulate knowledge-intensive investment and support the productive capacities and innovation potential of the domestic economy

- Ensure that financial support to stimulate knowledge-intensive investment addresses well-identified market failures (e.g. information asymmetries, risks arising from engaging in innovation, high fixed costs of technology-intensive activities) and that the conditions and criteria for its granting are clearly defined, transparent and subject to regular reviews.

- Use financial and technical support (e.g. supplier development programmes, skills development policies, technology extension services, financing, capacity building) to strengthen the absorptive capacities of domestic firms, in particular SMEs, and improve their chances of becoming suppliers and partners of foreign investors.
- Promote quality infrastructure (e.g. ICT, transport and logistics, energy) through a national infrastructure plan, public investment in infrastructure development and public-private partnerships to support productive investment that creates linkages with the domestic economy.
- Establish intermediary organisations and specialised facilities (e.g. technology transfer offices, collaborative laboratories, knowledge centres, business incubators, science and technology parks) to support business-to-business and science-to-business collaboration.
- Implement comprehensive cluster development programmes that facilitate business linkages, foster cross-sectoral interactions and take into account place-based capabilities.

4. Facilitate knowledge and technology spillovers from FDI by eliminating information barriers and administrative hurdles

- Implement investment promotion strategies that allow to identify, prioritise and attract productivity-enhancing and knowledge-intensive investment, including through intelligence gathering (e.g. market studies), sector-specific events (e.g. business fairs, country missions), and pro-active investor engagement (e.g. one-to-one meetings, campaigns, enquiry handling).
- Provide comprehensive investment facilitation and aftercare services to foster greater embedding of foreign investors in local economies including by facilitating supplier linkages, strategic partnerships and collaboration with actors of the domestic entrepreneurial and innovation ecosystem.
- Ensure that information pertaining to the host country's innovation ecosystem and the productive capabilities of domestic firms is made readily available, or available upon request, to foreign investors.

2.1. Global productivity slowdown amid rising inequalities

Productivity reflects a country's stage of economic development, and its resulting competitive edge and economic structure. As an economy develops, its structure typically shifts from agriculture, to light manufacturing, to heavier manufacturing, and eventually to high technology manufacturing and services, reflecting increasing levels of productivity and innovation capacity (OECD, 2014[1]). While productivity varies considerably across sectors, different value chain functions within sectors and the efficiency to conduct such activities involve varying levels of labour intensity and thus productivity levels (Box 2.1. for definitions of productivity and innovation in this policy toolkit).

Productivity and innovation figure prominently in the Sustainable Development Goals (SDGs), particularly in SDG 8 (economic growth) and SDG 9 (industry and innovation). These goals encompass boosting overall competitiveness, reducing regional disparities, and raising productivity and innovation capacity of the typically more constrained small and medium-sized enterprises (SMEs). Enhanced productivity and innovation are closely tied to better-paid and more stable jobs and greater human capital and skills (Chapter 3). Productivity and innovation capacity is also closely tied with the transition towards a low-carbon economy (Chapter 4). Productivity and innovation may thus support progress across a broader set of sustainability objectives (e.g. employment generation, green transition, skills development), although causality is likely to go in both directions (OECD, 2019[2]).

Productivity growth has decelerated globally as shown in recent OECD work on 'The Future of Productivity' (OECD, 2015[3]). The main source of the productivity slowdown is not so much a decline in innovation, but rather a drop in the pace at which innovations spread throughout the economy. Productivity growth of the globally most productive and innovative firms has remained robust in recent years but the gap between these highly productive and innovative firms and the rest has widened. For instance, although in some niche markets SMEs are more productive and innovative than large firms (Marchese et al., 2019[4]), in a number of countries a fat tail of low productivity micro and small firms usually co-exists with large multinational enterprises (MNEs), which are very productive and exposed to international competition.

SMEs are key actors for building more inclusive and sustainable growth, increasing economic resilience and improving social cohesion. Across the OECD, for instance, SMEs account for about 60% of employment and between 50% and 60% of value added and are the main drivers of productivity and innovation in many regions and cities where other global frontier innovators are absent (OECD, 2019[5]). Smaller firms face long-standing size-related barriers in dealing with stringent business conditions or accessing strategic resources such as finance, skills, knowledge, technology and infrastructure. SMEs are a very heterogeneous population whose performance in terms of productivity, wages paid and international competitiveness, vary considerably across sectors, regions and firms. Enterprise creation in the OECD has picked up over the last decade, especially in services, but newly created jobs are concentrated in low-productivity and low-wage sectors, and have increased over time, even if SMEs outperform large enterprises in the services sector in many countries (OECD, 2019[2]; 2021[6]). More lower-productivity jobs have resulted in more lower-paid jobs. SMEs, even the larger ones, typically pay employees around 20% less than large firms and the gap with foreign firms is even larger.

Innovation is key to boost productivity, and digitalisation offers SMEs new opportunities to take part in the next production revolution. Emerging digital technologies, such as big data analytics, artificial intelligence and 3D printing, enable greater product differentiation and mass customisation, better integrated supply chain systems and, overall, new digitally enhanced business models that leverage shorter distance and time to markets (OECD, 2019[7]). This is likely to benefit smaller and more responsive businesses. Digitalisation also supports open sourcing and open innovation, with large – and foreign – firms contributing to the transformation of business ecosystems through business accelerators and innovation labs that provide start-ups, innovative SMEs and R&D organisations with access to resources and markets. Digitalisation creates a range of innovative financial services for SMEs and eases SME access to skills through better job recruitment sites, outsourcing and online task hiring, or by connecting them with knowledge partners.

Digitalisation can also help SMEs integrate in global value chains (GVCs). Digitalisation has created effective mechanisms to reduce size disadvantages in international trade, such as by reducing the absolute costs associated with transport and border operations. In addition, the fragmentation of production worldwide has provided smaller businesses with significant scope for competing in specialised GVC segments and scaling up activities abroad, while capturing international knowledge spillovers and capitalising on more robust growth in emerging markets. In fact, wage gaps with large foreign firms are smaller for exporting SMEs and for highly productive SMEs, particularly those at the frontier of the digital revolution (OECD, 2021[8]).

Box 2.1. Defining productivity and innovation

This policy toolkit defines **productivity** in terms of value added per unit of labour (labour productivity), where labour is measured as total hours worked or number of employees (OECD, 2019[2]). It is important to stress that labour productivity is an incomplete gauge of efficiency. Labour productivity can rise due to increased capital spending (e.g. giving workers more machines), but does not mean all factors of production are being used more efficiently (e.g. using better machines). Labour productivity measures in services come with caveats as measures of output are often in terms of costs of labour and thus value added is difficult to measure (Triplett and Bosworth, 2008[9]). Total factor productivity or measures of return on capital (e.g. incremental capital-output ratios) would better capture efficiency improvements for capital-intensive industries like mining.

Innovation is defined as the implementation of a new or improved product (good or service) or business process (or combination thereof) that differs significantly from the firm's previous products or business processes and that has been introduced on the market or brought into use by the firm (OECD/Eurostat, 2018[10]). Innovation activities include all developmental, financial and commercial activities undertaken by a firm that are intended to result in an innovation. Patented intellectual property is sometimes used as an indicator for innovation output, although not all innovations are protected with patents. A broad set of tangible and intangible assets with embedded knowledge – ranging from human and organisational capital, existing technologies to R&D – need to be accumulated and combined to yield innovation outputs (Cirera and Maloney, 2017[11]). This Policy Toolkit makes predominantly reference to two measures of innovation: process innovation and R&D intensity, or R&D per unit of value added (OECD, 2019[2]).

2.2. FDI impacts on productivity and innovation

FDI can contribute to enhanced productivity and innovation through the activities of foreign firms (direct impact) and via knowledge and technology spillovers that arise from market interactions with domestic firms (indirect impact). The impacts of FDI may not materialise automatically, and depend on a number of economic, market and firm-specific factors. These framework conditions underpin the channels through which FDI affects domestic productivity and innovation and shape the magnitude and direction of spillovers in the host economy (Figure 2.1). Examining the performance of transmission channels and their framework conditions can shed light on the trends and complexities of the relationship between FDI and productivity, triggering dialogue and facilitating the identification of policy priorities and possible trade-offs. Annex Table 2.A.1 provides a detailed checklist of questions for governments to self-assess the impacts of FDI on productivity and innovation.

2.2.1. FDI can contribute directly to productivity enhancement

Foreign firms' direct impact relates to their own activities and how they contribute to aggregate and sectoral productivity and innovation (Cadestin et al., 2018[12]). FDI directly relates to improved productivity and innovation at the industry or aggregate level if foreign firm activity is concentrated in sectors that are typically more productive and innovative. The opposite holds if FDI is concentrated in low-value added, less innovative, sectors. Thus, FDI can shift the sectoral composition towards more or less productive or innovative activities.

Figure 2.1. Conceptual framework: Impacts of FDI on productivity and innovation

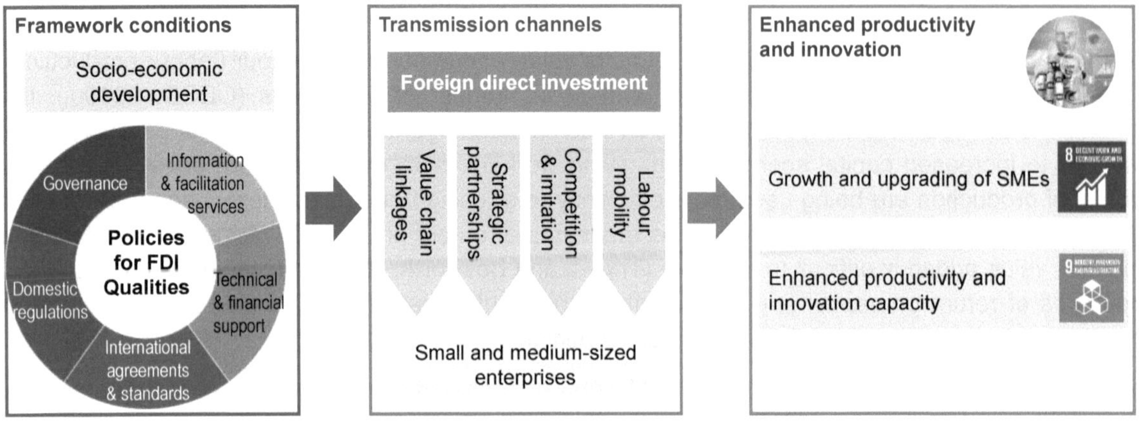

The OECD FDI Qualities Indicators suggest that, in OECD economies, sectors receiving more FDI tend to have higher labour productivity and R&D intensity levels. They also experience higher growth in labour productivity than other sectors (Figure 2.2.). The extent of FDI concentration in highly productive sectors varies across OECD countries, but tends to be greater in those with large natural resources industries (e.g. Norway, the Netherlands, Canada) where highly profitable and capital-intensive mining and extraction activities attract significant foreign MNE activity (OECD, 2019[2]). In some OECD countries, R&D-intensive manufacturing (e.g. computer equipment and electronics, chemicals, machinery) and services sectors (e.g. logistics, finance, and communications) are also associated with higher FDI activity. In the US, these high-tech and R&D-intensive sectors account for more than 50% of greenfield FDI. Expanding the analysis to developing countries reveals a rather mixed picture; foreign manufacturers do not always operate in sectors with higher average labour productivity or sectors in which process innovation is more common. This is mainly due to the large concentration of FDI in labour-intensive industries, such as food processing and garments, where the intensity of innovation is expected to be lower than in capital-intensive manufacturing.

Besides the fact that foreign investors tend to invest in sectors that are typically more technology intensive, FDI's direct impact on productivity growth is also the result of foreign firms being on average more productive than domestic firms (Figure 2.3). Accordingly, FDI can raise overall productivity even in low value-added sectors if it is more productive than local firms are. The FDI Qualities Indicators show that productivity gaps between foreign and domestic firms exhibit considerable variation across OECD and developing economies, with substantial gaps in some countries and negligible gaps in others (Figure 2.3). A recent study for the United Kingdom shows that foreign firms are around twice as productive as domestic companies are (Batten and Jacobs, 2017[13]). This is linked to foreign affiliates operating on a larger scale and having stronger access to technology, better managerial skills and more adequate resources for capital investment than domestic firms (Javorcik, 2004[14]; 2020[15]). Size also matters, since foreign affiliates are larger than the average domestic enterprise and can therefore harness economies of scale, including through their relationship with the parent company, which are not available to domestic companies (Alfaro and Chen, 2012[16]; Desai, Foley and Forbes, 2007[17]).

Figure 2.2. Concentration of FDI based on sectoral productivity and R&D performance

FDI is concentrated in relatively higher performing sectors if score > 0

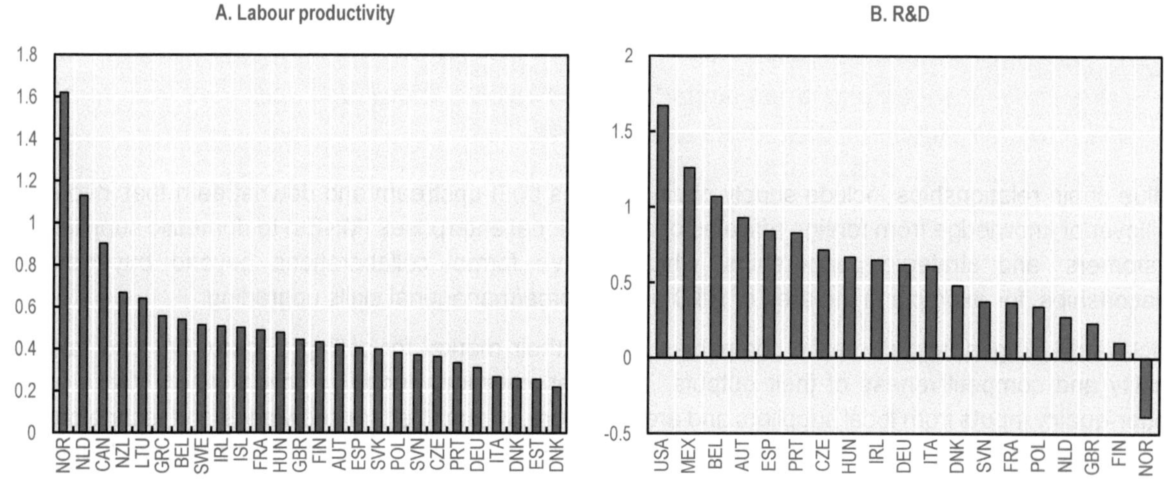

Note: See OECD (2019[2]) for a description of the methodology and data. Labour productivity = value added per employee; R&D intensity = R&D expenditures per unity of value added; wages = wage per employee.

Source: OECD (2019[2]), *FDI Qualities Indicators: Measuring the sustainable development impacts of investment*, www.oecd.org/fr/investissement/fdi-qualities-indicators.htm

Figure 2.3. Productivity premium of foreign firms in OECD and non-OECD economies

Average labour productivity premium of foreign relative to domestic firms, in percentage

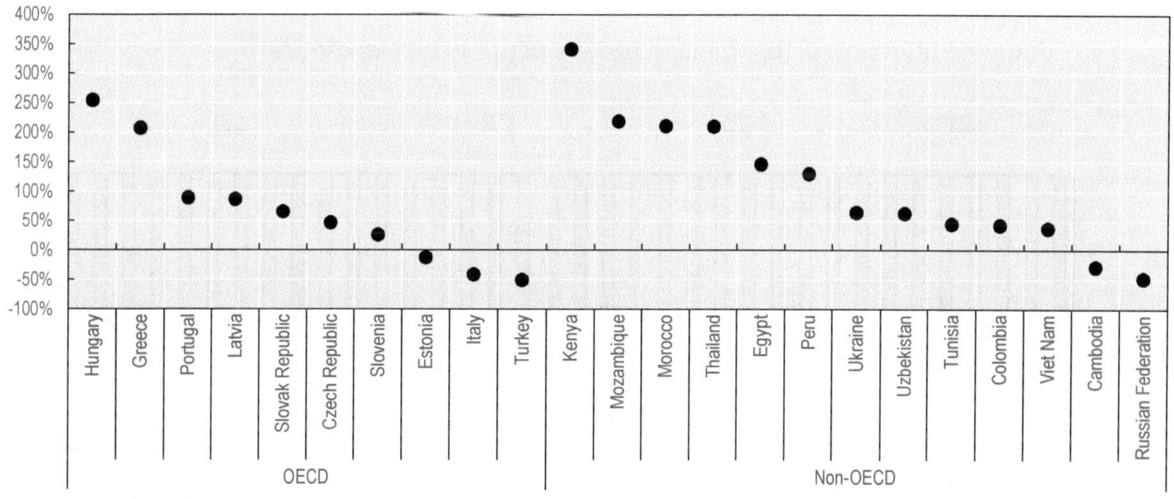

Note: See methodology in OECD (2019[2]), ; labour productivity = value added per employee.

Source: OECD (2019[2]), *FDI Qualities Indicators: Measuring the sustainable development impacts of investment*, www.oecd.org/fr/investissement/fdi-qualities-indicators.htm.

2.2.2. FDI can involve productivity and innovation spillovers on host economy firms

Due to foreign firms' performance premium relative to domestic firms, policy makers often expect FDI to generate knowledge and technology spillovers that will result in increased productivity of domestic firms, especially SMEs (Caves, 2007[18]; Blomstrom and Kokko, 1998[19]). Domestic firms can benefit from knowledge and technology spillovers through various transmission channels – such as value chain linkages, strategic partnerships, competition and imitation effects, and labour mobility. These channels are themselves enabled through specific contextual factors, notably the characteristics of FDI, capabilities of domestic firms as well as broader policy and non-policy framework conditions (Gorg and Strobl, 2001[20]; Crespo and Fontoura, 2007[21]; Smeets, 2008[22]; OECD, 2022[23]).

Value chain linkages and strategic partnerships involve knowledge spillovers from foreign MNEs to their suppliers, customers and partners

Value chain relationships include supply chain linkages both upstream and downstream that involve the spillover of knowledge from foreign affiliates of multinational enterprises (MNEs) to domestic suppliers and customers; and strategic partnerships, which involve formal collaborations beyond buyer-supplier relationships, for example in the area of R&D or workforce/managerial skills upgrading.

Backward linkages help domestic companies extend their market for selling (Figure 2.4) and raise the quality and competitiveness of their outputs. They generate knowledge spillovers when MNEs require better-quality inputs from local suppliers and are, therefore, willing to share knowledge and technology with them to encourage their adoption of better practices (OECD, 2022[23]). A recent study of New Zealand, for example, found that small firms do benefit from economies of scale when they supply foreign MNEs and, thereby catch up technologically with foreign firms (Doan, Maré and Iyer, 2014[24]). For such technology spillovers to happen, domestic firms require a certain level of absorptive capacity often defined in terms of technological proximity with foreign firms (see next sub-section). FDI spillovers are more commonly found in these vertical supply relationships than in the relationship between foreign MNEs and potential local competitors (horizontal spillovers), as rivalry is more naturally embedded in the latter (Rojec and Knell, 2017[25]; Javorcik, 2004[14]; Blalock and Gertler, 2008[26]) (see section on competition and imitation effects). Finally, having strong linkages with domestic firms can embed foreign affiliates more deeply into the economy, making it less likely that they will move operations elsewhere (OECD, 2022[23]).

Figure 2.4. Sourcing structure of foreign affiliates, by supplier type/origin, 2016

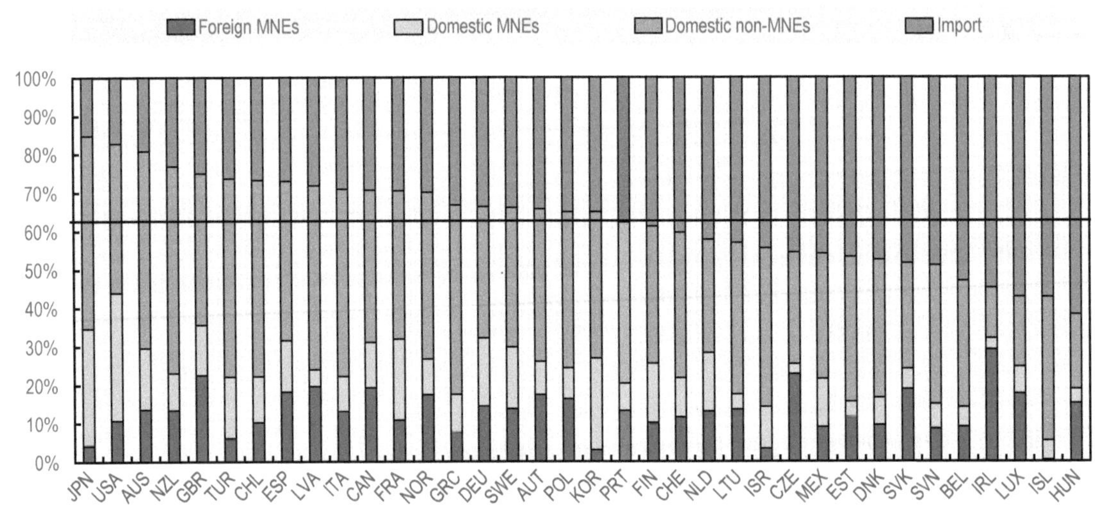

Source: OECD based on the OECD Analytical AMNE database, 2019, https://www.oecd.org/sti/ind/analytical-AMNE-database.htm

Affiliates of foreign MNEs operate in host countries as buyers of intermediate goods and as suppliers to domestic companies (forward linkages). Forward linkages between MNEs and local buyers have a positive impact on local enterprise productivity mostly through the acquisition of better quality inputs, which were not locally available before (Criscuolo and Timmis, 2017[27]). In addition, many MNEs, especially in industrial sectors such as machinery, often offer training to their customers on the use of their products as well as information on international quality standards (Jindra, 2006[28]).

The emergence of GVCs has brought new types of FDI-SME partnerships, especially in high technology and knowledge-intensive industries, which are based on the transfer of technology and the development of cross-border R&D projects. These strategic partnerships can take many forms, including joint ventures, licensing agreements, contract manufacturing, research collaborations as well as R&D and technology alliances (Andrenelli et al., 2019[29]; OECD, 2008[30]). Strategic partnerships are the result of a shift towards an open mode of innovation, which, as noted above, has made innovation more accessible to SMEs (OECD, 2019[5]). Open innovation has increasingly been seen as a way for accelerating internal innovation and expanding the markets for external use of innovation (Chesbrough, 2003[31]). Large firms have increasingly taken part in the open innovation transformation by developing strategic partnerships with smaller enterprises or by setting up innovation labs and accelerators where start-ups and other small firms can nurture new business ideas and business models. Foreign MNEs, in particular, often seek talent and specialised knowledge in local SME and start-up ecosystems.

A recent study based on firm-level data of OECD and developing economies finds that productivity spillovers from strategic partnerships, such as manufacturing/marketing agreements and joint ventures, depend on firm-level characteristics, such as firm size, (foreign) ownership, internationally recognised certifications and staff training. Larger and foreign-owned firms as well as firms that have internationally recognised certifications and engage in staff training are more likely to improve their productivity when foreign MNEs engage in partnerships. This is consistent with studies showing that knowledge and technology spillovers from foreign MNEs depend on SME absorptive capacities (see below).

The movement of skilled workers from foreign MNEs to domestic firms can bring new knowledge and skills to local economies

Labour mobility can be an important source of knowledge spillovers in the context of FDI, notably through the movement of MNE workers to domestic firms – either through temporary arrangements such as detachments and long-term arrangements such as open-ended contracts – or through the creation by MNE workers of start-ups (i.e. corporate spin-offs).

Existing evidence suggests that firms established by MNE managers are more productive than other local firms are (Görg and Strobl, 2005[32]). Similarly, evidence from manufacturing in Norway suggests that workers who moved from foreign-owned to domestic firms retain part of their knowledge and contribute 20% more to the productivity of their firm than workers without foreign firm experience (Balsvik, 2011[33]). Recent OECD research on Ireland shows that over the period 2009-2015 more than one in four employees at foreign-owned companies either moved to a domestic firm or became self-employed. In addition, more than one in three start-up founders had previously worked at a foreign-owned company (OECD, 2020[34]). Labour mobility within Ireland is also very common among highly skilled researchers who have produced patents. One out of two patent inventors changed employer at least once during the period 2006-2016. As most inventors are based in foreign-owned companies, FDI spillovers related to inventor mobility play an important role in Ireland (OECD, 2020[34]).

On the other hand, research on Portugal provides a more sceptical perspective on potential productivity spillovers on domestic firms resulting from the mobility of workers from foreign to domestic firms (Martins, 2011[35]). Domestic firms in Portugal tend to hire 'below-average' workers from foreign firms who take, on average, pay cuts (which is consistent with involuntary mobility). It suggests that worker mobility is unlikely to be a major source of productivity spillovers from foreign to domestic firms. However, movements from domestic to foreign firms translate into considerable pay increases in Portugal but also in other EU Member States (Becker et al., 2020[36]). This pay increase is consistent with a generally greater 'generosity' in the remuneration practices of foreign firms vis-à-vis their domestic counterparts (see Chapter 3). As foreign firms attract some of the best workers in domestic firms where they experience a wage increase and acquire new knowledge, productivity spillovers from worker mobility may also (or rather) occur from domestic to foreign firms.

Competition with foreign MNEs and imitation of their business practices provide significant learning and upgrading opportunities for domestic firms

The entry of foreign firms heightens the level of competition on domestic companies, putting pressure on them to become more innovative and productive – not least to retain skilled workers (Becker et al., 2020[36]). The new standards set by foreign firms – in terms of product design, quality control or speed of delivery – can stimulate technical change, the introduction of new products, and the adoption of new management practices in local companies, all of which are possible sources of productivity growth. Foreign firms can also become a source of emulation for local companies, for example by showing better ways to run a business. Imitation and tacit learning can therefore become a channel to strengthen firm productivity at the local level.

However, if local companies are not quick to adapt, competition from foreign companies may also result in the exit of some domestic firms. Increased competition for talent may also make it more difficult for local companies to recruit skilled workers (Lembcke and Wildnerova, 2020[37]). These effects are more likely to happen to local companies operating in the same sector or value chain of the foreign company. This is the main reason why horizontal spillovers from FDI are so rare and, when they happen, they mostly involve larger domestic companies (Gorodnichenko, Svejnar and Terrell, 2014[38]; Farole and Winkler, 2014[39]; Crespo and Fontoura, 2007[21]).

2.2.3. Magnitude and direction of FDI impacts depend on contextual factors

The magnitude and direction of FDI impacts depend on contextual factors, including the structure of the economy, the type of FDI that a country attracts, the capacity of domestic firms, in particular SMEs, to absorb knowledge from foreign firms, and economic geography factors.

The industrial structure, specialisation and internationalisation of the domestic economy influence the potential to benefit from FDI's presence

The industrial structure, economic specialisation and technological sophistication of the host country are primary determinants of FDI inflows. Differences in the comparative advantage of economies result in differing FDI profiles, with some countries attracting more knowledge-intensive investment than others do. Economies driven by sectors with higher average productivity levels and technological intensity are expected to have greater potential to absorb and utilise the knowledge and technology brought by foreign MNEs. Countries with more advanced industrial structures tend to attract FDI in higher value added activities, involving more productive and technology-intensive activities that allow them to further advance the industrialisation process (Benfratello and Sembenelli, 2006[40]; Criscuolo and Martin, 2003[41]). Conversely, countries at early stages of the industrialisation process may benefit more from investments in lower value added sectors where local producers, often SMEs, have a comparative advantage, allowing them to move up the value chain within those sectors into activities that are more complex.

Economic specialisations may differ even within countries, leading to different FDI impacts across regions. Specialisation patterns are often driven by natural endowments and regional assets that cannot be changed or can only be changed in the long run, such as geographic location, natural resources, urban or rural settings and demographics (OECD, 2007[42]). They are often the outcome of natural configurations, market dynamics and past economic and policy choices. For instance, metropolitan regions tend to have greater endowments of human and physical capital, including more favourable demographic structure, higher intensity of skills, and better infrastructure facilities. This leads to a high concentration of knowledge-intensive FDI in urban areas and therefore greater potential for market interactions with domestic firms compared to rural areas. Within OECD countries, there are rural regions that have higher rates of growth than urban regions (OECD, 2009[43]). These regions have found ways to exploit their resource endowment in an efficient manner – for instance through specialisation that takes into account place-based capabilities. Regional economies can, therefore, attract productivity-enhancing FDI with strong spillover potential based on location-specific comparative advantages.

Beyond economic specialisations, the exposure of an economy to international markets also matters for FDI impacts on productivity and innovation. Integration into GVCs is an important driver of aggregate productivity growth and can have important consequences on the ability (and incentives) of firms to exploit the knowledge transmitted through international production networks (Gal and Witheridge, 2019[44]). Domestic firms that are exposed to international markets (through forward and backward GVC participation) may be better equipped to develop linkages and partnerships with foreign investors.

The magnitude of knowledge spillovers often depends on the characteristics of FDI

There is emerging evidence that FDI concentration in high technology manufacturing is particularly beneficial for local SMEs. For example, in three Eastern European countries (i.e. Bulgaria, Poland and Romania), a recent study found that horizontal FDI spillovers (e.g. as a result of imitation and competition effects) are observed in labour-intensive sectors, while vertical FDI spillovers (e.g. related to buy and supply linkages) are mostly observed in high technology sectors (Nicolini and Resmini, 2010[45]). In the context of the United States, FDI spillovers are particularly strong in high technology sectors, while they are largely absent in low technology sectors (Keller and Yeaple, 2009[46]). Furthermore, low-productivity small firms benefit more from FDI spillovers than high-productivity larger firms do. FDI can however be isolated from the rest of the economy in high technology manufacturing. For example, Israel has succeeded in attracting many ICT R&D labs from large US-based MNEs (e.g. Intel, IBM, etc.); however, these labs are often self-contained and have developed limited relationships with the rest of the economy (OECD, 2016[47]; OECD, 2019[5]).

The type of FDI – greenfield investment or mergers/acquisitions – that a country attracts has implications on the extent of FDI linkages with the local economy. A greenfield investment is more likely to involve the implementation of a new technology in the host country and is therefore accompanied by a direct transfer of knowledge and technology from the parent firm to the new affiliate (Farole and Winkler, 2014[48]). On the other hand, the acquisition of a domestic firm allows foreign investors to primarily access the host country's technology as well as the already established business networks and knowledge sharing relationships possessed by the acquired firm. In this case, the deployment of the foreign investor's technology would be implemented more gradually, thus making knowledge spillovers to domestic firms less likely in the short term but may still occur in the longer term (Crespo and Fontoura, 2007[21]; Braconier, Ekholm and Knarvik, 2001[49]; Branstetter, Fisman and Foley, 2006[50]).

The degree and structure of foreign ownership is also an important factor affecting the strength of linkages between domestic and foreign firms. Empirical evidence shows that MNEs with fully foreign-owned affiliates exert greater control upon the technologies they transfer to their foreign locations and seek to avoid knowledge and technology leakages, thereby limiting the potential for FDI spillovers (Konwar et al., 2015[51]). In contrast, MNEs with more domestic participation may have greater potential for linkages with the local economy due to better knowledge of, and well-established relations with, domestic supplier networks (Farole and Winkler, 2014[39]). This is particularly the case for joint venture agreements, which have been found to have positive horizontal spillovers on local firms (Abraham, Konings and Slootmaekers, 2010[52]). However, as highlighted in the following sections, restrictions on foreign ownership as a means to achieve knowledge spillovers should be generally avoided as they have been found to deter FDI, especially when intellectual property rights are not protected (OECD, 2021[53]).

Turning to the motives of investments, foreign investors may enter a country to expand sales in a new, often large, market (i.e. market-seeking); to tap into natural resources (resource-seeking), which is often the case in commodity sectors and agribusiness; or to achieve efficiency (efficiency-seeking), either by reducing costs (e.g. labour costs) or by seizing new local assets in the form of technology, innovation and related skills. In general, FDI motives are often interlinked, so that they cannot be fully separated but rather emerge in combination.

Domestic firms with strong absorptive capacities are better positioned to integrate new knowledge and technologies into their production processes

Global production networks and the presence of foreign MNEs provide domestic firms with an important opportunity to increase their productivity and acquire new knowledge. Technology transfers are more effective when domestic firms possess previously accumulated knowledge and innovative capabilities. This set of knowledge and capabilities is generally identified by the literature as absorptive capacity (OECD, 2022[23]). More specifically, absorptive capacity is defined as the ability of the firm to acquire, assimilate and exploit the available information, knowledge and technology that comes through interaction with other firms (Cohen and Levinthal, 1990[54]; Todorova and Durisin, 2007[55]). It largely depends on the financial, human and knowledge-based capital of companies and their ability to access the strategic resources they need to adapt to market conditions, become more productive and innovate (i.e. access to finance, skills and innovation assets, including technology, data and networks).

Empirical evidence shows that the absorptive capacity of domestic firms is an important determinant of knowledge spillovers. Domestic suppliers with better technical capabilities tend to develop more knowledge-intensive types of linkages with foreign firms (Saliola and Zanfei, 2009[56]). FDI is also found to have a positive effect on domestic productivity growth when the technology gap between domestic and foreign firms is not too large (Nicolini and Resmini, 2010[45]). The absorptive capacity is typically measured in terms of performance gaps (e.g. productivity gaps) between foreign and domestic companies as illustrated in Figure 2.3 (OECD, 2019[2]; Gal and Witheridge, 2019[44]; Farole and Winkler, 2014[48]).

However, domestic firms vary in terms of size, business model, performance and ability to access and make use of the necessary strategic resources for their growth and upgrading. This heterogeneity means that different types of firms have different chances to enter into knowledge-sharing relationships with foreign MNEs. For instance, SMEs typically have greater difficulty in attracting skilled workers, face internal and external barriers in accessing finance, and often struggle to find the technology, information and networks that would enable them to participate in innovative activities with foreign MNEs (OECD, 2019[5]; 2020[57]; 2021[58]). Given that SMEs account for almost all enterprises in both OECD and developing economies, strengthening their absorptive capacities is key to enhancing FDI's spillover potential for domestic productivity and innovation (OECD, 2022[23]).

Recent OECD work on FDI-SME linkages and spillovers in Portugal and the Slovak Republic shows that cross-country differences in SME productivity and innovation performance can explain differences in the sourcing strategies of foreign MNEs. In Portugal, foreign investors source extensively from the domestic market, reflecting the fact that SMEs are relatively more innovative and digitally savvy than those in many other OECD economies (OECD, 2022[59]). In contrast, foreign investors in the Slovak Republic rely mainly on imports for the sourcing of inputs, which could be linked to the poor productivity performance and innovation capacity of the Slovak SME population.

Economic geography factors shape agglomeration and network dynamics, which are key for domestic firms to benefit from FDI's presence

Economic geography factors generate spatial and agglomeration effects. The localised nature of FDI means that geographical and cultural proximity between foreign and domestic firms affects the likelihood of knowledge spillovers, which often involve tacit knowledge, and whose strength decays with distance (Audretsch and Feldman, 1996[60]). Recent work confirms that when there are productivity spillovers from FDI, these are concentrated in the same region of the investment (Lembcke and Wildnerova, 2020[37];

Girma, Görg and Pisu, 2008[61]). When deciding where to invest, foreign firms are considering the specific factor endowment of a region – rather than just of the country. SME activity and performance are also unevenly distributed within countries, with high concentration of R&D and innovation activities and investments in few regions, and large cross-regional disparities in SME productivity (OECD, 2016[62]).

Agglomeration effects, notably through the presence of local industrial clusters, have been also reported to affect the volume of FDI and its potential for knowledge spillovers. Clusters embed characteristics such as industrial specialisation (through specialised skilled workers and suppliers) and geographical proximity that make knowledge spillovers more likely to happen, including from MNE operations. For the same reasons, MNEs can also expect to benefit from investing in local clusters, notably through the sourcing of local knowledge and technology. Evidence from the United Kingdom, Italy, Poland and Romania shows that firms located in clusters benefit from FDI, both in the same sector of the foreign affiliate and in other sectors. However, these benefits do not materialise for companies located outside the clusters (De Propris and Driffield, 2005[63]; Menghinello, De Propris and Driffield, 2010[64]; Franco and Kozovska, 2008[65]).

2.3. Policies that influence FDI impacts on productivity and innovation

Productivity and innovation impacts of FDI may not materialise automatically. Besides economic and market conditions, public policies and institutional arrangements play an important role in fostering positive FDI impacts. Policies and institutions are also essential to avoid negative implications that may result from the presence of foreign firms, such as crowding out of local SMEs and jobs (see Chapter 3). Most public policies do not specifically target foreign firms; they treat foreign and domestic investors alike. Yet, the extent to which they affect the two groups, and with that their outcomes on sustainable development, can vary. Laws, regulations and public support schemes directly affect foreign firms' choice of location, incentivise specific types of foreign firms to invest and keep away others.

The OECD Policy Framework for Investment (PFI) provides guidance on investment climate reforms that are concurrent with enabling investment for productivity growth (OECD, 2015[66]). Yet, ensuring that FDI leads to higher productivity levels and supports the competitiveness and innovation of domestic firms, in particular SMEs, requires more tailored policy considerations and increased focus on complementary policies outside the PFI, including industrial, innovation, SME and entrepreneurship policies. Given the important role that FDI can play in meeting territorial development objectives and alleviating (or sometimes exacerbating) regional disparities in economic growth and competitiveness, regional development policies are also key in shaping the economic geography of FDI impacts on productivity and innovation.

Interest in industrial policies has grown over the past decade as both OECD and developing economies are looking at how to strengthen their domestic industrial capacities, advance technological development, address the structural productivity slowdown and improve their global positioning in higher value-added segments of production (OECD, 2016[67]). There is a growing consensus that the risks associated with selective industrial policy and the influence of vested interests could be minimised. New industrial policies are increasingly focusing on market failure-correcting interventions that help build systems, create networks, develop institutions and align strategic priorities (Warwick, 2013[68]). OECD work on the role that industrial policies (including innovation and general business framework policies) can play in advancing the SDGs demonstrates that a diverse set of policy instruments (e.g. rewards and incentives, government assistance policies, compliance instruments), adequate business framework conditions, and enhanced focus on SMEs, innovative startups and local entrepreneurial ecosystems are needed to improve domestic productive capacities (OECD, 2021[69]).

This Policy Toolkit aims to provide a thorough assessment of policy initiatives, from national strategies and regulations to financial incentives and technical assistance programmes, at the intersection of these policy areas to help policy makers enhance the impacts of FDI on productivity and innovation (Table 2.1). It explains what institutional settings, regulatory conditions, policies and programmes are important ingredients of a policy mix that enables positive FDI impacts – both directly and through spillovers. The policy guidance provided in the following sections also incorporates OECD research on the contribution of FDI-SME linkages and spillovers to the productivity of local economies, based on evidence from policy approaches implemented in EU countries and regions (OECD, 2022[23]). The Policy Toolkit is structured around four broad principles and the policy instruments that support these principles (Table 2.1). Annex Table 2.A.2 provides a detailed checklist of questions for governments to self-assess their policy frameworks.

Table 2.1. Overview of the FDI Qualities Policy Toolkit for strengthening the impacts of FDI on productivity and innovation

Principle 1: Provide strategic direction and promote policy co-ordination and coherence on investment, innovation and SME development	Governance	National strategies and plans
		Oversight and co-ordination bodies
		Policy dialogue and evaluation of policy impacts
Principle 2: Ensure that domestic and international regulations create a conducive business environment for FDI-driven productivity growth and innovation	Domestic regulations	Legal framework for investment
		Competition policy and intellectual property rights protection
		Labour and financial market laws and regulations
		Regulatory incentives
		Regulatory impact assessments
	International agreements and standards	Innovation and SME policy provisions in IIAs
		Provisions on intellectual property rights, the digital economy, and competition in IIAs
Principle 3: Stimulate knowledge-intensive investment and support the productive capacities and innovation potential of the domestic economy	Financial support	Incentives for knowledge-intensive investment
		Financial support for SME internationalisation and innovation
		Incentives for business-to-business and science-to-business collaboration
	Technical support	Business and supplier development services
		Training and skills development services
		Network and knowledge infrastructure
		Cluster policies
Principle 4: Facilitate knowledge and technology spillovers from FDI by eliminating information barriers and administrative hurdles	Information & facilitation services	Investment promotion activities
		Investment facilitation and aftercare
		Information services, networking and knowledge exchange activities

2.3.1. Provide strategic direction and ensure policy co-ordination and coherence on investment, innovation and SME development

Ensure that national strategies can foster policy coherence and a whole-of-government approach to investment promotion, innovation and SME development

The institutional framework that governs the investment, innovation and SME development policy areas differs from country to country. Different governance arrangements are feasible as long as appropriate reporting mechanisms and communication channels are in place to ensure policy alignment among different institutions and tiers of government. To this end, clear responsibility and accountability among government institutions is a pre-condition for designing and implementing coherent and effective policies that strengthen the impact of FDI on productivity and innovation.

National strategies and action plans can be important instruments for policy coherence as they are crosscutting in nature and often require whole-of-government responses to ensure their effective implementation. Establishing a clear, overarching and comprehensive strategic framework for investment promotion policy allows to create an integrated vision across government and set out long-term strategic objectives, quantifiable targets, policy pillars, related programme actions and clearly defined roles for all the institutions involved in its implementation. Such a long-term and country-wide vision for inward investment attraction should sufficiently consider FDI's contribution to productivity growth, innovation promotion and SME development, and identify specific policy priorities, short-term and long-term targets, and policy interventions to achieve these objectives.

It is also critical that investment promotion strategies are not developed in silos, but are sufficiently aligned with and include cross-references to national strategies addressing innovation, SME and industrial policy issues. Many OECD countries have dedicated national strategies on these policy areas, while others mainstream relevant policy priorities in economic reform programmes, sectoral action plans and national development strategies. As part of their policy response to the supply chain disruptions caused by the COVID-19 pandemic, both Ireland and the Czech Republic have recently developed dedicated SME and entrepreneurship strategies, focusing on strengthening their productivity, internationalisation and innovation including through linkages with foreign MNEs (OECD, 2021[8]). Conversely, many investment and innovation promotion strategies increasingly consider the role that FDI can play in strengthening the domestic R&D ecosystem. The national investment strategies of Norway, Spain, Slovenia and the UK include specific measures aimed at supporting the upgrading of SMEs in GVCs, while the Czech Republic's National Research, Development and Innovation Policy Strategy (2016-20) foresees business support measures to help SMEs become more involved in international R&D collaborations (OECD, 2019[5]).

Ensure effective policy co-ordination and multi-level governance in the design and implementation of investment promotion, innovation and SME policies

Actions to improve the impact of FDI on productivity and innovation need to be aligned with the objectives and priorities set by government across different policy areas. This often entails co-operating with a number of government institutions at national and subnational levels. Although co-ordination is a fundamental and longstanding problem for public administration, much of the success or failure of attempts to co-ordinate appear to depend upon country contexts, including the complexity of the institutional setting and the co-ordination instruments at play. In many OECD and developing economies, the institutional framework governing investment promotion, innovation and SME policies is structured along lines reflecting different policy domains. In Belgium, Portugal and Canada, for instance, several implementing agencies operate across the three policy areas under the supervision of different ministries. Such institutional settings may induce more complex governance systems – i.e. higher risks of information asymmetry, transaction costs and trade-offs – and require strong inter-institutional co-ordination mechanisms to overcome potential policy silos. In contrast, other governments (e.g. Croatia, Finland, Lithuania, Luxembourg, and Slovenia) target the entire FDI-SME-innovation ecosystem through a single government entity to facilitate co-ordination and synergies among different policy domains.

Irrespective of the complexity of the institutional setting, the set-up of effective inter-institutional co-ordination mechanisms at the strategic and policy implementation level is key. Instruments of co-ordination can be formal or informal; based on regulation, incentives, norms and information sharing; top-down relying on the authority of a lead government body, or bottom-up and emergent. For instance, high-level government councils can bring together line ministries responsible for investment, SME, innovation and industrial policy issues, implementing agencies and regional and local governments to identify priority areas where cross-ministerial policy planning and decision-making is necessary. In many countries, some of these councils are also responsible for the co-ordination of national strategies while others have been given broader mandates to foster policy dialogue, convene stakeholders and issue opinions on legislative initiatives.

At the policy implementation level, the establishment of inter-agency working groups, committees and task forces can help policy makers pull resources from different parts of government to effectively advance specific policy agendas. Inter-agency joint programming can also facilitate the implementation of crosscutting measures that span several policy areas, in particular in countries with highly fragmented institutional settings (e.g. large number of public institutions involved in policy design and implementation). In these country contexts, the Centre of Government, i.e. the office serving the highest level of the executive branch of government (e.g. presidents, prime ministers), can also play an important role in bridging bureaucratic boundaries across ministries and improving the enforcement of policy decisions. Finally, informal channels of communication between officials or job circulation of civil servants can play an important role in improving co-ordination and often suggest a relatively well-developed culture of inter-agency trust and communication.

Beyond horizontal co-ordination, effective multi-level governance is also key to ensuring policy effectiveness. Given the localised nature of foreign MNEs' operations and the economic geography factors affecting FDI spillovers, policies aimed at strengthening FDI impacts on productivity and innovation require synergies among various levels of government and complementary expertise from regional and local actors. Responsibilities assigned to different tiers of government should therefore be clearly defined to reduce potential duplication and overlaps. Subnational governments (e.g. regional authorities, municipalities, regional development agencies) have better knowledge of local market needs and greater potential to interact with local business enterprises, foreign or domestic. Their active involvement in the design and implementation of investment promotion, innovation and SME support policies can help unlock the growth potential of the territories where these are implemented by drawing on the knowledge and expertise of local actors and linking investment promotion and SME development priorities to regional and local development strategies.

Assess the impact of FDI and relevant policies on the productivity and innovation of the domestic economy and promote policy dialogue to enhance the effectiveness of policy interventions

Monitoring and evaluation (M&E) practices have been at the centre of governance frameworks as a result of the emergence of multi-dimensional policy issues and the increasing expectations over the effectiveness of public policy. The systematic collection of disaggregated data for the assessment of FDI impacts on productivity and innovation can help governments assess the economic and market conditions that underpin FDI-driven productivity growth, identify market failures and possible policy responses. The OECD FDI Qualities Indicators allow policy makers to make the necessary link between investment and host economy impacts, and assess how FDI supports national policy objectives with regard to productivity, innovation, SME growth and upgrading (OECD, 2019[2]).

Furthermore, a comprehensive framework for evaluating the impact of policies on foreign direct investors, local SMEs and other actors of the domestic research and innovation ecosystem (e.g. R&D organisations, technology parks, applied research centres, collaborative laboratories, universities) could play a crucial role as an "early warning mechanism" to identify potential policy gaps and take corrective action. For line ministries and implementing agencies responsible for investment promotion, it is critical that impacts on innovation, R&D and the capacities of domestic firms are sufficiently considered when measuring success in reaching the policy objectives of related investment promotion measures. In fact, 53% of OECD IPAs and 60% of MENA IPAs use innovation and R&D-related performance indicators when measuring the impact of their policy actions in the economy (OECD, 2018[70]). Policy impacts on the capacities of domestic firms are also evaluated by 22% of OECD IPAs and 60% of MENA IPAs.

For many OECD and developing countries, the development of better systems to track and collect reliable statistical data based on international standards is a pre-requisite to the development of more robust outcome indicators, including on productivity and innovation. The use of qualitative evaluation methodologies (e.g. surveys, benchmarking, consultations), and the establishment of data tracking tools and feedback processes can ensure that relevant and reliable data on the impact of policy interventions are available. Co-ordination and collaboration between investment promotion, innovation and SME agencies can facilitate the exchange of data, experiences and expertise. Apart from the use of quantifiable outcome-based performance indicators, a reliable assessment of policy impacts also requires strong internal capacity to plan, prepare and execute ex ante and ex post evaluations. Setting up dedicated evaluation units within implementing agencies and involving specialised staff with technical knowledge of M&E principles and implementation tools could strengthen internal competences and improve the effectiveness of their programmes.

Active engagement and consultation with foreign direct investors, local SMEs and R&D organisations is necessary for the effective implementation of relevant policies. Through their interactions with the private sector, public institutions are able to understand the challenges and expectations of foreign and domestic firms, receive feedback on the relevance of their policy programmes, and enrich policy making processes with insights from various stakeholders of the domestic research and innovation ecosystem. Mechanisms for regular public-private dialogue within specific sectors and supply chains should be combined with bottom-up communication processes to ensure that local level market needs and perspectives are fed into higher-level policy processes.

2.3.2. Ensure that domestic and international regulations create a conducive business environment for FDI-driven productivity growth and innovation

Ensure an open, transparent and non-discriminatory regulatory environment for productive and knowledge-intensive investment

An open and non-discriminatory regulatory environment can increase the amount and spillover potential of FDI and strengthen the absorptive capacities of domestic firms, in particular SMEs (Figure 2.5). Fewer restrictions for investments in more productive, innovative and knowledge-intensive sectors can increase the direct impact that foreign firms have through their own activities on sectoral and aggregate productivity growth. Openness to FDI may not only affect productivity in industries that get market access, but also those in downstream sectors that benefit from potentially better access to high quality inputs and services domestically. Recent OECD work on Southeast Asia shows that liberalising FDI in services is positively associated with productivity in downstream manufacturing industries, where SMEs benefit in particular (OECD, 2019[71]).

FDI spillovers also tend to be larger in countries that are more open towards trade (Meyer and Sinani, 2009[72]; Havranek and Irsova, 2011[73]; Du, Harrison and Jefferson, 2011[74]). A study on Thailand's manufacturing sector, found that technology spillovers from FDI to the domestic economy happen predominantly in sectors with low trade restrictions, while evidence from China's entry into the World Trade Organisation (WTO) suggests that vertical backward spillovers increased after its accession when tariffs were lowered and domestic content restrictions relaxed (Du, Harrison and Jefferson, 2011[74]). Trade openness can also shape the absorptive capacity of domestic firms, which are more exposed to international competition in an open trade regime, and therefore more likely to access new markets, participate in GVCs, and produce intermediate goods required by foreign investors (Havranek and Irsova, 2011[73]).

FDI-driven productivity growth and innovation may not automatically materialise just because a country is able to attract FDI (Alfaro, 2017[75]). Competition rules that ensure a level playing field for foreign and domestic firms facilitate the entry of foreign investors and, at the same time, incentivise domestic firms to become more productive, innovate and improve the quality of their products (Lembcke and Wildnerova, 2020[37]). Firms exposed to stronger competition might also be better prepared to imitate good practices from foreign firms. As described in Section 2.2, competition and imitation effects are an important channel through which knowledge and technology spillovers from FDI take place in the host economy. In this context, it is important to assess the degree to which laws and policies promote or inhibit competition in areas of the product and services markets where competition is viable.

Figure 2.5. FDI openness in services and productivity in downstream manufacturing sectors

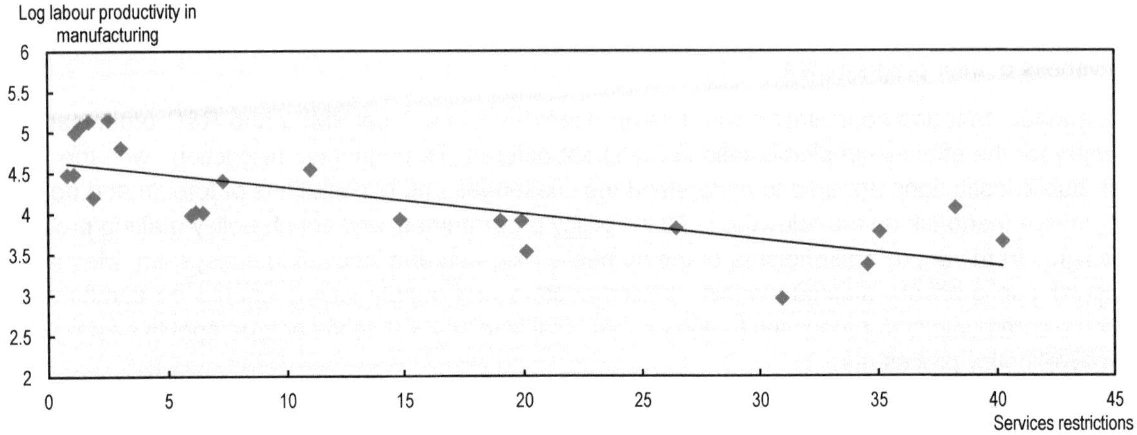

Note: Analysis is based on firm-level data from 23 OECD and developing countries; see methodology in OECD (2019[71]). Services restrictions are based on the OECD FDI Regulatory Restrictiveness Index.
Source: OECD (2019[71]), *OECD Investment Policy Reviews: Southeast Asia*, http://www.oecd.org/investment/oecd-investment-policy-review-southeast-asia.htm

Policies that ensure intellectual property rights (IPR) protection are also important as they guarantee the appropriability of knowledge and innovation benefits, and determine the qualities of FDI that can be attracted. Empirical evidence suggests that where rights are strong, foreign firms are not only more likely to invest but are also more likely to engage in local R&D and more willing to share new technologies with local partners through joint ventures and licensing agreements (OECD, 2015[66]). Branstetter et al. (Branstetter, Fisman and Foley, 2006[50]) find that US MNEs respond to changes in IPR regimes abroad by increasing technology transfer to their affiliates in countries that undertake reforms to strengthen IPRs. Similarly, Javorcik (2004[14]) finds that, in Central and Eastern Europe, the strength of patent laws as well as the overall level of IPR protection increases the likelihood of attracting FDI in several high technology sectors where IPRs play an important role. Foreign investors are also found to be more likely to engage in local production, as opposed to focusing solely on setting up distribution networks, in countries with stronger IPR regimes, increasing therefore the potential for more linkages with the local economy.

Several countries have chosen to introduce local content requirements (LCRs) to induce foreign firms to use domestically manufactured goods or domestically supplied services in exchange for market access in certain strategic sectors. Recent OECD work shows that, while LCRs may help governments achieve certain short-term objectives in targeted industries (e.g. potential learning and technological spillovers, economies of scale), they undermine long-term competitiveness and may prove to be detrimental for FDI attraction and productivity growth in the long run (Stone, Messent and Flaig, 2015[76]). LCRs may restrain competition from imports, which might contribute to higher production costs and ultimately higher prices to downstream industries and consumers. The literature on the potential effects of LCRs also points to potential market distortions and inefficiencies arising from a suboptimal allocation of resources. They may undermine the original goals for imposing LCRs. Targeted incentives that generate less negative economy-wide effects and do not impede market access may be preferable to incentivise linkages between FDI and domestic firms (see section on financial support and technical assistance).

Consider the impact of laws and regulations on business capacity and incentives to engage in innovation and technology development

Firm size is a determinant of absorptive capacity and a critical factor shaping a firm's ability to move towards high value added, knowledge-based production. OECD and developing economies are often dominated by SMEs with low productivity, which may find it difficult to grow and obtain a critical scale that would allow them to join GVCs, participate in innovation activities and become suppliers and partners of foreign firms. Overly burdensome regulations often perpetuate informality, particularly of smaller and less productive firms, which have less capacity to screen the regulatory landscape and allocate the necessary resources to address legal and regulatory requirements (OECD, 2018[77]). It is important that a conducive business environment is created and regulatory hurdles removed to enable small businesses to expand. These include areas such as the ease of registering a business, dealing with reporting and tax compliance requirements, trading across borders, resolving insolvency and dealing with licence and permit systems.

Stringent regulations can also deter innovation by imposing high compliance costs that reduce the attractiveness of R&D and limit the capacity of domestic entrepreneurs and foreign firms to experiment with alternative business and production models (Davidson, Kauffmann and de Liedekerke, 2021[78]). One option for encouraging FDI-driven productivity growth and innovation is to develop laws and regulations that are sufficiently flexible and forward-looking to anticipate and adapt to fast-changing technologies. This is particularly the case for regulations addressing issues related to digital innovation (e.g. use of AI applications, robotics, Internet of Things). Related technological standards should be also updated regularly to catch up with the latest market developments. Finally, regulatory impact assessment (RIA) tools and processes should move beyond assessing the economic impacts of regulations (e.g. impacts on competition, economic growth, etc.) to also cover impacts on SME competitiveness, innovation and the internationalisation of the economy.

In many countries, the simplification of the regulatory framework is often combined with targeted easing of the regulatory burden for certain types of investment. This usually comes in the form of special investment regimes granted to FDI projects that are deemed to be of strategic importance for the host economy, giving access to expedited administrative and licensing procedures. These special regimes are usually predicated on certain conditions such as creating a number of jobs, investing in knowledge-intensive and productivity-enhancing sectors, or benefitting specific geographic areas. In Portugal, for instance, the government has introduced several special regulatory regimes allowing investors to benefit from simplified licensing procedures, conditional to introducing innovative and technology-based production processes in co-operation with domestic R&D institutions (OECD, 2022[59]). Many developing countries have also established special economic zones (SEZs) as a tool to attract FDI that creates linkages with the local economy.

Evidence on the effectiveness of these regulatory measures has been mixed. Anecdotal evidence on their impacts, in particular of the SEZs, shows that they have often failed to sustain innovation and competitiveness over time, delivering little technological upgrading or new firm creation. In many instances, SEZs have been criticised for negative social and environmental impacts as a result of excessive competition between regions and a misuse of resources and land where the SEZs are located (Farole and Akinci, 2011[79]; OECD, 2018[80]). In principle, regulatory concessions should not be used as a substitute for improving the general investment climate but instead be embedded in broader national development strategies. Accompanying measures need to be in place to generate productivity spillovers on the rest of the economy, including supplier development programmes, business matchmaking services, and initiatives to engage the private sector and local education institutions in cluster building activities.

It is also critical that policy efforts to reduce the regulatory burden on business do not lead to a "race to the bottom" in terms of social and environmental standards (see chapters 3, 4 and 5). This becomes even more crucial for industries driven by digital innovation, which rely on alternative business models and often lead to new and more precarious forms of employment or weakened social protection conditions (OECD,

2020[81]). In fact, regulation should mitigate the potential socio-economic risks arising from the adoption of new, innovative and digitally enabled business models while at the same time ensuring that regulatory responses are proportional, set out some level of certainty and predictability, and do not stifle the innovation potential of the economy.

Ensure that labour market regulations facilitate FDI spillovers through labour mobility

Labour market regulations shape FDI impacts on productivity and innovation by affecting the potential for knowledge and technology spillovers through labour mobility (see section 2.2) and the availability of skills in the local labour force. Recent evidence from EU countries shows that less rigid labour markets with strong absorptive capacities are better positioned to moderate any adverse labour market effects of FDI, in particular the crowding out of employees in domestic firms, which occurs when foreign and domestic firms compete for the same scarce labour resources (Becker et al., 2020[36]). In contrast, the benefits for a local economy from FDI are lowest where there exist a combination of stringent employment protection legislation and low absorptive capacities. This is because foreign firms seek to attract local talent by offering higher wages that less productive domestic firms are unable to match. Increased wage disparities coupled with rigid labour market conditions limit the ability of domestic firms to retain and attract skilled workers, holding back labour mobility and the potential for knowledge spillovers that this entails.

These findings highlight the need to examine labour market regulations and their role in FDI-driven productivity growth by looking at how they relate to other drivers of FDI impacts, namely domestic SME performance and the availability (or lack) of skills in the local labour force. Spillovers from labour mobility cannot be fully leveraged unless structural challenges related to the absorptive capacities of domestic firms, in particular SMEs, are addressed, and the complexity of hiring regulations reduced (and with that the disproportionate impact they may have on small businesses). Targeted measures that allow micro and small firms to be exempted from certain procedural requirements or other hiring restrictions of the labour legislation can facilitate the movement of highly skilled workers from foreign affiliates to the domestic entrepreneurial ecosystem.

Encouraging the uptake of permanent employment can also have a positive impact on domestic firms' willingness to invest in job training of their employees, which is an important component of a firm's absorptive capacity. Evidence on the role of employment protection regulations in shaping the incentives of firms to invest in formal training shows that enforcing stricter hiring regulations for temporary contracts and less rigid regulations for dismissals of permanent workers is associated with higher investment by firms in the human capital of their employees (Almeida and Aterido, 2011[82]). Similarly, a stricter enforcement of employment protection regulation is found to have a positive impact on firms' willingness to upskill their employees. This is mainly because firms have greater incentive to invest in firm-specific knowledge and skills for employees who stay longer on the job and seek to exploit the career advancement opportunities provided by the firm (OECD, 2020[83]). Chapter 3 provides a detailed analysis of the positive impacts that labour market regulations can have on human capital formation.

Linked to the need for a skilled labour force is the increasing number of governments that introduce regulatory incentives to encourage workforce skills development and facilitate the immigration of business talent as a way to help domestic economies address labour shortages. Some OECD countries have introduced statutory rights for employees for training leave – however, their take-up is generally not high with less than 2% of employees benefitting from such measures (OECD, 2019[5]). In recent years, there has been also an increase of entrepreneur visa programmes (e.g. Startup Visa, Tech Visa), which seek to attract innovative entrepreneurs and highly skilled workers by allowing them to obtain residence and employment rights. For the visa to be granted, entrepreneurs usually have to demonstrate solid business and financial plans and undertake innovative activities in knowledge-intensive sectors. The impact of these schemes on the productivity and innovation of domestic economies is not clear yet, but other factors such as labour market conditions, the presence of a thriving startup ecosystem, and the quality of the business environment are thought to be key determinants.

Ensure that financial market laws and regulations facilitate access to finance for innovative and technology-intensive activities

Well-functioning financial markets can facilitate FDI spillovers by enabling SMEs to access supply chain finance and secure investments for entrepreneurial activity. Studies find that well-developed financial markets can strengthen the absorptive capacity of domestic firms and provide the liquidity that SMEs need to export, develop new products and invest in technology upgrading (Farole and Winkler, 2014[48]). For many SMEs, the high fixed costs of establishing a distribution network and adjusting their products for overseas standards, often require external finance (OECD, 2020[57]). Similarly, access to finance is an important condition for foreign firms that seek to finance collaborative technology-based projects or enter into partnerships with domestic firms (for instance, through joint ventures).

Financial stability risks (e.g. low bank profitability, high sovereign and corporate debt) and structural market deficiencies (e.g. underdeveloped equity markets and credit rating systems, insufficient market liquidity, weak contract enforcement, inefficiencies in the judicial system, etc.) are often the most common causes that hold back the necessary capital that foreign and domestic firms need to expand their operations. Governments can play an important role in improving access to credit by creating a regulatory environment that provides flexible collateral options and transparent legal recourse in cases of default, and by establishing easily accessible financial support schemes (OECD, 2019[5]). Regulatory reforms that facilitate market-based long-term debt financing, increase the availability of alternative financing instruments, and promote access to equity capital through the stock market can help free up capital for innovative business projects. Raising awareness about alternative forms of financing such as crowdfunding, venture capital and business angels, and encouraging firms to source finance from equity markets can also further stimulate innovative business activities.

Integrate innovation and SME policy considerations into international investment agreements

Most investment treaties in force today do not contain provisions that seek expressly to promote productivity and innovation. Rather, they have tended to focus almost exclusively on providing legal protections to investors. Recent international investment agreements (IIAs) concluded in the past decade, especially free trade agreements (FTAs) that address investment issues, have covered broader policy areas beyond investment protection that pertain to fostering international co-operation on science, technology and innovation (STI) policy and strengthening the capacities of SMEs to engage in international trade and investment.

Recent IIAs address regulatory issues affecting host country SMEs by envisaging international co-operation and dialogue to promote investment opportunities for SMEs in the economies of the treaty parties (Clicteur et al., 2021[84]). SME-specific provisions may take the form of standalone chapters, or be mainstreamed across FTA chapters dealing with e-commerce, trade facilitation, procurement, investment and trade in services (Box 2.2). The degree of commitment that they require varies; from general principles emphasising the importance of SMEs in international trade and investment, to binding agreements on simplified administrative procedures for SMEs trading or investing abroad, and commitments to the establishment of dedicated SME Committees to ensure co-operation and information sharing among treaty signatories (UKTPO, 2020[85]; Lodrant and Cernat, 2017[86]). These initiatives may help SMEs to overcome a lack of familiarity with foreign markets as well as logistical, managerial and other challenges when trading or investing abroad. By facilitating the internationalisation of host country SMEs, these provisions can also increase the exposure of SMEs to international competition and improve their capacities to become suppliers and partners of foreign firms, including foreign direct investors located in their own countries.

The inclusion of STI provisions in bilateral investment treaties (BITs) and regional trade agreements (RTAs) is another channel through which governments often seek to signal their readiness to attract FDI in high-technology areas, promote international co-operation on technology transfer issues and strengthen domestic innovation capabilities. Provisions on intellectual property rights (IPRs) are the most commonly found STI provisions in IIAs (Stone, Kim and Engen, 2017[87]). They often include general principles stressing the importance of IPRs for innovation and economic growth; binding commitments on specific IP issues (e.g. minimum standards for IP protection, use and enforcement of IPRs, settlement of IP disputes); and bilateral or multilateral co-operation provisions. The economy-wide effects of including IPR provisions in RTAs or BITs have seldom been quantified, but it is widely accepted that they can support innovation in the treaty party economies to the extent that they lead to improvements in domestic laws in these areas (WTO, 2014[88]). New IIAs concluded over the past few years have been also increasingly incorporating more general provisions on the digital economy (e.g. data protection, cybersecurity, data localisation and online consumer protection rules) as well as STI co-operation (Stone, Kim and Engen, 2017[87]). The latter usually seek to facilitate the exchange of information on cross-border innovation programmes, the joint conduct of R&D projects; the exchange of country visits of specialised delegations, industry representatives, universities and research centres; and the promotion of public-private sector partnerships for the development of innovative products and services (Box 2.2).

Another feature of some recent IIAs that can affect productivity and innovation is disciplines on performance requirements. These provisions, inspired by the WTO TRIMs Agreement, prohibit treaty parties from imposing mandatory performance requirements on incoming foreign investors such as forced technology transfers, local content or R&D quotas. As outlined in the previous section, performance requirements have been found to deter FDI inflows and undermine the long-term competitiveness of the domestic economy. Some IIAs adopt a more nuanced approach by creating express exceptions or reservations in some areas (e.g. allowing governments to impose technology transfers on foreign investors as part of investment screening review processes) or allowing governments to attach certain conditions to non-mandatory advantages offered under domestic law (e.g. incentive schemes, tax breaks, subsidies, etc.) that would require foreign investors to perform in some way to benefit the domestic economy (e.g. locate production, train or employ workers, carry out R&D locally, etc.). The impacts of such policies need to be carefully weighed and examined alongside other factors that drive FDI spillovers such as the productive capacities of domestic firms and the availability (or lack) of skills in the local labour market.

Some recent IIAs also contain government commitments on market access, investment facilitation and promoting fair competition that may generate tangible impacts for productivity and innovation. Through the elimination of regulatory barriers to investment based on nationality, IIAs can stimulate more potential FDI primarily based on market considerations, which in turn can generate many benefits for host economies as described above. Greater openness to foreign competition can lead to new competition for local SMEs, which may stimulate greater productivity or lead to crowding-out effects depending on the maturity of the domestic market. In addition to market access barriers, businesses can face myriad other obstacles to effective entry and success of FDI in foreign markets. Recent IIAs have sought to alleviate these barriers through rules to address problems such as transfers and visas for personnel, clarity on different environmental and technical standards, a lack of transparency in regulatory procedures, or logistics issues.

Box 2.2. STI co-operation and SME facilitation provisions in international trade and investment agreements

The EU-Canada Comprehensive Economic and Trade Agreement (CETA)

Article 25.5: Enhanced co-operation on science, technology, research and innovation

1. The Parties acknowledge the interdependence of science, technology, research and innovation, and international trade and investment in increasing industrial competitiveness and social and economic prosperity.
2. Building upon this shared understanding, the Parties agree to strengthen their co-operation in the areas of science, technology, research and innovation.
3. The Parties shall endeavour to encourage, develop and facilitate co-operative activities on a reciprocal basis in support of, or supplementary to the Agreement for Scientific and Technological Co-operation between the European Community and Canada, done at Halifax on 17 June 1995. The Parties agree to conduct these activities on the basis of the following principles: (a) the activities are of mutual benefit to the Parties; (b) the Parties agree on the scope and parameters of the activities; and (c) the activities should take into account the important role of the private sector and research institutions in the development of science, technology, research and innovation, and the commercialisation of goods and services thereof.
4. The Parties also recognise the importance of enhanced co-operation in science, technology, research and innovation, such as activities initiated, developed or undertaken by a variety of stakeholders, including the Canadian federal government, the Canadian Provinces and Territories, the European Union and its Member States.
5. Each Party shall encourage, in accordance with its law, the participation of the private sector, research institutions and civil society within its territory in activities to enhance co-operation.

The Trans-Pacific Partnership (TPP) Agreement

Article 24.2: Committee on SMEs

1. The Parties hereby establish a Committee on SMEs (Committee), composed of government representatives of each Party.
2. The Committee shall: (a) identify ways to assist SMEs of the Parties to take advantage of the commercial opportunities under this Agreement; (b) exchange and discuss each Party's experiences and best practices in supporting and assisting SME exporters with respect to, among other things, training programmes, trade education, trade finance, identifying commercial partners in other Parties and establishing good business credentials; (c) develop and promote seminars, workshops or other activities to inform SMEs of the benefits available to them under this Agreement; (d) explore opportunities for capacity building to assist the Parties in developing and enhancing SME export counselling, assistance and training programmes; (e) recommend additional information that a Party may include on the website referred to in Article 24.1 (Information Sharing); (f) review and co-ordinate the Committee's work programme with those of other committees, working groups and any subsidiary body established under this Agreement, as well as those of other relevant international bodies, in order not to duplicate those work programmes and to identify appropriate opportunities for co-operation to improve the ability of SMEs to engage in trade and investment opportunities provided by this Agreement; (g) facilitate the development of programmes to assist SMEs to participate and integrate effectively into the global supply chain; (h) exchange information to assist in monitoring the implementation of this Agreement as it relates to SMEs; (i) submit a report of its activities on a regular basis and make appropriate recommendations to the

Commission; and (j) consider any other matter pertaining to SMEs as the Committee may decide, including any issues raised by SMEs regarding their ability to benefit from this Agreement.

3. The Committee shall meet within one year of the date of entry into force of this Agreement, and thereafter as necessary.

Source: (European Commission, 2021[89]; USTR, 2021[90])

2.3.3. Stimulate knowledge-intensive investment and support the productive capacities and innovation potential of the domestic economy

Implement clearly defined, transparent and rules-based investment incentive schemes that target FDI in productive and knowledge-intensive activities

Investment incentives are widely used by governments to attract investors, promote investment in specific sectors or locations, and encourage or discourage certain types of business activities (Box 2.3). They can take many forms, including direct financial support, tax relief and regulatory concessions.[1]

Direct funding (e.g. grants, loans and guarantees, provision of infrastructure and land, other subsidised goods and services) is often used to compensate foreign investors for the perceived disadvantages of a particular location or subsidise the actual costs of relocating corporate units (e.g. job training costs, expatriation support, temporary wage subsidies). It represents a more selective form of public support as it allows governments to target investment projects that they consider to generate public goods (e.g. green technology, social innovation and other novel areas) or have a high potential for knowledge spillovers (OECD, 2015[91]; 2021[92]). Grants and other forms of direct support may therefore be valuable to promote mission-oriented innovation that offers high economic and social returns. Tax incentives, on the other hand, such as tax holidays, tax credits, accelerated depreciation allowances, consist of an easing of the tax burden on the investing companies (Table 2.2). They are usually granted to all firms that qualify for a set of pre-defined conditions, leaving the selection of supported projects to firms. In principle, their non-discretionary nature makes it easier and less costly for governments to administer.[2] Ultimately, the optimal mix of investment incentives (i.e. direct versus indirect financial support) depends on the specific policy goals, market conditions and country contexts.

Investment incentives are not always aligned with the objective to enhance domestic resource mobilisation for productivity and innovation. They can distort competition and resource allocation, reduce the revenue-raising capacity of the public administration, increase administrative and compliance costs, and are not always cost-effective in attracting investment that creates linkages with the host economy (Celani, Dressler and Wermelinger, 2022[93]; IMF-OECD-UN-World Bank, 2015[94]). Transparency around investment incentives is also often lacking as responsibility for their granting is usually spread among multiple agencies and stipulated in numerous pieces of legislation. If used, governments should ensure that incentives address a well-identified market failure such as information asymmetries between foreign and domestic firms, the inherent risks and uncertainty arising from engaging in innovation, or the high fixed costs of undertaking technology-intensive activities (Martin and Scott, 2000[95]). The design, eligibility conditions, sectoral targeting and administration of incentive schemes should be also taken into consideration. Different types of incentives present advantages and disadvantages related to their financial and administrative costs, their impact on economic and social conditions, and their effectiveness in attracting productivity-enhancing FDI.

Box 2.3. Investment incentives for knowledge- and technology-intensive activities in Thailand and Rwanda

Thailand

Following the development of its investment promotion strategy in 2015, Thailand moved from a system of location-based investment incentives (economic zones) to an activity- and merit-based one, with emphasis on SME linkages, R&D investments and skills development (OECD, 2021[53]). Thailand's investment promotion policy aims to attract investment into research and development (R&D) projects in 10 target sectors and particularly in areas that involve technologies in which Thailand is considered to have potential to enhance the country's overall competitiveness. Supported investment projects must involve a component on technology transfer by co-operating with educational and research institutions, for example via programmes of the National Science and Technology Development Agency (NSTDA) or the Thailand Institute of Scientific and Technological Research.

Activity-based incentives are granted for knowledge-based activities as well as investment projects that strengthen supply chain development. Merit-based incentives provide an add-on to the basic scheme with additional corporate income tax (CIT) exemptions and tax deductions if a project undertakes R&D or skills development activities or locates in specific regions and industrial zones. In 2017, the government amended the Investment Promotion Act to introduce an additional set of technology-based incentives that grant CIT exemption for up to 10 years to projects with targeted core technology development such as biotechnology, nanotechnology, advanced materials technology and digital technology.

Rwanda

In January 2021, Rwanda enacted a new Investment Promotion and Facilitation Law, which introduces new priority sectors and various tax incentives aimed at improving the competitiveness and productivity of the economy and make Kigali, the country's capital, a hub for innovative investors and startups (Government of Rwanda, 2021[96]). Investments in the construction of specialised industrial and innovation parks, R&D and skills development facilities, creative arts, e-mobility and high-value horticulture figure among the new priority economic activities that will drive Rwanda's investment promotion policy in the coming decade. Foreign firms that establish a R&D facility, ICT training centre, software build and test lab, ICT specialised institution or a business incubator benefit from a 15% preferential CIT rate. The incentives apply for investments that take place in the Kigali Innovation City, a technology cluster area located in Kigali's special economic zone.

Rwanda's new investment law also exhibits a strong focus on the role that small investors and startups can play in spurring innovation and productivity growth. Small, medium and emerging investors are given access to a Seed Innovation Fund that will provide grants, loans and equity for training costs, technology acquisition, professional services and costs incurred on intellectual property rights. A 150% tax deduction also applies to expenditures relating to internationalisation activities (e.g. exports, participation in overseas trade fairs and business missions, etc.). In an effort to attract business talent, innovative foreign entrepreneurs are eligible for a two-year entrepreneurship visa to start or move their business to Rwanda, while highly skilled international students can apply for a two-year talent visa to gain access to the local labour market.

Table 2.2. Tax incentives targeting SME linkages, exports/GVC linkages, SEZs, R&D and high-tech activities in ASEAN countries

	Local sourcing, SME linkages	R&D and other strategic sectors	High-tech activities	Exports, GVC linkages	Less developed regions and SEZs
Brunei Darussalam		Deduction	Deduction		
Cambodia				Trade tax exemption	Trade tax exemption
Indonesia			Tax holiday		Deduction, trade tax exemption
Laos				Trade tax exemption	Tax holiday
Malaysia	Tax holiday, reduction	Tax holiday, reduction	Tax holiday, reduction	Trade tax exemption	Reduction
Myanmar		Deduction		Trade tax exemption	Reduction
Singapore		Deduction	Tax holiday, deduction		Trade tax exemption
Thailand	Deduction	Deduction			Tax holiday
Viet Nam		Deduction	Deduction		Tax holiday, reduction, trade tax exemption

Note: Tax holiday = total income tax exemption over defined period; reduction = income tax rate reduction over defined period; deduction = deductions of certain expenses from taxable income; tax credits = deduction of certain expenses from payable taxes (loss carried forward and accelerated depreciation also fall under this category for simplicity); trade tax exemption = exemption from import duties, export taxes or VAT.
Source: OECD (2019[71]), *OECD Investment Policy Reviews: Southeast Asia*, http://www.oecd.org/investment/oecd-investment-policy-review-southeast-asia.htm

For instance, cross-country differences in the generosity of R&D tax incentives can lead to differences in the cost of capital faced by firms – and subsequently encourage or discourage them from increasing their R&D investment or locating their R&D functions in a given country (González Cabral, Appelt and Hanappi, 2021[97]; OECD, 2021[98]). Moreover, there is growing anecdotal evidence suggesting that income-based tax incentives (e.g. tax holidays, preferential tax rates), which reduce the rate applied to profits/income already secured, tend to attract mobile activities rather than long-term FDI projects that are more likely to create linkages with the local economy and generate knowledge spillovers (OECD, 2019[71]). Income-based tax incentives may also have limited effectiveness in attracting new investment and often come at a substantial cost to a country by resulting in windfall gains for projects that would already have taken place in the absence of the incentive. In contrast, expenditure-based tax incentives – such as tax deductions, tax credits, and accelerated depreciation – that lower the cost of specific inputs of production factors allow to link investments to performance criteria that support progress towards specific development objectives, including innovation promotion and linkages with domestic firms.

Beyond the type of incentive, more targeted approaches in terms of supported sectors and activities should be preferred (OECD, 2021[99]). Governments could consider making the granting of direct financial support and tax relief conditional to creating linkages with domestic SMEs, undertaking R&D locally, or investing in more productive, knowledge-intensive and high-tech sectors. Recent OECD evidence from 36 developing economies shows that an increasing number of countries are adopting tax incentives that include outcome conditions associated with the SDGs (e.g. export promotion, skills development, local linkages) (Celani, Dressler and Wermelinger, 2022[93]). The conditions and criteria for the granting of incentives should be transparent, clearly defined and rules-based to facilitate their verification, avoid discretionary and distortive granting decisions, and strengthen the link to the intended policy goal of increasing productivity gains for the domestic economy. When the provision of financial support depends on discretionary decisions by government agencies, selection processes must be competitive and designed so as to ensure efficiency, avoid rent-seeking activities and alleviate problems of adverse selection (OECD, 2015[91]).

Given the ever-changing nature of innovation and the fast pace of technological developments, investment incentives targeting R&D and high-tech activities should be also reviewed periodically to ensure that they continue to reflect the latest market developments and that their costs – in terms of revenue forgone and potential economic distortions – outweigh their benefits. Cost-benefit analysis prior to introducing incentives, robust monitoring frameworks, and systematic ex-post impact evaluations are crucial to ensure the continuing validity of their objectives and whether their targeting and design remain appropriate. One option to ensure periodic reviews is to make them mandatory by law or integrate them into the monitoring and evaluation framework of national investment promotion strategies.

Effective targeting may come at the cost of significant financial and administrative resource requirements. Serious policy consideration should be given to the impact that incentive schemes have on the complexity of the tax system and the capacity of the public administration to implement more targeted policy approaches. Targeted tax incentives, for example, require higher tax administration capacities and the necessary resources to monitor the compliance of beneficiaries to outcome-based criteria, carry out regular audits to avoid fraudulent behaviour, measure their costs and value-for-money and assess their overall effectiveness over time. Country contexts and institutional arrangements discussed in the previous section should be taken into account. For developing countries, where institutional capacities are lagging, a simple and unspecific incentives scheme (i.e. applying to all types of firms uniformly, targeting all types of activities, not requiring discretionary decisions by government agencies) may bring longer-term benefits to the domestic economy by creating more certainty for potential investors.

Provide financial support and technical assistance to strengthen the absorptive capacities of domestic firms, in particular SMEs

Governments can strengthen the absorptive capacity of domestic firms, in particular SMEs, not only by ensuring that the regulatory environment is conducive to business growth but also by implementing targeted measures that support the development of strategic assets and resources at the firm level (e.g. access to skills, finance, innovation and digitalisation, etc.) (OECD, 2021[8]). Such measures often involve financial support and technical assistance in diagnosing weaknesses in business performance, experimenting with and adopting alternative business models, and undertaking innovative, technology-based activities with foreign firms. In many cases, financial and technical support is supplemented with training and guidance on the skills, managerial and organisational changes that are required to strengthen firm productivity and innovation (Table 2.3).

Supplier development programmes can play a crucial role in enhancing the absorptive capacity of local SMEs and increasing their chances of becoming partners and suppliers of foreign firms. These programmes usually assess the need for upgrading SME capabilities in various aspects of their performance – management, production, sales and commercialisation, innovation, human resources and overall productivity – and provide coaching and training in quality control, product certification and foreign market standards. As part of these programmes, government agencies organise seminars, workshops and courses (e.g. SME academies) to help domestic firms become familiar with foreign markets, enhance their export capacities and explore alternative sales strategies based on the use of ICT tools (e.g. e-commerce). To maximise the effectiveness of supplier development programmes, it is critical that their scope is aligned with the investment facilitation and aftercare services offered to foreign firms to ensure that the goods and services of domestic suppliers respond to the needs of foreign direct investors, especially in FDI-intensive sectors.

Table 2.3. Technical support to strengthen the absorptive capacities of domestic firms, in particular SMEs, in selected OECD and developing countries

Country	Policy initiative	Description
Portugal	Internationalisation Academy	Training programmes and online courses developed in partnership with Portuguese universities and business schools to help companies acquire knowledge of overseas product certification standards and processes.
	Innovation Scoring Tool	A performance assessment platform that allows companies to measure the degree of innovation of their business activities, receive a score and a set of recommended actions.
Costa Rica	Chain Acceleration Programme	Tailored support through managerial and technical training to SMEs that have a high potential to become suppliers of export-oriented companies based in Costa Rica.
	Digital Check-up Platform	Providing companies with a diagnosis of their digital maturity in 8 areas, and offering recommendations according to the level of maturity in each area.
Morocco	Mowakaba programme	Financial and technical support covering domestic companies' development strategy, financial optimisation, operational resilience, skills as well as product design and development for domestic and international markets.
	Skills Transfer Platform	Matchmaking platform comprising more than 1 000 entrepreneurship advisors and technical experts that seek to support SMEs upgrade the managerial skills of their employees.
Turkey	SME Technology Support Programme	Providing professional services (coaching, consultancy, mentoring) to enterprises through Technology Development Centres (TEKMER).
	KOBIGEL/SME Development Support Programme	Increasing SME productivity and competitiveness with the help of digital technologies, with a focus on the manufacturing sector.

Source: OECD (2022[100]), FDI Qualities mapping: A survey of policies and institutions that can strengthen sustainable investment.

Given the increasing digitalisation of supply chain management processes, supplier development programmes should be combined with technology extension services (TES) to improve the use of "new-to-firm" innovation by SMEs (Shapira, Youtie and Kay, 2011[101]). The main objective of these services is to facilitate the adoption of existing technology through diagnostic assessments of a firm's operations, processes and technological maturity; information services to bring awareness of new business models and digitally enabled sale practices; benchmarking to identify areas for improvement; consulting, training and technical assistance to implement internal organisational changes.

Addressing the financing challenges of SMEs across all stages of their business cycle is also of particular importance to help them invest in technology upgrading and improve the quality of their products and services in line with the needs of foreign investors. Public support to SME financing can take a variety of forms, from loans and credit guarantees to grants, equity and quasi-equity schemes, which help SMEs invest in R&D, acquire new technologies, adopt digital tools and processes, and engage in innovation and internationalisation activities (OECD, 2019[5]). Tax relief measures can be also provided to support subgroups of the SME population such as young high-growth firms and startups to expand their business operations and join GVCs. Many of these financial support schemes often include additional financial incentives for the development of products and services through science-to-business (S2B) and business-to-business (B2B) collaboration, including with foreign firms, reflecting the importance of networks and strategic partnerships for FDI-driven knowledge transmission.

The G20/OECD High-Level Principles on SME Financing provide guidance to G20 and OECD governments for the development of cross-cutting policy strategies on SME financing, highlighting in particular the need for a diverse range of bank-based and alternative financing instruments and the importance of safeguarding financial stability, transparency and investor protection (G20/OECD, 2015[102]). Diversifying the finance mix of SMEs requires government action to address both demand-side barriers (i.e. insufficient market incentives for investors) and supply-side barriers (i.e. lack of financial knowledge and guarantees among SMEs). Given the challenges that many SMEs face in accessing traditional bank financing, governments should promote alternative financing instruments such as equity, venture capital and fintech solutions. Policymakers can provide incentives for collaboration between banks and other private investors; capacity building to improve the way SME managers present their business model to potential funders; public tenders to encourage joint financing between several investors; and establishing platforms with easily accessible information on financing tools for growth-oriented SMEs.

Measures that facilitate access to qualified human capital should be also available to domestic firms to strengthen their capabilities in areas that require highly specialised expertise and skillsets such as those involving the use of innovative production processes, automation and digitalisation. Small businesses tend to offer fewer training and upskilling opportunities than large firms due to the increased financial costs of organising tailored training programmes, the lack of internal organisational capacities, and lower levels of resources to anticipate skill needs. Many OECD countries provide tax exemptions to encourage small businesses to provide on-the-job training to their employees, while others offer direct subsidies such as training vouchers that allow SMEs to purchase training hours from accredited training and educational institutions (OECD, 2021[8]).

Managerial skill development programmes in the form of seminars, workshops and individual consulting should be part of technical support packages provided by investment promotion and enterprise development agencies. Canada's Operational Efficiency Programme, for example, strengthens operational efficiency in manufacturing SMEs by enabling participating companies to benchmark and monitor their operational performance against the industry average (OECD, 2019[103]). Linking the development of SME workforce skills to vocational education and training (VET) frameworks can also foster greater collaboration between employers and vocational schools and help SMEs access highly skilled young employees through apprenticeship programmes. By combining school-based education and on-the-job training, apprenticeships can stimulate company productivity and profitability. Evidence from countries for which data are available show that more than half of all apprentices work in companies with 50 employees or fewer (Kergroach, 2021[104]). Work placement, employee exchange programmes and wage subsidies for highly skilled or R&D workers should be also used to ensure that SMEs have access to high quality human capital. For instance, the Portuguese investment promotion agency, AICEP, manages the INOV Contacto programme, which gives the opportunity to highly skilled graduates to conduct a short-term internship in a Portuguese company, followed by a long-term internship in a multinational company abroad. Such programmes play a crucial role in strengthening labour mobility and facilitating the transfer of knowledge and skills to domestic firms.

Ensure access to quality infrastructure to promote productive investment that creates linkages with the domestic economy

Infrastructure is a key enabler of agglomeration and connectivity and a pre-condition for the attraction of investment that contributes to productivity and innovation (OECD, 2015[105]). A well-functioning network infrastructure (e.g. transport and logistics, energy, ICTs) ensures secure and cost-efficient use of the host country's resources, reduces operational costs and facilitates access to local and international markets for foreign and domestic firms.

The quality of the transport infrastructure influences the decisions of foreign MNEs about where to locate their investment projects. It also allows economically weaker regions of the host country to benefit from the concentration of FDI in more urban and developed areas (OECD, 2019[5]). By expanding commuting opportunities for workers and facilitating the integration of rural regions into the labour market of the cities located in their proximity, transport infrastructure can foster FDI spillovers through labour mobility and increase productivity gains for remote local economies. Information and communication technologies (ICT) infrastructure is also critical for promoting technology-intensive investment and attracting digital economy MNEs that can make use of the domestic IT infrastructure to set up their supply chain operations (Gestrin and Staudt, 2018[106]). High-speed digital networks also enable small domestic firms to build digital capacity and become suppliers and partners of foreign MNEs operating in high-tech sectors. Energy infrastructure also matters for MNE operations (see chapter 5). Affordable energy supply can influence the cost of doing business and improve energy efficiency at the firm level. The quality of the energy infrastructure also has implications for FDI location decisions. Recent commitments to green and renewable energy production mean that foreign MNEs involved in green innovation could be put off by the lack of sustainable and affordable green energy in a specific country or region.

The OECD Compendium of Policy Good Practices for Quality Infrastructure Investment provides a set of international good practices and measures relevant to policymakers and practitioners in both developed and developing economies to pursue quality infrastructure investment (OECD, 2020[107]). In order to develop quality infrastructure that helps attract productivity-enhancing FDI, governments need to establish procedures to assess infrastructure needs, build robust policy coordination mechanisms (e.g. through dedicated administrative units, inter-ministerial task forces), promote a diverse mix of financial instruments for infrastructure investment and ensure a credible regulatory and legal environment for contract enforcement and the functioning of infrastructure partnerships (OECD, 2015[66]). Developing comprehensive national infrastructure plans, communicating priorities and identifying infrastructure projects across sectors aligned with development objectives can make infrastructure networks attractive for private participation and increase value for money in the use of public funds for infrastructure development.

Although ensuring access to quality infrastructure is a joint challenge of all levels of government, subnational governments can play a vital role in the infrastructure landscape since they are often responsible for key policy areas such as spatial planning, local public transport networks, the energy grid, broadband and telecommunications systems (OECD, 2019[5]). Strengthening the involvement of regional authorities and municipalities in the design and implementation of local infrastructure development plans can help ensure that infrastructure planning is linked to an assessment of regional (or local) characteristics, competitive advantages, growth and innovation potential.

Mobilising sufficient financial resources is also important. In many countries, where the government owns a range of key economic and social infrastructure assets, the public sector will be a key driver of infrastructure investment. Developing economies, however, do not often have the fiscal capacity to increase public investment significantly. Private investment can supplement public investment including through public-private partnerships (PPPs). Securing the necessary financial resources and making infrastructure networks more attractive for private involvement is possible by improving the efficiency of public service delivery, facilitating investor access to land, and establishing a more level playing field between State-owned infrastructure operators and private investors (OECD, 2015[105]). A diverse range of financing instruments and vehicles, along with appropriate risk mitigation approaches, can broaden the investor base and reduce investment risks.

Establish intermediary organisations and specialised facilities to support business-to-business and science-to-business collaboration

The impact of FDI on productivity and innovation is also influenced by the domestic knowledge infrastructure, which may include technology transfer offices, applied research centres, collaborative laboratories, universities and other facilities that contribute to the creation and diffusion of knowledge through synergies. Knowledge co-creation, i.e. the joint production of innovation between industry, research and possibly other stakeholders of the entrepreneurial ecosystem, is increasingly acknowledged as an important mechanism to bring together complementary expertise and facilitate the transfer of tacit knowledge (Kreiling and Paunov, 2021[108]). The establishment of facilities that provide a physical environment for foreign firms to interact, network, exchange knowledge and collaborate with domestic actors can be instrumental for the development of knowledge-intensive partnerships. Local SMEs can also gain access to technological premises, equipment, manpower and activities provided by universities and public research institutes that they could not afford independently (OECD, 2019[5]).

Over the past decade, there has been a rapid increase of intermediary technology transfer organisations in many OECD countries (Rossi et al., 2020[109]). These infrastructures seek to address the market failure, which exists in taking innovative ideas forward to commercial application by providing resources, competences and expertise that SMEs often lack. Their role is to provide from the earliest possible moment hands-on support in innovation processes and help SMEs undertake foresight exercises, technology development, and manage intellectual assets. Governments should ensure that particular emphasis is placed on supporting collaborative projects that involve foreign firms, domestic entrepreneurs and R&D institutions. These intermediary organisations can play the role of an innovation broker and create “communities of innovators” that undertake joint R&D and product development activities.

Furthermore, establishing and operating business incubators and accelerators in regions and sectors with high innovation potential allows entrepreneurs and early-stage startups to experiment with new business models, access frontier expertise, and technologies that they can use to further develop their innovative ideas, often in collaboration with foreign firms. Business facilities and services supporting the startup ecosystem can also further boost knowledge-intensive FDI by facilitating acquisitions of innovative startups by foreign multinationals. In fact, startup acquisitions are a common practice among MNEs that seek to maintain their position in digital economy sectors by acquiring and exploiting the technological “inventions” and valuable data and information held by young high-growth firms. In Israel, for example, the number and value of M&As and buyouts involving innovative startups has continuously grown over the past decade to reach a total value of USD 21.7 billion in 2019, as local players and multinational corporations expanded open innovation activities in a wide variety of sectors (OECD, 2020[110]).

Implement cluster development programmes that facilitate business linkages, foster cross-sectoral interactions and take into account place-based capabilities

The development of effective network and knowledge infrastructure can foster the spatial proximity of firms, thereby generating agglomeration externalities that reduce production costs through economies of scale and network effects. Well-designed cluster development policies may encourage companies to group together for the development of joint projects, foster industry-science linkages, and enhance cross-sectoral interactions. When foreign direct investors are located in such clusters, they are likely to be more willing to collaborate with other local firms and organisations (Potter, 2001[111]). From a policy perspective, this means that cluster policies should be aligned with FDI promotion, SME and regional development policies to increase the potential of FDI for local productivity gains. Cluster policies can achieve meaningful impacts when they integrate sectoral priorities, keep regional and local actors involved (e.g. businesses, municipalities, universities), and provide support (e.g. technical assistance, funding, capacity building) that takes into account the diversity of regional economies and FDI-SME ecosystems.

Public support can take many forms depending on the stage of development of a country (or region) and the level of maturity of the cluster itself – ranging from mature export-oriented clusters in metropolitan areas and technology-centred clusters built around R&D organisations, to smaller agglomerations in niche fields and small-scale networks in less mature ecosystems. Recent evidence from France shows that cluster policies are more effective in promoting knowledge diffusion when they are implemented in regions with a minimum degree of specialisation (N’Ghauran and Autant-Bernard, 2020[112]). This means that other types of policy interventions may be needed in economically weaker regions before cluster policies are implemented (e.g. strengthening SME absorptive capacities or establishing basic infrastructure). Intra-regional effects should be also taken into consideration. Knowledge spillovers arising from cluster policies in one region may negatively affect innovation diffusion in other locations, in particular neighbouring regions (i.e. ‘beggar-thy-neighbour’ effects). Subnational governments can play a strong role in the design and implementation of cluster policies by pooling resources, mobilising local actors and ensuring that public action is aligned with local market characteristics.

The establishment of industrial, science and technology parks can also facilitate FDI spillovers by fostering agglomeration economies. These parks are location-specific and target both foreign and domestic firms, providing them with land or office space to set up their business activities. Apart from providing basic infrastructure, many industrial parks are often associated with the provision of other services such as incentives for entrepreneurs to grow, business diagnostic tools, and programmes involving public-private partnerships. The co-location of companies facilitates the development of networks and information sharing among firms and can be an important source of knowledge and technology spillovers. Evidence on the effectiveness of science and technology parks in attracting FDI and promoting intra-firm linkages is overall positive, at least through tacit learning and informal interactions among park tenants (Vásquez-Urriago, Barge-Gil and Modrego Rico, 2016[113]; Cantù, 2010[114]; Vaidyanathan, 2007[115]). Specialised parks that apply rigorous selection criteria and target sector-specific firms in line with the sectoral make-up of the local economy have been found to be more effective in facilitating knowledge spillovers, promoting on-park relationships and spurring innovation (Kocak and Can, 2013[116]; Lamperti, Mavilia and Castellini, 2015[117]).

2.3.4. Facilitate knowledge and technology spillovers from FDI by eliminating information barriers and administrative hurdles

Implement effective investment promotion strategies geared towards productive and knowledge-intensive investment with strong spillover potential

IPAs are key players in promoting productive and knowledge-intensive investment. Effective investment promotion includes raising potential investors' awareness of the host country's strengths, branding the country as an attractive investment destination, and directly reaching out to potential investors to generate leads and investment projects (OECD, 2018[70]). IPAs should review and identify specific economic activities where they see a potential to enhance productivity growth and strengthen the technological sophistication and knowledge base of the economy. On this basis, they can design investment promotion packages geared towards productivity-enhancing activities, combining a variety of investment generation tools such as intelligence gathering (e.g. raw data analysis, market studies), sector-specific events (e.g. road-shows, business fora and fairs, country missions), and pro-active investor engagement (one-to-one meetings, email/phone campaigns, enquiry handling). These activities should provide potential investors with information that allows them to identify investment opportunities with the highest potential for knowledge spillovers, including information on the host country's knowledge infrastructure and the productive capabilities of domestic firms.

Implementing prioritisation strategies aligned with the economy's industrial capabilities and innovation potential is another way through which IPAs can influence the impact of FDI on productivity and innovation. Most IPAs prioritise certain types of investments over others by selecting priority sectors, countries or investment projects, and allocating resources accordingly (OECD, 2018[70]). Such an approach allows governments to focus on investments that have a higher probability of being realised and may bring unique benefits to the host economy. Evidence from 97 IPAs worldwide shows that the prioritisation of specific economic activities translates into higher levels of FDI in the targeted sectors (Harding and Javorcik, 2011[118]). Recent OECD evidence from 32 OECD IPAs also shows that investment policy makers increasingly take into account sustainable development considerations when setting their prioritisation strategy, with 90% of them using productivity and innovation-related indicators to prioritise investment attraction (Sztajerowska and Volpe Martincus, 2021[119]).

To leverage the potential of FDI for productivity, IPAs can prioritise FDI in knowledge- and technology-intensive sectors, target potential investors in countries with higher average productivity levels, or focus on specific types of foreign firms such as top R&D performers. Targets and promotion activities should be coherent with policy priorities set out in national investment promotion, innovation and SME development strategies, and reasonably reflect the country's production capacities and innovation potential. The use of prioritisation tools such as sustainability-related KPIs, scoring mechanisms, surveys and big data analytics, can help IPAs focus their limited resources on the most valuable deals (Sztajerowska and Volpe Martincus, 2021[119]).

Provide comprehensive investment facilitation and aftercare services to foster greater embedding of foreign firms in local economies

Investment facilitation and aftercare services can be instrumental in encouraging greater embedding of foreign affiliates in local economies and building relationships that contribute to greater use of local SME suppliers. They often involve accompanying investors in their project definition and during their establishment phase, ensuring that they identify local suppliers and clients, providing additional assistance once the project is implemented and encouraging expansions and reinvestments through aftercare. The aim of these services is to maximise the socio-economic benefits from investment.

Practically, IPAs have several options to bring down information barriers and help foreign firms identify local suppliers for future collaboration. Matchmaking services and B2B meetings allow representatives of foreign and domestic firms to meet and discuss potential local sourcing and business partnership opportunities. Many IPAs also use supplier databases to help foreign firms find information on domestically manufactured goods and domestically supplied services. Online matchmaking platforms can also serve as a single access point for B2B technology offers and requests, allowing companies to receive information on collaborative R&D projects. Measures to improve the quality of facilitation and aftercare services should therefore be at the centre of policy efforts to foster knowledge spillovers from FDI. IPAs should have sufficient resources and dedicated staff that is trained to identify the sourcing needs of foreign investors and steer FDI projects toward locations with the greatest potential for supporting supplier linkages. The development of clear objectives, a strategy and an action programme for embedding foreign investors in the local economy can help create policy momentum and mobilise public resources and relevant government actors.

Investment facilitation and aftercare services should be aligned with the priorities and objectives of supplier development programmes (see previous section) and combined with other types of support such as capacity building for local firms, training programmes for local staff, and cluster building initiatives. Evidence from OECD and developing economies shows that MNE-SME linkage programmes and other matchmaking services are often combined with policy initiatives aimed at promoting supply chain development and strengthening SME absorptive capacities. This mix of policy instruments allows aligning domestic supplier capabilities with the needs of foreign investors. It is therefore critical that governments increase the focus of investment promotion policy on FDI's potential for supply chain development by strengthening the IPA's policy footprint on issues that shape the capacities of domestic firms. This can be done either directly by integrating SME development into the mandate and mission of IPAs – as is the case with many European IPAs such as Enterprise Estonia, Business Finland, SPIRIT Slovenia – or indirectly by strengthening co-ordination and promoting joint programming between IPAs and government agencies responsible for SME and innovation policy.

MNE-SME linkage programmes and matchmaking services should be also integrated into wider regional development initiatives. Linkages between foreign and domestic firms are often location-specific and therefore depend on the availability of facilitation services at the local level. Recent findings from EU countries show that FDI responds better to the activity of IPAs operating in closer proximity to investors' operations (Crescenzi, Di Cataldo and Giua, 2019[120]). Similarly, the availability of appropriate business development services is a local issue because SMEs and entrepreneurs generally access the services within a narrow local area. There are, however, wide cross-country disparities in the way national agencies operate at the subnational level. In some countries where inter-institutional co-ordination is limited, local presence in the form of secondary offices may be crucial to ensure the effectiveness of aftercare. In some countries, such as France and Canada, investment facilitation and aftercare services are provided by local autonomous agencies such as local regional development agencies, who possess knowledge of the local context. In these cases, co-ordination and collaboration with subnational governments and regional development agencies is necessary to ensure an end-to-end service to foreign investors.

The organisation of networking and knowledge exchange events is a common practice among government agencies responsible for investment promotion, SME and innovation policies. Such events strengthen FDI spillovers arising from the imitation of MNE activities by local firms. The demonstration effect resulting from the improved visibility of foreign firm practices and technologies and the informal sharing of views and ideas during conferences, seminars and site visits involves significant learning opportunities for local SMEs. For instance, Enterprise Ireland, the Irish SME agency, organises Best Practice Study Visits that allow Irish firms to visit the manufacturing plants of foreign firms and get first-hand experience on their business practices and processes. Similarly in Portugal, the national SME agency, IAPMEI, implements the Open Days i4.0 initiative, which aims to present the technological capabilities of innovative companies during stakeholder events and promote the sharing of experiences between market actors operating in the same value chain (OECD, 2022[59]). These public events include, in addition to moments of networking and information sharing, visits to the most advanced industrial plants in Portugal, presentations of innovative technologies, exhibitions of technological products and hands-on discussions between business representatives and other market stakeholders.

References

Abraham, F., J. Konings and V. Slootmaekers (2010), "FDI spillovers in the Chinese manufacturing sector", *Economics of Transition*, Vol. 18/1, pp. 143-182, https://doi.org/10.1111/j.1468-0351.2009.00370.x. [52]

Alfaro, L. (2017), "Gains from foreign direct investment: Macro and micro approaches", *World Bank Economic Review*, https://doi.org/10.1093/wber/lhw007. [75]

Alfaro, L. and M. Chen (2012), "Surviving the Global Financial Crisis: Foreign Ownership and Establishment Performance", *American Economic Journal: Economic Policy*, Vol. 4/3, pp. 30-55, https://doi.org/10.1257/pol.4.3.30. [16]

Almeida, R. and R. Aterido (2011), "On-the-job training and rigidity of employment protection in the developing world: Evidence from differential enforcement", *Labour Economics*, Vol. 18, pp. S71-S82, https://doi.org/10.1016/j.labeco.2011.05.001. [82]

Andrenelli, A. et al. (2019), "Micro-Evidence on Corporate Relationships in Global Value Chains: The Role of Trade, FDI and Strategic Partnerships", *OECD Trade Policy Papers*, No. 227, OECD Publishing, Paris, https://doi.org/10.1787/f6225ffb-en. [29]

Appelt, S., F. Galindo-Rueda and A. González Cabral (2019), "Measuring R&D tax support: Findings from the new OECD R&D Tax Incentives Database", *OECD Science, Technology and Industry Working Papers*, No. 2019/06, OECD Publishing, Paris, https://doi.org/10.1787/d16e6072-en. [121]

Audretsch, D. and M. Feldman (1996), "R&D Spillovers and the Geography of Innovation and Production", *American Economic Review*, Vol. 86/3, pp. 630-40. [60]

Balsvik, R. (2011), "Is Labor Mobility a Channel for Spillovers from Multinationals? Evidence from Norwegian Manufacturing", *The Review of Economics and Statistics*, Vol. 93/1, pp. 285-297. [33]

Batten, S. and D. Jacobs (2017), *Foreign-owned firms and productivity*, https://bankunderground.co.uk/2017/08/17/foreign-owned-firms-and-productivity/. [13]

Becker, B. et al. (2020), "FDI in hot labour markets: The implications of the war for talent", *Journal of International Business Policy (2020)*, pp. 107–133. [36]

Benfratello, L. and A. Sembenelli (2006), "Foreign ownership and productivity: Is the direction of causality so obvious?", *International Journal of Industrial Organization*, Vol. 24/4, pp. 733-751, https://doi.org/10.1016/j.ijindorg.2005.07.012. [40]

Blalock, G. and P. Gertler (2008), "Welfare gains from Foreign Direct Investment through technology transfer to local suppliers", *Journal of International Economics*, Vol. 74/2, pp. 402-421, https://doi.org/10.1016/j.jinteco.2007.05.011. [26]

Blomstrom, M. and A. Kokko (1998), "Multinational Corporations and Spillovers", *Journal of Economic Surveys*, Vol. 12/3, pp. 247-277, https://doi.org/10.1111/1467-6419.00056. [19]

Braconier, H., K. Ekholm and K. Knarvik (2001), "In search of FDI-transmitted R&D spillovers: A study based on Swedish data", *Review of World Economics*, Vol. 137/4, pp. 644-665, https://doi.org/10.1007/bf02707427. [49]

Branstetter, L., R. Fisman and C. Foley (2006), "Do Stronger Intellectual Property Rights Increase International Technology Transfer? Empirical Evidence from U. S. Firm-Level Panel Data", *The Quarterly Journal of Economics*, Vol. 121/1. [50]

Cadestin, C. et al. (2018), "Multinational enterprises and global value chains: New Insights on the trade-investment nexus", *OECD Science, Technology and Industry Working Papers*, No. 2018/05, OECD Publishing, Paris, https://doi.org/10.1787/194ddb63-en. [12]

Cantù, C. (2010), "Exploring the role of spatial relationships to transform knowledge in a business idea — Beyond a geographic proximity", *Industrial Marketing Management*, Vol. 39/6, pp. 887-897, https://doi.org/10.1016/j.indmarman.2010.06.008. [114]

Caves, R. (2007), *Multinational Enterprise and Economic Analysis*, Cambridge University Press, Cambridge, https://doi.org/10.1017/cbo9780511619113. [18]

Celani, A., L. Dressler and M. Wermelinger (2022), "Building an Investment Tax Incentives database: Methodology and initial findings for 36 developing countries", *OECD Working Papers on International Investment*, No. 2022/01, OECD Publishing, Paris, https://doi.org/10.1787/62e075a9-en. [93]

Chesbrough, H. (2003), "Open Innovation: The New Imperative for Creating and Profiting from Technology", *Harvard Business School Press, Boston (MA).* [31]

Cirera, X. and W. Maloney (2017), *The Innovation Paradox: Developing-Country Capabilities and the Unrealized Promise of Technological Catch-Up*, Washington, DC: World Bank, https://doi.org/10.1596/978-1-4648-1160-9. [11]

Clicteur, T. et al. (2021), *Benefits of EU trade agreements for small and medium-sized enterprises (SMEs)*, https://www.europarl.europa.eu/RegData/etudes/BRIE/2021/653628/EXPO_BRI(2021)653628_EN.pdf. [84]

Cohen, W. and D. Levinthal (1990), "Absorptive Capacity: A New Perspective on Learning and Innovation", *Administrative Science Quarterly*, Vol. 35/1, pp. 128-152. [54]

Crescenzi, R., M. Di Cataldo and M. Giua (2019), *FDI inflows in Europe: does investment promotion work?*, The London School of Economics and Political Science, http://www.lse.ac.uk/iga/assets/documents/research-and-publications/FDI-inflows-in-Europe-does-investment-promotion-work.pdf. [120]

Crespo, N. and M. Fontoura (2007), "Determinant Factors of FDI Spillovers – What Do We Really Know?", *World Development*, Vol. 35/3, pp. 410-425, https://doi.org/10.1016/j.worlddev.2006.04.001. [21]

Criscuolo, C. and R. Martin (2003), *Multinationals, foreign ownership and US productivity leadership: Evidence from the UK*, Royal Economic Society Annual Conference 2003 50, Royal Economic Society. [41]

Criscuolo, C. and J. Timmis (2017), "The Relationship Between Global Value Chains and Productivity", *International Productivity Monitor, Centre for the Study of Living Standards*, Vol. 32, pp. 61-83. [27]

Davidson, P., C. Kauffmann and M. de Liedekerke (2021), "How do laws and regulations affect competitiveness: The role for regulatory impact assessment", *OECD Regulatory Policy Working Papers*, No. 15, OECD Publishing, Paris, https://doi.org/10.1787/7c11f5d5-en. [78]

De Propris, L. and N. Driffield (2005), "The importance of clusters for spillovers from foreign direct investment and technology sourcing", *Cambridge Journal of Economics*, Vol. 30/2, pp. 277-291, https://doi.org/10.1093/cje/bei059. [63]

Desai, M., C. Foley and K. Forbes (2007), "Financial Constraints and Growth: Multinational and Local Firm Responses to Currency Depreciations", *Review of Financial Studies*, Vol. 21/6, pp. 2857-2888, https://doi.org/10.1093/rfs/hhm017. [17]

Doan, T., D. Maré and K. Iyer (2014), "Productivity spillovers from foreign direct investment in New Zealand", *New Zealand Economic Papers*, Vol. 49/3, pp. 249-275, https://doi.org/10.1080/00779954.2014.945229. [24]

Du, L., A. Harrison and G. Jefferson (2011), *Do Institutions Matter for FDI Spillovers? The Implications of China's "Special Characteristics"*, The World Bank, https://doi.org/10.1596/1813-9450-5757. [74]

European Commission (2021), *The EU-Canada Comprehensive Economic and Trade Agreement (CETA)*, https://ec.europa.eu/trade/policy/in-focus/ceta/. [89]

Farole, T. and G. Akinci (2011), "Special Economic Zones: Progress, Emerging Challenges, and Future Directions, Washington, D.C.: World Bank". [79]

Farole, T. and D. Winkler (eds.) (2014), *Making Foreign Direct Investment Work for Sub-Saharan Africa:Local Spillovers and Competitiveness in Global Value Chains*, The World Bank, https://doi.org/10.1596/978-1-4648-0126-6. [48]

Farole, T. and D. Winkler (2014), *Quantitative Studies The Role of Mediating Factors for FDI Spillovers in Developing Countries: Evidence from a Global Dataset*, World Bank, https://doi.org/10.1596/978-1-4648-0126-6. [39]

Franco, C. and K. Kozovska (2008), "Mutual Productivity Spillovers and Clusters in Eastern Europe: Some Empirical Evidence", *SSRN Electronic Journal*, https://doi.org/10.2139/ssrn.1317334. [65]

G20/OECD (2015), *G20/OECD High-level Principles on SME Financing*, https://www.oecd.org/finance/G20-OECD-High-Level-Principles-on-SME-Financing.pdf. [102]

Gal, P. and W. Witheridge (2019), "Productivity and innovation at the industry level: What role for integration in global value chains?", *OECD Productivity Working Papers*, No. 19, OECD Publishing, Paris, https://doi.org/10.1787/a5cec52c-en. [44]

Gestrin, M. and J. Staudt (2018), *The digital economy, multinational enterprises and international investment policy*, OECD, http://www.oecd.org/investment/the-digital-economy-mnes-and-international-investment-policy.htm. [106]

Girma, S., H. Görg and M. Pisu (2008), "Exporting, linkages and productivity spillovers from foreign direct investment", *Canadian Journal of Economics/Revue canadienne d'économique*, Vol. 41/1, pp. 320-340, https://doi.org/10.1111/j.1365-2966.2008.00465.x. [61]

González Cabral, A., S. Appelt and T. Hanappi (2021), "Corporate effective tax rates for R&D: The case of expenditure-based R&D tax incentives", *OECD Taxation Working Papers*, No. 54, OECD Publishing, Paris, https://doi.org/10.1787/ff9a104f-en. [97]

Gorg, H. and E. Strobl (2001), "Multinational Companies and Productivity Spillovers: A Meta-Analysis", *The Economic Journal*, Vol. 111/475, pp. F723-F739, https://doi.org/10.1111/1468-0297.00669. [20]

Görg, H. and E. Strobl (2005), "Spillovers from Foreign Firms though Worker Mobility: An Empirical Investigation", *Scandinavian Journal of Economics*, Vol. 107(4), pp. 693-709. [32]

Gorodnichenko, Y., J. Svejnar and K. Terrell (2014), "When does FDI have positive spillovers? Evidence from 17 transition market economies", *Journal of Comparative Economics*, Vol. 42/4, pp. 954-969, https://doi.org/10.1016/j.jce.2014.08.003. [38]

Government of Rwanda (2021), "Rwanda's Law on investment promotion and facilitation N° 006/2021 of 05/02/2021", *Official Gazette n° 04 bis of 08/02/2021*, https://gazettes.africa/archive/rw/2021/rw-government-gazette-dated-2021-02-08-no-4bis.pdf. [96]

Harding, T. and B. Javorcik (2011), "Roll Out the Red Carpet and They Will Come: Investment Promotion and FDI Inflows", *The Economic Journal*, Vol. 121/557, pp. 1445-1476, https://doi.org/10.1111/j.1468-0297.2011.02454.x. [118]

Havranek, T. and Z. Irsova (2011), "Estimating vertical spillovers from FDI: Why results vary and what the true effect is", *Journal of International Economics*, Vol. 85/2, pp. 234-244, https://doi.org/10.1016/j.jinteco.2011.07.004. [73]

IMF-OECD-UN-World Bank (2015), *Options for Low Income Countries' Effective and Efficient Use of Tax Incentives for Investment*, A report prepared for the G-20 Development Working Group by the IMF, OECD, UN and World Bank, https://www.oecd.org/ctp/tax-global/background-document-options-for-low-income-countries-effective-and-efficient-use-of-tax-incentives-for-investment.pdf. [94]

Javorcik, B. (2020), "Global supply chains will not be the same in the post-COVID-19 world", *Chapter 8 in R Baldwin and S Evenett (eds.)*, https://voxeu.org/content/covid-19-and-trade-policy-why-turning-inward-won-t-work. [15]

Javorcik, B. (2004), "Does Foreign Direct Investment Increase the Productivity of Domestic Firms? In Search of Spillovers Through Backward Linkages", *American Economic Review*, Vol. 94/3, pp. 605-627, https://doi.org/10.1257/0002828041464605. [14]

Jindra, B. (2006), "The Theoretical Framework: FDI and Technology Transfer", in *Technology Transfer via Foreign Direct Investment in Central and Eastern Europe*, Palgrave Macmillan UK, London, https://doi.org/10.1057/9780230524484_2. [28]

Keller, W. and S. Yeaple (2009), "Multinational Enterprises, International Trade, and Productivity Growth: Firm-Level Evidence from the United States", *Review of Economics and Statistics*, Vol. 91/4, pp. 821-831, https://doi.org/10.1162/rest.91.4.821. [46]

Kergroach, S. (2021), ""SMEs Going Digital: Policy challenges and recommendations", Going Digital Toolkit Note, No. 15", https://goingdigital.oecd.org/data/notes/No15_ToolkitNote_DigitalSMEs.pdf. [104]

Kocak, O. and O. Can (2013), "Determinants of inter-firm networks among tenants of science technology parks", *Industrial and Corporate Change*, Vol. 23/2, pp. 467-492, https://doi.org/10.1093/icc/dtt015. [116]

Konwar, Z. et al. (2015), "Do Foreign Ownership Modes Matter for FDI Spillovers?", in *The Rise of Multinationals from Emerging Economies*, Palgrave Macmillan UK, London, https://doi.org/10.1057/9781137473110_14. [51]

Kreiling, L. and C. Paunov (2021), "Knowledge co-creation in the 21st century: A cross-country experience-based policy report", *OECD Science, Technology and Industry Policy Papers*, No. 115, OECD Publishing, Paris, https://doi.org/10.1787/c067606f-en. [108]

Lamperti, F., R. Mavilia and S. Castellini (2015), "The role of Science Parks: a puzzle of growth, innovation and R&D investments", *The Journal of Technology Transfer*, Vol. 42/1, pp. 158-183, https://doi.org/10.1007/s10961-015-9455-2. [117]

Lembcke, A. and L. Wildnerova (2020), "Does FDI benefit incumbent SMEs?: FDI spillovers and competition effects at the local level", *OECD Regional Development Working Papers*, No. 2020/02, OECD Publishing, Paris, https://doi.org/10.1787/47763241-en. [37]

Lodrant, M. and L. Cernat (2017), *SME Provisions in Trade Agreements and the Case of TTIP*, Oxford University Press, https://doi.org/10.1093/acprof:oso/9780198795650.003.0007. [86]

Marchese, M. et al. (2019), "Enhancing SME productivity: Policy highlights on the role of managerial skills, workforce skills and business linkages", *OECD SME and Entrepreneurship Papers*, No. 16, OECD Publishing, Paris, https://doi.org/10.1787/825bd8a8-en. [4]

Martins, P. (2011), "Paying More to Hire the Best? Foreign Firms, Wages, and Worker Mobility", *Economic Inquiry*, Vol. 49/2, pp. 349-363, https://doi.org/10.1111/j.1465-7295.2010.00301.x. [35]

Martin, S. and J. Scott (2000), "The nature of innovation market failure and the design of public support for private innovation", *Research Policy*, Vol. 29/4-5, pp. 437-447, https://doi.org/10.1016/s0048-7333(99)00084-0. [95]

Menghinello, S., L. De Propris and N. Driffield (2010), "Industrial districts, inward foreign investment and regional development", *Journal of Economic Geography*, Vol. 10/4, pp. 539-558, https://doi.org/10.1093/jeg/lbq012. [64]

Meyer, K. and E. Sinani (2009), "When and where does foreign direct investment generate positive spillovers? A meta-analysis", *Journal of International Business Studies*, Vol. 40/7, pp. 1075-1094, https://doi.org/10.1057/jibs.2008.111. [72]

N'Ghauran, K. and C. Autant-Bernard (2020), "Effects of cluster policies on regional innovation networks: Evidence from France", https://halshs.archives-ouvertes.fr/halshs-02482565/document. [112]

Nicolini, M. and L. Resmini (2010), "FDI spillovers in new EU member states", *Economics of Transition*, Vol. 18/3, pp. 487-511, https://doi.org/10.1111/j.1468-0351.2009.00379.x. [45]

OECD (2022), *FDI Qualities mapping: A survey of policies and institutions that can strengthen sustainable investment.* [100]

OECD (2022), *Strengthening FDI and SME Linkages in Portugal*, OECD Publishing, Paris, https://doi.org/10.1787/d718823d-en. [59]

OECD (2022), *Strengthening FDI and SME Linkages: A Policy Toolkit*, https://www.oecd.org/industry/smes/fdi-sme.htm. [23]

OECD (2021), *Industrial Policy for the Sustainable Development Goals: Increasing the Private Sector's Contribution*, OECD Publishing, Paris, https://doi.org/10.1787/2cad899f-en. [69]

OECD (2021), *Middle East and North Africa Investment Policy Perspectives*, OECD Publishing, Paris, https://doi.org/10.1787/6d84ee94-en. [99]

OECD (2021), *OECD Investment Policy Reviews: Thailand*, OECD Investment Policy Reviews, OECD Publishing, Paris, https://doi.org/10.1787/c4eeee1c-en. [53]

OECD (2021), "OECD R&D Tax Incentives Database", http://oe.cd/rdtax. [98]

OECD (2021), *OECD Science, Technology and Innovation Outlook 2021: Times of Crisis and Opportunity*, OECD Publishing, Paris, https://doi.org/10.1787/75f79015-en. [92]

OECD (2021), *OECD SME and Entrepreneurship Outlook 2021*, OECD Publishing, Paris, https://doi.org/10.1787/97a5bbfe-en. [8]

OECD (2021), *SME and Entrepreneurship Policy in the Slovak Republic*, OECD Studies on SMEs and Entrepreneurship, OECD Publishing, Paris, https://doi.org/10.1787/9097a251-en. [6]

OECD (2021), *The Digital Transformation of SMEs*, OECD Studies on SMEs and Entrepreneurship, OECD Publishing, Paris, https://doi.org/10.1787/bdb9256a-en. [58]

OECD (2020), *FDI Qualities Assessment of Ireland*, http://www.oecd.org/investment/FDI-Qualities-Assessmentof-Ireland.pdf. [34]

OECD (2020), *Financing SMEs and Entrepreneurs 2020: An OECD Scoreboard*, OECD Publishing, Paris, https://doi.org/10.1787/061fe03d-en. [57]

OECD (2020), *OECD Compendium of Policy Good Practices for Quality Infrastructure Investment*, http://www.oecd.org/finance/oecd-compendium-of-policy-good-practices-for-quality-infrastructure-investment.htm. [107]

OECD (2020), *OECD Digital Economy Outlook 2020*, OECD Publishing, Paris, https://doi.org/10.1787/bb167041-en. [81]

OECD (2020), *OECD Employment Outlook 2020: Worker Security and the COVID-19 Crisis*, OECD Publishing, Paris, https://doi.org/10.1787/1686c758-en. [83]

OECD (2020), "Start-ups, killer acquisitions and merger control – Note by Israel, 133rd OECD Competition Committee meeting", *OECD Directorate for Financial and Enterprise Affairs*, https://one.oecd.org/document/DAF/COMP/WD(2020)17/en/pdf. [110]

OECD (2019), *FDI Qualities Indicators: Measuring the sustainable development impacts of investment*, http://www.oecd.org/fr/investissement/fdi-qualities-indicators.htm. [2]

OECD (2019), *Going Digital: Shaping Policies, Improving Lives*, OECD Publishing, Paris, https://doi.org/10.1787/9789264312012-en. [7]

OECD (2019), *OECD Investment Policy Reviews: Southeast Asia*, http://www.oecd.org/investment/oecd-investment-policy-review-southeast-asia.htm. [71]

OECD (2019), *OECD SME and Entrepreneurship Outlook 2019*, OECD Publishing, Paris, https://doi.org/10.1787/34907e9c-en. [5]

OECD (2019), *Strengthening SMEs and Entrepreneurship for Productivity and Inclusive Growth: OECD 2018 Ministerial Conference on SMEs*, OECD Studies on SMEs and Entrepreneurship, OECD Publishing, Paris, https://doi.org/10.1787/c19b6f97-en. [103]

OECD (2018), *Improving the business environment for SMEs through effective regulation*, https://www.oecd.org/cfe/smes/ministerial/documents/2018-SME-Ministerial-Conference-Parallel-Session-1.pdf. [77]

OECD (2018), *Mapping of Investment Promotion Agencies in OECD Countries*, http://www.oecd.org/investment/Mapping-of-Investment-Promotion-Agencies-in-OECD-Countries.pdf. [70]

OECD (2018), *OECD Investment Policy Reviews: Viet Nam 2018*, OECD Investment Policy Reviews, OECD Publishing, Paris, https://doi.org/10.1787/9789264282957-en. [80]

OECD (2016), "New industrial policies", in *OECD Science, Technology and Innovation Outlook 2016*, OECD Publishing, Paris, https://doi.org/10.1787/sti_in_outlook-2016-27-en. [67]

OECD (2016), *OECD Regions at a Glance 2016*, OECD Publishing, Paris, https://doi.org/10.1787/reg_glance-2016-en. [62]

OECD (2016), *SME and Entrepreneurship Policy in Israel 2016*, OECD, https://doi.org/10.1787/9789264262324-en. [47]

OECD (2015), *Fostering investment in infrastructure: Lessons learned from OECD Investment Policy Reviews*, https://www.oecd.org/daf/inv/investment-policy/Fostering-Investment-in-Infrastructure.pdf. [105]

OECD (2015), *Policy Framework for Investment, 2015 Edition*, OECD Publishing, Paris, https://doi.org/10.1787/9789264208667-en. [66]

OECD (2015), *The Future of Productivity*, OECD Publishing, Paris, https://doi.org/10.1787/9789264248533-en. [3]

OECD (2015), *The Innovation Imperative: Contributing to Productivity, Growth and Well-Being*, OECD Publishing, Paris, https://doi.org/10.1787/9789264239814-en. [91]

OECD (2014), *Perspectives on Global Development 2014: Boosting Productivity to Meet the Middle-Income Challenge*, OECD Publishing, Paris, https://doi.org/10.1787/persp_glob_dev-2014-en. [1]

OECD (2009), *Investing for Growth: Building Innovative Regions, Background report for the Meeting of the Territorial Development Policy Committee (TDPC) at Ministerial Level*, https://www.oecd.org/regional/ministerial/42531915.pdf. [43]

OECD (2008), *Open Innovation in Global Networks*, OECD Publishing, Paris, https://doi.org/10.1787/9789264047693-en. [30]

OECD (2007), *OECD Regions at a Glance 2007*, OECD Publishing, Paris, https://doi.org/10.1787/reg_glance-2007-en. [42]

OECD/Eurostat (2018), *Oslo Manual 2018: Guidelines for Collecting, Reporting and Using Data on Innovation, 4th Edition*, The Measurement of Scientific, Technological and Innovation Activities, OECD Publishing, Paris/Eurostat, Luxembourg, https://doi.org/10.1787/9789264304604-en. [10]

Potter, J. (2001), "Embedding foreign direct investment, Paris: OECD", https://www.oecd.org/cfe/regionaldevelopment/2489910.pdf. [111]

Rojec, M. and M. Knell (2017), "WHY IS THERE A LACK OF EVIDENCE ON KNOWLEDGE SPILLOVERS FROM FOREIGN DIRECT INVESTMENT?", *Journal of Economic Surveys*, Vol. 32/3, pp. 579-612, https://doi.org/10.1111/joes.12207. [25]

Rossi, F. et al. (2020), ""Public innovation intermediaries and digital co-creation. Research contribution to the OECD TIP Co-creation project"", https://stip.oecd.org/assets/TKKT/CaseStudies/49.pdf. [109]

Saliola, F. and A. Zanfei (2009), "Multinational firms, global value chains and the organization of knowledge transfer", *Research Policy*, Vol. 38/2, pp. 369-381, https://doi.org/10.1016/j.respol.2008.11.003. [56]

Shapira, P., J. Youtie and L. Kay (2011), ""Building capabilities for innovation in SMEs: A cross-country comparison of technology extension policies and programmes"", Vol. 3, pp. 254-272. [101]

Smeets, R. (2008), "Collecting the Pieces of the FDI Knowledge Spillovers Puzzle", *The World Bank Research Observer*, Vol. 23/2, pp. 107-138, https://doi.org/10.1093/wbro/lkn003. [22]

Stone, S., S. Kim and L. Engen (2017), *Science, technology, and innovation in international investment agreements in the Asia-Pacific region*, https://www.unescap.org/sites/default/d8files/knowledge-products/STI%20in%20IIAs%20in%20the%20A-P%20region-30%20Oct%202017_1.pdf. [87]

Stone, S., J. Messent and D. Flaig (2015), "Emerging Policy Issues: Localisation Barriers to Trade", *OECD Trade Policy Papers*, No. 180, OECD Publishing, Paris, https://doi.org/10.1787/5js1m6v5qd5j-en. [76]

Sztajerowska, M. and C. Volpe Martincus (2021), *Together or apart: investment promotion agencies' prioritisation and monitoring and evaluation for sustainable investment promotion*, https://www.oecd.org/daf/inv/investment-policy/Investment-Insights-Investment-Promotion-Prioritisation-OECD.pdf. [119]

Todorova, G. and B. Durisin (2007), "Absorptive capacity: Valuing a reconceptualization", *Academy of Management Review*, Vol. 32/3, pp. 774-786, https://doi.org/10.5465/amr.2007.25275513. [55]

Triplett, J. and L. Bosworth (2008), "The state of data for services productivity measurement in the United States", *International Productivity Monitor*, Vol. 16, pp. 53-70. [9]

UKTPO (2020), *The Representation of SME Interests in Free Trade Agreements: Recommendations for Best Practice*, https://blogs.sussex.ac.uk/uktpo/files/2020/01/FSB-Trade-TPO-Report.pdf. [85]

USTR (2021), *Trans-Pacific Partnership Agreement*, https://ustr.gov/trade-agreements/free-trade-agreements/trans-pacific-partnership/tpp-full-text. [90]

Vaidyanathan, G. (2007), "Technology parks in a developing country: the case of India", *The Journal of Technology Transfer*, Vol. 33/3, pp. 285-299, https://doi.org/10.1007/s10961-007-9041-3. [115]

Vásquez-Urriago, Á., A. Barge-Gil and A. Modrego Rico (2016), "Science and Technology Parks and cooperation for innovation: Empirical evidence from Spain", *Research Policy*, Vol. 45/1, pp. 137-147, https://doi.org/10.1016/j.respol.2015.07.006. [113]

Warwick, K. (2013), "Beyond Industrial Policy: Emerging Issues and New Trends", *OECD Science, Technology and Industry Policy Papers*, No. 2, OECD Publishing, Paris, https://doi.org/10.1787/5k4869clw0xp-en. [68]

WTO (2014), "Intellectual Property Provisions in Regional Trade Agreements: Revision and Update", *WTO Working Papers*, No. 2014/14, World Trade Organization, Geneva, https://doi.org/10.30875/6e577b22-en. [88]

Annex 2.A. Assessing the impact of FDI on productivity and innovation

Annex Table 2.A.1. Core questions to assess the impact of FDI on productivity and innovation

Dimension	Questions	Potential data sources
Structure and characteristics of the economy	What is the industrial structure and specialisation of the economy? What sectors and value chains are driving growth, productivity and innovation?	OECD STAN Database for Structural Analysis; World Bank Enterprise Surveys; OECD Analytical AMNE Database
	Is economic activity concentrated in high technology and/or knowledge-intensive sectors?	
	What is the level of GVC integration (both through backward and forward linkages)? What sectors are better integrated into GVCs?	OECD Trade in Value Added Database; World Bank Enterprise Surveys; OECD Trade in Goods and Services Indicators
	How vulnerable is the economy, including SME and FDI performance, to economic shocks?	OECD Economic Outlook; OECD FDI Statistics
FDI characteristics	What is the sectoral composition of FDI inflows? Is FDI concentrated in sectors with higher average productivity and R&D intensity levels?	OECD FDI Qualities Indicators; Refinitiv Database on cross-border M&A; Financial Times' fDi Markets Database; OECD FDI Statistics
	What type of FDI is more prevalent (e.g. greenfield investment, M&As) and what are the key investment motives of foreign MNEs (e.g. technology-exploiting, market-seeking, efficiency-seeking FDI)?	Refinitiv Database on cross-border M&A; Financial Times' fDi Markets Database (for greenfield FDI); World Bank Enterprise Surveys
	What is the contribution of foreign investors to value added, employment and exports? To what extent does FDI drive the economy's participation in GVCs?	OECD Analytical AMNE database; World Bank Enterprise Surveys
	What are the main countries of origin of FDI (e.g. higher or lower-productivity economies)?	OECD FDI Statistics
Domestic absorptive capacities	Is there a productivity (performance) gap between foreign and domestic firms? In what sectors are these gaps larger?	OECD FDI Qualities Indicators
	What are the characteristics of the SME population in terms of size, location, sector and position in GVCs?	OECD Structural and Demographic Business Statistics (SDBS)
	What is the contribution of SMEs to value added, employment and exports?	OECD Structural and Demographic Business Statistics (SDBS); OECD Trade by Enterprise Characteristics
	How do domestic firms, in particular SMEs, perform in terms of access to finance, skills, knowledge and technology? What are the main internal and external barriers that SMEs face in accessing these strategic resources?	OECD SME and Entrepreneurship Outlook; OECD Financing SMEs and Entrepreneurship Scoreboard; OECD Entrepreneurship Financing Database; OECD Skills for Jobs database; OECD ICT use by Businesses Database; OECD R&D Statistics Database; OECD Education database
	How dynamic is the startup and entrepreneurial ecosystem?	Global Entrepreneurship Report; Flash Eurobarometer on Entrepreneurship
Economic geography factors	Are there regional disparities in economic growth, labour productivity and innovation performance? What is the industrial structure and specialisation of regions?	OECD Regional Statistics
	What is the geographic distribution of FDI within the country?	Refinitiv Database on cross-border M&A; Financial Times' fDi Markets Database (greenfield FDI); World Bank Enterprise Surveys
	In what regions are productivity (performance) gaps between foreign and domestic firms more pronounced?	OECD FDI Qualities Indicators

Dimension	Questions	Potential data sources
	To what extent does SME performance varies across regions (in terms of innovation capacity, digitalisation, access to finance, skill-intensity, etc.)?	OECD Regional Statistics; EU Regional Innovation Scoreboard; EC Regional Entrepreneurship and Development Index
	Is there any evidence of market-driven industrial clustering either at the sectoral or regional level?	World Economic Forum Global Competitiveness Index
FDI transmission channels	To what extent do foreign investors source intermediate goods and services from domestic firms, in particular SMEs?	OECD Analytical AMNE database
	To what extent do domestic firms, in particular SMEs, purchase inputs from foreign investors?	OECD Analytical AMNE database
	How common are strategic partnerships between foreign investors and local SMEs (e.g. joint ventures, licensing agreements, R&D collaborations)?	World Bank Enterprise Surveys; Factset
	How common and likely is the mobility of workers from foreign investors to domestic firms? What is the wage premium of foreign investors compared to domestic firms?	OECD Job Quality Database; World Bank Enterprise Surveys; Eurostat CIS surveys
	Is there any evidence of tacit learning/imitation by domestic firms of foreign investors operating in the same sector or value chain? Does market competition hamper innovation in SMEs?	National statistics and empirical research; Eurostat CIS surveys

Annex Table 2.A.2. Core questions to assess policies that influence the impact of FDI on productivity and innovation

Dimension	Instrument	Policy questions
Governance	National strategies and plans	Are the country's strategic priorities in terms of productivity growth and innovation performance clearly defined in a national strategy or action plan?
		Does the country's investment promotion strategy articulate the government's vision on the contribution of investment to productivity and innovation? If yes, does the strategy set specific goals, identify priority policy actions and clarify responsibilities of institutions in order to maximise FDI impacts on productivity and innovation?
		Do national development or economic plans provide coherent and strategic directions on investment promotion, innovation and SME development? Are investment considerations integrated into innovation, SME and entrepreneurship strategies and vice versa?
	Oversight and co-ordination bodies	Are responsibilities across line ministries and government agencies on investment, SMEs and innovation clearly defined, balanced and mutually understood by all government actors?
		Is there horizontal strategic co-ordination between different ministries and operational co-ordination between implementing agencies involved in the design and implementation of investment promotion, innovation and SME development policies? Are co-ordination mechanisms formal (e.g. inter-ministerial councils, working groups, inter-agency committees, joint programming) or informal?
		Are the mandates and internal governance structures of co-ordinating bodies clearly defined and supported with sufficient human and financial resources?
		What is the role of subnational governments in the design and implementation of investment promotion, innovation and SME development policies? What governance frameworks and institutional arrangements are in place to ensure effective multi-level governance?
	Policy dialogue and evaluation of policy impacts	Do relevant government institutions systematically monitor and evaluate the impact of FDI, and relevant policies and programmes, on domestic productivity and innovation?
		Do relevant government institutions have the necessary analytical capacities, tools and frameworks in place to collect information on the implementation of their policy initiatives and regularly conduct comprehensive impact assessments?
		Have relevant government institutions established policy dialogue mechanisms, processes and frameworks to consult with foreign investors, local SMEs and other actors of the domestic research and innovation ecosystem?
Domestic regulation	Legal framework for investment	Are there regulatory restrictions on FDI and trade in sectors that drive labour productivity and innovation?
		What steps has the government taken to ensure that the laws and regulations dealing with investments, and their implementation and enforcement, are clear, transparent, readily accessible and do not impose unnecessary burdens?

Dimension	Instrument	Policy questions
	Competition policy	Do competition rules ensure a level playing field for foreign and domestic firms alike? Is there a robust legal framework that prohibits anti-competitive conduct by dominant companies, and that provides the necessary tools to uncover and deter such illegal practices?
	Intellectual property rights protection	Are intellectual property rights (IPR) protected by adequate laws and regulations? Is the IPR legislation effectively enforced?
	Regulatory impact assessments	How does the government ensure that laws and regulations do not impose an unnecessary burden on foreign and domestic firms' innovation activities? Are there built-in mechanisms or processes such as SME tests and regulatory impact assessments (RIAs) to periodically review these burdens?
	Regulatory incentives	Does the government grant regulatory incentives (e.g. eased licensing procedures, SEZs) to foreign investors that invest in productive and knowledge-intensive activities? If yes, are there accompanying measures and standards in place to avoid a regulatory "race to the bottom" and mitigate potential socio-economic risks?
	Labour market laws and regulations	Do labour market laws and regulations provide a level of employment stability that encourages learning in the workplace while allowing for enhanced mobility of workers from foreign to domestic firms? How do these regulations take into account other drivers of labour mobility such as the availability (or lack) of skills in the labour market and the absorptive capacities of domestic firms?
		What regulatory measures are in place to address skills shortages in the economy, in particular in FDI-intensive sectors and regions (e.g. tax relief on training expenses, statutory training leave, and entrepreneur visas)?
	Financial market laws and regulations	Do financial market laws and regulations facilitate access to finance for foreign and domestic firms' innovation activities, in particular by addressing financial stability risks, increasing the availability of alternative financing instruments and facilitating access to equity capital?
International agreements & standards	Innovation and SME policy provisions in IIAs	Is the country party to international investment agreements (IIAs) that include provisions on fostering international co-operation and dialogue on science, technology and innovation (STI) policy and facilitating SMEs' participation in international trade and investment?
	Provisions on IPRs, the digital economy and competition in IIAs	Is the country party to international investment agreements with provisions that strengthen domestic legal frameworks for competition, intellectual property rights protection and the digital economy?
Financial & technical support	Investment incentives	Has the government enacted investment incentive schemes targeting productive and knowledge-intensive activities or sectors where domestic absorptive capacities are strong? Are the criteria for the granting of incentives clearly defined, transparent, rules-based and subject to regular reviews?
		What types of investment incentives are provided (e.g. grants, subsidised loans, income-based tax incentives, expenditure-based tax exemptions) and what eligibility criteria or performance requirements apply (e.g. R&D, supplier linkages, skills development, size)?
	Financial support to SMEs	Do government institutions provide targeted financial support (e.g. training vouchers, R&D grants, technology-upgrading loans) to strengthen the competitiveness, productivity and innovation capacity of domestic firms, in particular SMEs? Do financial support schemes support collaborative business-to-business and science-to-business projects involving foreign firms?
	Business and supplier development services	Do government institutions provide technical assistance to domestic firms, in particular SMEs, to improve their productive capacities and help them become suppliers/partners of foreign investors, including through supplier development programmes, technology extension services, product certification, business diagnostics and advisory services?
	Training and skills development services	What measures are in place to address potential skills shortages in FDI-intensive sectors and improve foreign and domestic firms' access to innovation-related skills and capabilities in the domestic labour market (e.g. digital skills, managerial skills and management practices, workforce skills)?
	Network infrastructure	Has the government developed a coherent and comprehensive infrastructure plan, delineating its policy goals and priorities for the development of the country's network infrastructure (e.g. transport, energy, ICTs)? Has the government enacted policies to mobilise public and private investments in infrastructure?
	Knowledge infrastructure	Are knowledge transfer organisations and other facilities in place (e.g. technology centres, collaborative laboratories, business incubators, applied research centres, technology transfer offices) to provide knowledge exchange and innovation services and support FDI-SME collaboration?
	Cluster policies	What initiatives are in place to promote industrial clusters and business networks involving foreign investors, local SMEs and actors of the domestic research and innovation ecosystem (e.g. industrial parks, science and technology parks, financial support to business networks)? How does the government ensure that cluster policies are aligned with sectoral priorities and place-based capabilities?
	Investment promotion	Within the investment promotion agency (IPA), are there clear goals and targets defined to help attract productivity-enhancing and knowledge-intensive FDI? Are there sufficient staff and resources available

Dimension	Instrument	Policy questions
Information & facilitation services	activities	to achieve these goals?
		Are specific sectors, markets and investors targeted as part of the investment promotion activities? If so, what are the prioritisation criteria (e.g. R&D investors) used for the implementation of these activities?
	Investment facilitation and aftercare	Does the IPA provide comprehensive investment facilitation and aftercare services? Does the IPA have sufficient resources and dedicated staff that is trained to identify the sourcing needs of foreign investors and promote linkages with local suppliers?
		Are investment facilitation and aftercare services aligned with the priorities and sectoral scope of supplier development programmes?
	Information services, networking and knowledge exchange activities	Does the IPA provide matchmaking services between foreign and domestic firms? Is there a local suppliers database? If so, is it regularly updated and easy to access for interested firms?
		What information pertaining to the host country's innovation ecosystem and the productive capabilities of domestic firms is made readily available, or available upon request, to foreign investors? What are the main vehicles of information to foreign investors?
		Does the IPA or other government agency organise networking and knowledge exchange events involving foreign and domestic firms?

Notes

1 Regulatory incentives are examined in the previous section as part of the regulatory framework conditions.

2 Since 2007, the OECD has worked to extend the international evidence on tax incentives for R&D and innovation (https://oe.cd/rdtax) and has developed methodologies and data infrastructures in this area. This includes indicators on direct government support for business R&D and on expenditure-based R&D tax incentives (Appelt, Galindo-Rueda and González Cabral, 2019[121]; González Cabral, Appelt and Hanappi, 2021[97]). This work is now being extended to cover income-based tax incentives for R&D and innovation. The STIP Compass is a joint European Commission and OECD database that compiles qualitative information on R&D and innovation policies, covering both tax and non-tax incentives (https://stip.oecd.org/stip/).

3 Policies for improving FDI impacts on job quality and skills

This chapter provides a Policy Toolkit to help governments boost the impacts of foreign direct investment (FDI) on job quality and skills. It describes the main transmission channels of FDI impacts on labour market outcomes and related policies and institutions that can act upon these channels. It builds on the OECD Policy Framework for Investment and is aligned with other OECD instruments and strategies such as the *Guidelines for Multinational Enterprises* and the *2018 Jobs Strategy*.

Main policy principles

1. Provide strategic directions and promote policy coherence and co-ordination on investment, employment and skills development

- Ensure that national development or economic plans provide coherent and strategic directions on investment, employment and skills development objectives and that investment considerations are integrated in employment and skills strategies and vice versa.
- Develop a dedicated strategy that articulates the government's vision on the contribution of investment to job quality and skills development. The strategy sets the goals, identifies priority policy actions and clarifies responsibilities of institutions and co-ordinating bodies.
- Strengthen co-ordination both at strategic and implementing levels by establishing, if inexistent, appropriate co-ordinating bodies or by considering to expand the mandate and composition of existing ones, such as boards of investment promotion agencies and national skills councils.
- Use public-private consultations and inclusive decision-making processes, including social dialogue, to negotiate, receive feedback and build consensus around reforms or programmes at the intersection of investment, employment and skills development.
- Involve investment bodies in labour market information and skill needs and anticipation exercises to reduce information gaps and inform the design, implementation, monitoring and evaluation of employment and skills policies that are better targeted.

2. Ensure that regulations support investment and labour market adjustments while promoting high-quality jobs and protecting the most vulnerable

- Promote labour provisions in international investment and trade agreements that raise labour standards, including by referring to ILO's international conventions and the OECD Guidelines for Multinational Enterprises (MNEs), allow for sufficient domestic policy space and establish institutional mechanisms to promote co-operation and monitoring of labour commitments
- Ensure adaptability of product and labour markets to foreign investors' entry and operations, and that the costs and benefits are fairly shared between workers and firms, by fostering competition and labour mobility while providing a level of employment stability that encourages learning in the workplace.
- Periodically assess existing regulatory restrictions on FDI against evolving public policy objectives on job creation and skills development and, where relevant, consider streamlining or removing them. Involve relevant bodies and social partners in such assessments.
- Set and enforce labour standards that support better working conditions to ensure that those practiced by foreign firms are not less favourable than those by domestic firms and are applied with the same level of diligence in all businesses and regions, including special economic zones.
- Ensure the right to collective bargaining and workers' voice arrangements, including within foreign MNEs and in special economic zones, and that these are adapted to a changing world of work and can promote collective solutions to emerging issues and conflicts.

3. Stimulate labour demand and develop skills through higher investment and targeted active labour market policies and programmes

- Financial support, particularly corporate tax relief, which aims at attracting FDI in job-creating or skill-intensive sectors or in regions with low employment rates should be subject to regular reviews. If used, favour support that is tied to the performance of firms in terms of jobs created or trained workers, including workers of suppliers, and ensure that it addresses specific market failures and is developed through concerted efforts with all relevant bodies.

- Develop training programmes in line with development and investment strategies and in partnership with social partners, and that provide transferable, certifiable skills to facilitate labour mobility and help workers and job seekers move to better jobs, including those adversely affected by changing labour markets, the low-carbon transition and evolving needs of MNEs.

4. Align investment opportunities with labour market potential by addressing information failures and administrative barriers

- Adopt investment promotion activities based on the existing skill base and labour market potential that lower information barriers for investors. Support investors in identifying suppliers with high labour standards, and thereby also incentivise other companies to raise theirs.
- Ensure that job information and matching services reduce information gaps and lower search costs in labour and product markets and stimulate internal labour mobility, particularly of job seekers or workers in communities near foreign firms' activities. Develop these services through concerted efforts or jointly between investment bodies and public employment services.
- Raise awareness about labour standards and incentivise companies to disclose their compliance with them, including local suppliers engaging with foreign buyers that conduct due diligence checks to assess risks in their supply chain.
- Ensure transparency and consistency of procedures and requirements for obtaining permits from labour authorities, including permits for foreign workers.

3.1. Building more inclusive labour markets in a globalised economy

Achieving more inclusive labour markets are increasingly key priorities for governments – in developed and developing countries alike. While the global economy has been recovering from the global financial crisis for several years now, employment and wage growth remain sluggish, and levels of income inequality are unprecedentedly high in most countries. The COVID-19 pandemic has taken an additional toll on labour market resilience by causing activity to collapse and unemployment to soar. Poverty will rise for the first time since 1998, with hundreds of millions of jobs lost, and wage disparities will widen as income losses have been uneven across workers (OECD, 2020[1]).

Policies in favour of job quality and skills development can play a significant role in building forward more inclusive labour markets and ensuring a fair and sustainable recovery. They can help improve well-being of individuals as well as support labour force participation, productivity and growth. Creating better jobs and developing skills figure prominently in the Sustainable Development Goals (SDGs), particularly SDG4 (education) and SDG8 (economic growth). These goals aim to increase the number of people with relevant skills for employment and ensure that all can work productively and receive fair wages. Employment creation, social protection, rights at work, and social dialogue – the four pillars of ILO's Decent Work Agenda – are an integral element of the 2030 Agenda for Sustainable Development. Creating good jobs is also at the core of the OECD Jobs Strategy, which goes beyond job quantity and considers job quality, in terms of both wage and non-wage working conditions, as a key policy priority (Box 3.1). The Strategy also insists on the need to equip people with the right skills in a context of rapidly changing skills demands.

Yet governments still lack a comprehensive policy framework that can help them think about how private investment – a key driver of labour market outcomes – influences job creation and skill upgrading. Investment, and particularly foreign direct investment (FDI), together with international trade, technological change and digitalisation, have been shaping the world of work, with both positive and adverse impacts on host countries' labour markets (OECD, 2019[2]). The COVID-19 crisis is the most recent illustration of that, with the fall in global FDI adversely affecting job creation (Figure 3.1). Prior to the pandemic FDI flows were creating approximately 180 000 jobs every month, and considerably more in developing and emerging countries than in OECD countries. Between January and April of 2020, FDI-induced job creation contracted by over 60% globally. Furthermore, many of the jobs affected by the pandemic depend on the operations of MNEs and their suppliers in global value chains (GVCs). However, the pandemic has revealed how MNEs return to pre-crisis workforce levels more rapidly than domestic firms and adapt faster to new forms of work by ramping up remote working (OECD, 2020[1]; OECD, 2022[3]).

Figure 3.1. The impact of the COVID-19 crisis on jobs created through greenfield FDI

Direct jobs created in thousands (estimates)

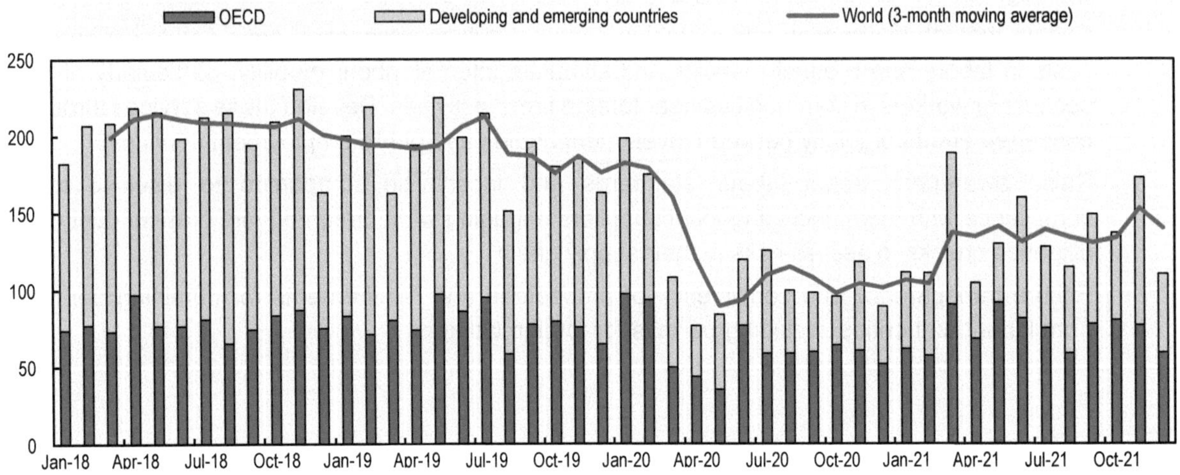

Source: OECD calculations from Financial Times fDi Markets.

3.2. FDI impacts on job quality and skills

FDI can have varying effects on host country labour market outcomes (Figure 3.2, right box). The establishment of a greenfield investment or a change in the nationality of a firm's ownership affects the demand for skilled and unskilled labour, with concomitant effects on employment and wages. Evidence shows that FDI has broadly positive impacts on job creation and earnings, but not all countries and all segments of the population benefit equally (OECD, 2019[2]). More FDI often leads to wage dispersions across firms and workers, mostly due to an increase in the skill premium. FDI can also affect other working conditions, including job security, occupational health and safety at work and core labour rights. Whether FDI improves or undermines working conditions depends on the type of activity of foreign firms and the extent to which they export home country practices and norms or adopt instead those of the host country.

Figure 3.2. Conceptual framework: FDI impacts on job quality and skills development

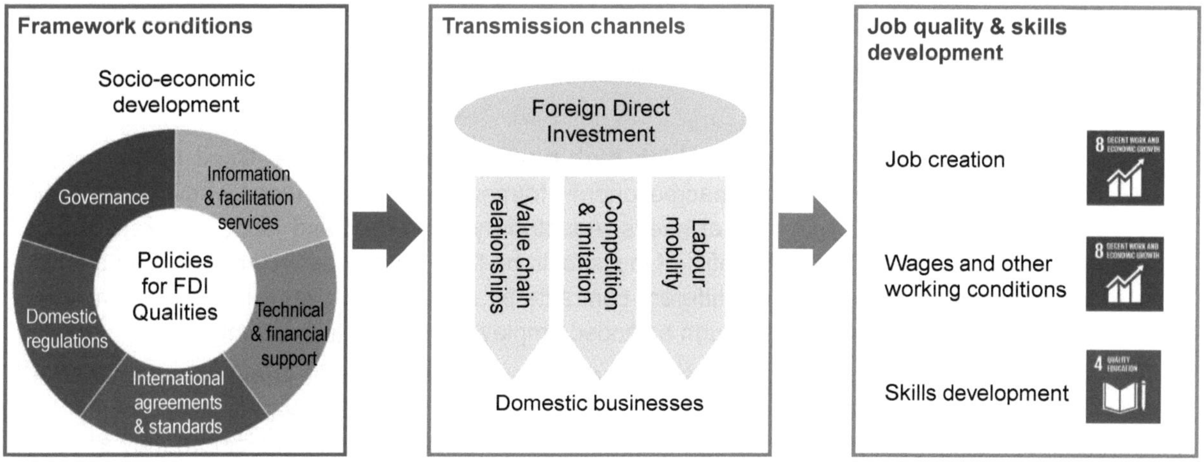

FDI effects on labour market outcomes involve several transmission channels (Figure 3.2, middle box). Outcomes can result from foreign firms' *direct* operations in the host country, such as hiring new workers or firing incumbents following a foreign takeover or offering better or worse working conditions than domestic firms. Foreign firms' direct operations have also *spillover effects* arising from:

1. Their value chain relationships with domestic firms, whether buyers or suppliers
2. Market interactions through competition and imitation (or learning) effects
3. Labour mobility of workers between foreign and domestic firms.

Value chain relationships or labour mobility between foreign and domestic firms can lead to knowledge sharing, and in turn raise productivity, wages and employment. The same spillovers occur when domestic firms imitate foreign competitors. FDI spillovers on labour market outcomes are often specific to certain segments of the workforce, industries, or locations. They are also not always positive if, for instance, foreign firms have irresponsible labour practices with their suppliers – particularly if the business relationship involves an activity with a higher risk of informal employment – or if competition for talent leads to lower quality of skilled labour in domestic firms. The intensity of such adverse impacts often depends on how fast the labour market adjusts to shocks. For instance, FDI does not increase the share of skilled workers and worsens wage disparities when skills shortages are severe and labour mobility is constrained.

The direction and magnitude of the combined direct and spillover effects of FDI on labour market outcomes ultimately depends on the economic structure of the host country and domestic firms' characteristics (size, productivity level, skill-intensity, business and labour practices), labour market characteristics (employment levels, skill base, unionisation rates, etc.) and the policies and institutions in place (Figure 3.2, left box). While the next section focuses on the policies, the following sub-sections describe how FDI affects specific outcomes, namely employment, wages and non-wage working conditions and skills. Annex Table 3.A.1 provides detailed questions for governments to self-assess the impacts of FDI on labour market outcomes.

Box 3.1. The OECD Jobs Strategy, Skills Strategy and Job Quality Framework

The key policy recommendations of the *2018 OECD Jobs Strategy* are organised around three principles:

I. **Promoting an environment in which high-quality jobs can thrive**. Good labour market performance requires a sound macroeconomic framework, a growth-friendly environment and skills evolving in line with market needs. Adaptability in product and labour markets is also needed, and the costs and benefits of this should be fairly shared between workers and firms, as well as among workers on different contracts by avoiding an over-reliance on temporary (often precarious) contracts through balanced employment protection schemes.

II. **Preventing labour market exclusion and protecting individuals against labour market risks**. Supporting the quick (re)integration of job seekers in employment is a top priority, but the new strategy also highlights the importance of addressing challenges before they arise by promoting equality of opportunities and preventing the accumulation of disadvantages over the life-course.

III. **Preparing for future opportunities and challenges in a rapidly changing economy and labour market**. People will need to be equipped with the right skills in a context of rapidly changing skills demands. Workers also need to remain protected against labour market risks in a world where new forms of work may arise.

The OECD also developed a framework for measuring and assessing job quality that guided its 2018 Jobs Strategy. The objective was to revise the 2006 Strategy, which had largely focused its recommendations on the quantity of jobs. The OECD Job Quality Framework measures three aspects of job quality: earning quality (including distributional aspects), labour market security and the quality of the working environment.

The key policy recommendations of the *2019 OECD Skills Strategy* are organised around three components:

I. **Developing relevant skills over the life course**. To ensure that countries are able to adapt and thrive in a rapidly changing world, all people need access to opportunities to develop and maintain strong proficiency in a broad set of skills. This process is lifelong, starting in childhood and youth and continuing throughout adulthood. It is also "life-wide", occurring not only formally in schools and higher education, but also non-formally and informally in the home, community and workplaces.

II. **Using skills effectively in work and society**. Developing a strong and broad set of skills is just the first step. To ensure that countries and people gain the full economic and social value from investments in developing skills, people also need opportunities, encouragement and incentives to use their skills fully and effectively at work and in society.

III. **Strengthening the governance of skills systems**. Success in developing and using relevant skills requires strong governance arrangements to promote co-ordination, co-operation and collaboration across the whole of government; engage stakeholders throughout the policy cycle; build integrated information systems; and align and co-ordinate financing arrangements.

Source: (Cazes, Hijzen and Saint-Martin, 2015[4]; OECD, 2018[5]; 2019[6])

3.2.1. FDI creates both direct and indirect job opportunities but not necessarily for all

FDI affects employment growth or contraction through changes in labour demand. Effects differ by investor entry mode (greenfield project versus M&A) and vary by workforce type (skilled vs. unskilled). Greenfield FDI has a positive and direct effect on the demand for labour, leading to job creation, at least in the short term. A foreign takeover of a domestic firm could either have a positive or negative direct effect on jobs, but evidence shows that it can boost employment as acquired firms' productivity and market share grow (Coniglio, Prota and Seric, 2015[7]; Ragoussis, 2020[8]). In contrast, a divestment by a foreign firm can lead to a drop in employment (Borga, Ibarlucea Flores and Sztajerowska, 2020[9]; Javorcik and Poelhekke, 2017[10]). Irrespective of the entry mode, foreign firms often have a higher demand for skilled workers than domestic firms due to technology advantages (Bandick and Karpaty, 2011[11]; Hijzen et al., 2013[12]).

Whether there will be net employment growth will also depend on FDI spillovers on domestic firms operating in the same value chain, industry or geographical area. Foreign firms could introduce labour-saving techniques that are then adopted by domestic firms through imitation effects, leading to a transitory decline in labour demand, but the progressive integration of foreign firms into the local economy can create a positive effect on jobs in the long run (Jude and Silaghi, 2016[13]; Lee and Park, 2020[14]). FDI may also raise employment at domestic firms in the same location, but only for higher-skilled workers (Setzler and Tintelnot, 2021[15]; Steenbergen and Tran, 2020[16]). FDI spillovers on employment growth are found to be negative, if domestic firms are geographically far from foreign firms as imitation effects are less likely to occur while market competition effects are less sensitive to distance (Lembcke and Wildnerova, 2020[17]).

Foreign and domestic firms' adjustments on the labour market are broadly, albeit not totally, comparable (OECD, 2019[2]). During the COVID-19 pandemic, the resulting decline in FDI as well as crippled MNEs operations adversely affected job creation, with knock-on effects on incomes. For instance, the decline in greenfield FDI reduced potential job creation by half in the first five months of 2020 (OECD, 2020[1]). Nonetheless, foreign businesses have cut jobs less than domestic firms, although many still had had to lay off workers or reduce working hours. Perhaps some MNEs are more resilient to disruptions by relying on a larger set of suppliers and buyers. In addition, foreign firms have managed better than their domestic peers to adapt their modus operandi to the new work realities by ramping up remote working.

3.2.2. FDI raises wages but can also exacerbate disparities if absorptive capacities are poor

In a competitive labour market, there is no reason why comparable foreign and domestic firms should pay different wages to workers with similar skills. Wage differences between the two groups arise, however, often because of other firm- and industry-specific characteristics (Hijzen et al., 2013[12]). Indeed, it is membership in a multinational production network – instead of foreignness – that generates the foreign-firm premium (Setzler and Tintelnot, 2021[15]). Characteristics include firms' size, productivity level, workforce skill intensity, product market power, and working conditions, such as job insecurity. Foreign firms may still pay higher wages to workers with similar skills and tasks, for example, to reduce turnover and lower the risk of technology transfer to competing firms through labour mobility.

The FDI Qualities Indicators and wider evidence confirm the role of productivity, technology and skills as engines to enhance living standards: foreign firms pay higher wages than domestic firms. This is true only to some extent, however. Labour productivity in foreign firms is on average 72% higher than in domestic firms, but foreign firms pay only 31% higher wages, and this gap is larger among non-OECD countries (Figure 3.3). This means that performance premia of foreign firms are not fully translated into wage benefits for workers, possibly because MNEs are more active in highly concentrated markets – which in turn can generate rents. Such rents, and how they are shared with workers, can be due to policy pitfalls, such as barriers to competition (Criscuolo et al., 2020[18]). In developing countries, the foreign wage premium is smaller when institutional quality is higher (Blanas, Seric and Viegelahn, 2019[19]).

Foreign companies do not necessarily lift wages in all sectors and for all workers. The largest wage gains often benefit skilled workers and, in the case of a foreign takeover, those moving from domestic to foreign firms, rather than incumbents, revealing the importance of labour mobility as a crucial transmission channel of FDI impact on wages, at least in the short-run (Hijzen et al., 2013[12]). Foreign firms in low-paid activities do not always pay higher salaries than their domestic peers, however (OECD, 2019[2]). Foreign firms also do not necessarily improve earning conditions of all workers within the firm. For instance, following a foreign takeover, workers at the bottom-end of the wage distribution may not experience as much wage growth as they would have, had their firm not been taken over by a foreign firm (OECD, 2008[20]).

Foreign entrants' competition for talent with domestic firms drives up wages, but potentially reduces the ability of the latter to hire or retain more skilled workers (Lu, Tao and Zhu, 2017[21]). This effect is stronger, and lasts longer, in industries facing skills shortages and in locations with limited labour mobility. Beyond raising the demand for labour, especially of skilled workers, FDI affects competitors' wages through skill-biased technological transfer (imitation effects). Studies point to increased wages in domestic firms as a result of FDI in the same industry or location, particularly in developing countries where skilled labour is scarcer and the technology gap more substantial (Hale and Xu, 2020[22]). In a geographically large country like the United States, foreign firms' operations substantially increase the wages of higher-earning workers in local domestic firms (Setzler and Tintelnot, 2021[15]). FDI effects on wages can also occur in upstream or downstream firms having value chain relationships with foreign firms, but empirical studies are inclusive on the direction of these effects. The FDI Qualities Indicators show, to some extent, that local sourcing by foreign firms amplifies positive spillovers of FDI on wages (OECD, 2019[2]).

Figure 3.3. Foreign firms' wage and productivity premia in OECD and emerging countries

Do foreign firms pay higher wages and are they more productive than their domestic peers? (yes if score > 0)

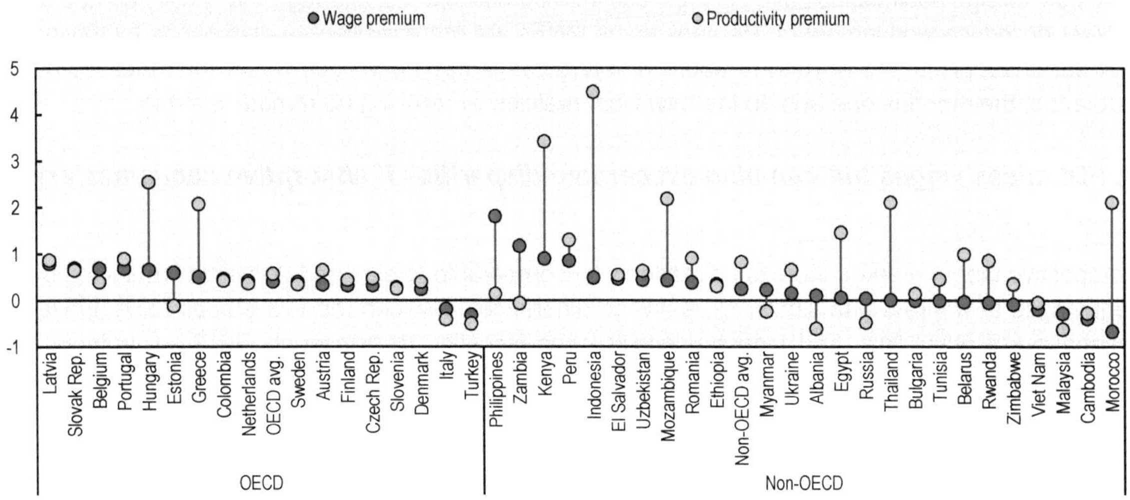

Note: The figure shows OECD and non-OECD countries for which World Bank Enterprise Surveys were available from 2015 and beyond.
Source:OECD (2022[3]), FDI Qualities Indicators: 2022.

If FDI can enhance living standards, it may nonetheless raise disparities through higher wage dispersion within the foreign firm and between foreign and domestic firms. In general, inequality between firms accounts for a sizeable share of the levels in overall wage inequality. Recent work shows that wage premia due to productivity-related rents is an increasingly important driver of between-firm inequality, even more than differences in workers' characteristics, such as skills or gender (Criscuolo et al., 2020[18]). This is relevant in a context where some MNEs are viewed as "superstar" or "winner-takes-most" firms with large market rents. FDI is likely to have a smaller impact on wage inequality in countries or regions with better absorptive capacity, including more adequate skills (Wu and Hsu, 2012[23]; Lin, Kim and Wu, 2013[24]).

3.2.3. FDI can improve non-wage working conditions but not in all sectors or value chains

Job quality also covers non-wage working conditions, including job security, occupational health and safety at work and core labour standards. Foreign and domestic firms may have differentiated impacts on these working conditions but, as for the foreign wage premium, differences often reflect firm- or industry-specific characteristics and are not specific to the ownership status. Foreign and domestic firms could be active in different sectors where companies have different survival rates, worker turnover rates, or propensities to use temporary contracts. Yet, other working conditions are shaped by foreign firms' intrinsic characteristics, such as more advanced management practices than in domestic firms, and good management can lead to higher job satisfaction and better health (Bloom and Van Reenen, 2016[25]). FDI effects on working conditions might also be contingent on foreign firms exporting their home country labour practices, and diffusing them to domestic firms, or responding instead to the host country's standards. Overall, there is little evidence that MNEs transmit their working conditions abroad (Almond and Ferner, 2007[26]).

Evidence on FDI impacts on job security is mixed. The FDI Qualities Indicators suggest that FDI is associated with lower job security. This could be due to the ability of MNEs to rapidly move activities across borders in response to wage movements or changes in regulations (Cuñat and Melitz, 2012[27]). The observed relationship could also reflect foreign firms' concentration in sectors with more exposure to trade fluctuations, or in areas with more flexible labour rules, such as in some special economic zones. Other findings show that, in the case of Sub-Saharan Africa, foreign firms provide more secure jobs, but not in countries with better governance and social policies (Blanas, Seric and Viegelahn, 2019[19]). The wider empirical literature examining these aspects does not provide a clear-cut response, however (Bernard and Sjoholm, 2005[28]; Bernard and Bradford Jensen, 2007[29]; Hijzen et al., 2013[30]; Javorcik, 2015[31]). There is also no evidence that foreign firms compensate workers for increased job insecurity or more difficult working conditions by paying higher wages (Hijzen et al., 2013[12]; OECD, 2017[32]).

There is a dearth of evidence relating FDI to occupational health and safety at work. Some studies suggest a positive correlation between fewer job accidents rates and FDI (Alsan, Bloom and Canning, 2006[33]) or find a negative effect of FDI on population health (Herzer and Nunnenkamp, 2012[34]). The FDI Qualities Indicators show that greenfield FDI tends to be concentrated in activities with higher risks of occupational injury, including in OECD countries, such as in manufacturing or infrastructure. During the COVID-19 pandemic, foreign firms managed better and faster than domestic business to adapt their modus operandi to the new work reality by ramping-up teleworking, potentially reducing workers' exposure to COVID-19 (OECD, 2020[1]). Fewer workers can telework in poorer economies, however – more skilled workers have higher odds to work remotely. MNEs could accelerate the adoption of new forms of work in host countries through competition and imitation effects, labour mobility, and relationships with their suppliers or buyers.

Evidence indicates that inward FDI and core labour standards, which cover the freedom of association, the abolition of forced and child labour and the eliminations of discriminations at work, are positively correlated, but not in all sectors (Kucera, 2002[35]; OECD, 2008[20]; Blanton and Blanton, 2012[36]). MNEs may shy away from investing in countries with low labour standards because of reputational risks and to fulfil international standards on responsible business conduct or core labour rights, sometimes adopted in home country regulations. This however does not say whether, once they are operating, foreign firms help improve working conditions, including in their relationships with local suppliers and buyers. Furthermore, while the positive relationship between FDI and core labour standards holds at the aggregate level, there are significant variation among sectors – mining, oil and gas and services may be important exceptions (Blanton and Blanton, 2012[36]). FDI mode of entry also matters. One study finds that M&As tend to have minimal, or slightly negative, effects on labour rights, whereas joint ventures and greenfield FDI can improve workers' rights. The sectors and motivations associated with the two modes of entry increase more labour demand, improving the bargaining power of workers (Biglaiser and Lee, 2019[37]).

FDI impacts on non-wage working conditions may also be increasingly affected by trends in digitalisation, which are themselves accelerated by cross-border investment. New business models are emerging, including the platform economy, in which self-employed workers provide services through online platforms often owned by foreign firms. These flexible working arrangements have created new jobs but also raised concerns about job security, poor working conditions and a weak bargaining position vis-à-vis platform firms (OECD, 2019[38]). Work through platforms is still a limited phenomenon in both developed and developing countries, and the exact impact of FDI on related working conditions is yet to be explored.

Another way FDI can affect job quality is through impacts on informal employment. In the absence of labour rights or social security, informal workers have more precarious working arrangements and worst working conditions. The evidence is clear that jobs in foreign firms are largely formal, but the wider effects of FDI on employment formalisation are less obvious. Transition to formal employment is often faster in countries with higher economic growth and exposure to global markets, including through higher FDI (La Porta and Shleifer, 2014[39]; McCaig and Pavcnik, 2015[40]). Evidence from Mexico, Turkey or Viet Nam shows that FDI leads to higher levels of formal employment, although this impact is not systematic across regions and sectors (Escobar and Dougherty, 2013[41]; Cao, 2020[42]; Steenbergen and Tran, 2020[16]). Other evidence suggest that FDI leads to higher demand for informal labour through increased outsourcing from foreign to non-formal firms (Beladi, Dutta and Kar, 2016[43]). MNEs are increasingly seeking to enforce compliance with labour standards in their supply chain relationships, however, which can lead to less sourcing from informal firms (Narula, 2019[44]). Overall, FDI positive spillovers are relatively weak in the informal sector as informal firms are mired in low productivity, with limited absorptive capacity (Narula, 2020[45]).

3.2.4. FDI increases the demand for and supply of skilled workers but labour market adjustments can be costly

Foreign firms – especially from more advanced economies – often bring new technologies that require complementary skills. If, as a result, skilled employment increases more than unskilled employment, the share of skilled workers in the host country will also grow. Many studies have shown that FDI raises the demand for skilled workers. The most salient example is Mexico's maquiladoras where FDI has accounted for over 50% of the increase in the skilled labour wage share that occurred in the late 1980s (Feenstra and Hanson, 1997[46]). Other studies have confirmed since then that FDI has led to an increase in the demand for skilled labour (Bandick and Karpaty, 2011[47]; Peluffo, 2014[48]).

That foreign firms raise the demand for skilled-labour in a specific industry does not necessarily imply they operate in high-skilled sectors of the host economy. The FDI Qualities Indicators show that FDI tends to be concentrated in sectors with lower shares of skilled workers in countries with competitive wages and labour-intensive manufacturing activities (OECD, 2019[2]). FDI could also affect the demand for specific tasks that parent companies want to offshore (Autor, Levy and Murnane, 2003[49]). For instance, routine tasks can be more easily offshored, thus explaining why foreign affiliates in developing countries may be less skill-intensive than their parent company (but not necessarily less than domestic firms in the same industry). Foreign investors can also increase the supply of skills by providing training to their employees or to those of domestic companies as part of support activities (Crespo and Fontoura, 2007[50]). They may also induce local firms to invest in upskilling in response to rising competitive pressure from their presence in the market (competition effects) or to imitate more profitable foreign firms' practices (imitation effects), including by training workers (Blomström and Kokko, 2002[51]).

Through impact on the demand and supply of skilled labour, FDI can enlarge the share of skilled workers in the host country, which, in turn, creates a virtuous circle as new investors will select the location for their knowledge-intensive projects. Ultimately, FDI impacts on skill development will depend on how fast the supply side can respond to increased demand for skilled labour. When skill shortages exist in a region or industry, labour market adjustments from an unskilled to a skilled labour force can be lengthy and costly (Hale and Xu, 2020[22]). In that case, foreign entrants will offer much higher wages to attract available talent, thus exacerbating wage disparities and crowding out employment in domestic firms, without raising the share of skilled workers in the host economy, at least in the short term. This illustrates the importance of addressing skill shortages and promoting labour mobility across regions and industries as ways to reap the benefits of FDI for skills while mitigating adverse distributional impacts (Becker et al., 2020[52]).

3.3. Policies that influence FDI impacts on job quality and skills

Policies that are conducive to investment in general influence FDI entering the host country and its labour market implications (OECD, 2015[53]). They are, however, not sufficient to act on the different – direct and indirect – transmission channels of FDI impacts on job quality and skills development. Beyond a conducive investment climate, policy makers must ensure that institutions, strategies and policies that are at the intersection of investment, labour and skills development create the conditions to improve FDI impacts while mitigating potential adverse effects (Table 3.1). These include product and labour market regulations that are adapted to foreign firms' entry and operations. But flexibility is not sufficient to deliver quality jobs and should be combined with measures that address specific market failures resulting from information failures or externalities resulting from FDI. Such interventions can cushion or amplify the spillover effects of foreign firms on the labour market, including distributional effects. Beyond measures implemented at national level, policy makers need to promote internationally agreed principles and conventions that can help ensure, inter alia, high labour standards in the operations of foreign firms.

Table 3.1. Policy instruments influencing the impact of FDI on job quality and skills development

Principle 1: Provide strategic directions and ensure policy coordination and coherence on investment, labour and skills development	Governance	Oversight and coordination bodies
		Public-private and social dialogues
		Labour market information and skills needs assessments
Principle 2: Ensure that regulations support investment and labour market adjustments while safeguarding quality jobs and protecting the most vulnerable	Domestic regulations	Product market regulations
		Labour market regulations and standards
		Collective bargaining rights and workers' voice
Principle 3: Adhere to and promote internationally-agreed principles that can help ensure high labour standards in the operations of foreign companies	International agreements & standards	Labour provisions in investment and trade agreements
		Adherence to OECD Guidelines on MNEs
		Global framework agreements
Principle 4: Stimulate labour demand and develop workers' skills through targeted investment and active labour market policies and programmes	Financial support	Corporate tax relief in targeted sectors or regions
		Corporate tax relief against job or training commitment
		Employment, wage or training subsidies
	Technical Support	Targeted training programmes, including for suppliers
		Training and skills development services (e.g. VET)
Principle 5: Align investment opportunities with labour market needs and skills base byaddressing information failures and administrative barriers	Information & facilitation services	Job search services
		Investment promotion and facilitation
		Corporate disclosure on labour standards
		Social support services (e.g. transport)
		Public awareness campaigns

The majority of policies do not explicitly target foreign firms, but they are particularly relevant to ensure that FDI has positive impacts on labour market outcomes. Indeed, the contribution of foreign firms to job quality and skills development is often linked to their performance, an aspect that does not justify developing specific policies for them. Nonetheless, the extent to which foreign and domestic firms react to the same policy setting can vary, together with their respective labour market outcomes. For instance, MNEs can choose to move production across subsidiaries following a policy change in one host country, an option that domestic firms do not have. Policymaking should take into consideration these differentiated impacts on foreign and domestic business, including through policy co-ordination. Policies considered in this Policy Toolkit build and expand on Chapter 8 "Developing human resources for investment" of the OECD Policy Framework for Investment (Box 3.2). Annex Table 3.A.2 provides detailed questions for governments to self-assess policies influencing the impacts of FDI on job quality and skills development.

Box 3.2. OECD Policy Framework for Investment: Core questions and principles for developing human resources for investment

1. Has the government established a coherent and comprehensive human resource development policy framework consistent with its broader development and investment strategy and its implementation capacity?
2. Is there an effective system for tackling discrimination that affects labour market outcomes?
3. What steps has the government taken to increase participation in basic schooling and to improve the quality of instruction so as to leverage human resource assets to attract and to seize investment opportunities?
4. Is the economic incentive sufficient to encourage individuals to invest in higher education and life-long learning, supporting improvements in the investment environment through a more qualified skill base?
5. To what extent does the government promote effective training programmes, including through involving the private sector?
6. Does the government have an affordable, effective and efficient overall health system?
7. What mechanisms are being put in place to promote and enforce core labour standards?
8. To what extent do labour market regulations support job creation and the government's investment attraction strategy?
9. How does the government assist large-scale labour adjustments? What role is business encouraged to play in easing the transition costs associated with labour adjustment?
10. What steps are being taken to ensure that labour market regulations support an adaptable workforce and maintain the ability of firms to modify their operations and investment planning?
11. To what extent does the government allow companies to recruit workers from abroad when they are unable to obtain the skills needed from the domestic labour market?

Source:OECD (2015[53]), Policy Framework for Investment, 2015 Edition, https://doi.org/10.1787/9789264208667-en

3.3.1. Provide strategic direction and ensure policy co-ordination and coherence on investment, labour and skills development

FDI that contributes to inclusive labour market outcomes can hardly be achieved through fragmented and isolated policy design, delivery and evaluation. Governments, together with the private sector and social partners, should articulate a clear vision on the contribution of FDI to job quality and skills by ensuring that national strategies provide coherent and interrelated directions on investment, employment and skills development objectives. It is equally important to strengthen co-ordination mechanisms – or establish them if inexistent – that can effectively support social dialogue and collective solutions to emerging labour market issues driven by FDI. Inter-agency collaboration can also improve data collection efforts to better monitor the impact of FDI and help inform the policy design and evaluation. In particular, involving investment bodies in skill needs assessments can help better anticipate future needs and adapt policies accordingly.

National strategies and plans can provide coherent and strategic directions by integrating investment considerations in employment and skills strategies and vice versa

Governments usually have no dedicated strategy relating FDI to job quality and skills, but most, if not all, set priorities and goals on investment, employment and skills development in various strategies and plans. Multi-year national development or growth plans provide overarching directions in a wide range of policy areas and, if well-articulated, a coherent vision to ensure that initiatives and reforms in one area (e.g. investment) support – or do not jeopardise – strategic goals in other areas (e.g. employment). Cross-cutting strategies can also steer policy action towards developing priority activities or value chains that are aligned with the country's aspirations and labour market realities. These national priorities, goals and policies ultimately affect the FDI transmission channels – the ways in which foreign firms have a direct and indirect impact on labour market outcomes – even when they are not strictly related to investment.

Coherent national development or growth plans also ensure alignment of objectives across specific strategies on investment, employment and skills development. In practice, this entails integrating investment considerations in, *inter alia*, employment and skills strategies and vice versa. This is the case of Rwanda, for instance, where the *2019 National Employment Strategy* includes specific goals on investment, such as to support investment with strong linkages in labour-intensive sectors (Table 3.2). The strategy clarifies responsibilities across a wide range of institutions, going well beyond the Ministry of Labour, and provides an estimated budget for each goal. Similarly, the *2011-20 Jordan National Employment Strategy* identifies FDI as a key driver of growth and delivers a diagnosis on its impact, indicating that FDI created mostly short-term job opportunities, often in the construction sector, with few long-term effects (OECD, 2022[54]). The strategy provides policy directions on investment, such as to align tax incentives to investors with the country's ambition of becoming a knowledge-based economy.

Table 3.2. Rwanda's 2019 National Employment Strategy includes specific actions on investment

Strategic goal: extend, prioritise and incentivise investment with strong linkages in employment-intensive sectors

Major Policy Actions	Lead implementing institution	Other implementing institutions
Place emphasis on choosing employment-intensive technologies	Ministry of Trade and Industry	Private Sector Federation; Rwanda Development Board
Consider the impact of investment on the number and quality of jobs created	Rwanda Development Board	Ministry of Trade and Industry; Private Sector Federation
Carry out comprehensive employment impact assessment of infrastructure investment	Ministry of Infrastructure	Rwanda Development Board; Private Sector Federation
Link incentive structures for FDI to the number and quality of jobs created and skills upgrading of local labour force	Ministry of Trade and Industry	Rwanda Development Board; Private Sector Federation
Target policy incentives to employment-intensive sectors and the participation of the poor in high-growth sectors	Ministry of Trade and Industry	Rwanda Development Board; Private Sector Federation

Source: OECD based on Rwanda's Revised 2019 National Employment Policy.

It is equally relevant to incorporate the labour market and skills dimensions into the country's investment strategy, and in a way that is adapted to the format of such documents. Some countries have comprehensive strategies that outline the government's objectives and reform plans to foster investment and the roles and responsibilities of all relevant government bodies. Such strategies could provide clear policy directions on labour market reforms adapted to investors' entry and operations or on promoting high labour standards through international investment and trade agreements. Most investment strategies are narrower in scope and set the government's FDI attraction targets (e.g. sectors), tools (e.g. fairs, tax incentives, aftercare services) and performance indicators (e.g. average wages in foreign firms). They are increasingly taking into consideration quality jobs and skills as outcomes of FDI (OECD, 2020[55]). For instance, the development of Ireland's 2021-24 investment promotion strategy was informed by *Future Jobs Ireland*, which itself seeks to address challenges and opportunities for FDI arising from changing skills demand. FDI that support upskilling is a new focus of the strategy and is addressed through various initiatives to promote investments in training.

Co-ordination bodies with clear mandates and inclusive public-private and social dialogue support policy delivery at the intersection of investment, employment and skills

The formulation and implementation of strategic objectives at the intersection of investment, employment and skills development are complex, and do not fit neatly within a single governmental department or agency. They require the involvement of several ministries, implementing agencies, social partners, and the private sector, including the foreign firms themselves. Given the multitude of actors with different interests, achieving a consensus between a broad range of stakeholders within and outside government is difficult. It is therefore important that responsibilities are balanced, explicit, sufficiently funded, and mutually understood by all actors. It is also crucial to establish, both at strategic and implementing levels, appropriate co-ordinating bodies with clear mandates or to adapt the governance structure of existing bodies, such as boards of investment promotion agencies or skills councils, to be more inclusive and support collaborative decision-making, while managing the risk of undue influence from special interests.

In most countries, mandates over investment are separated from employment and skills, which are themselves scattered across various ministries and agencies – yet they are reasonably more integrated than with investment. Mandates are often enshrined in law or spelled-out in national strategies that often also define governance relationships with other bodies. Labour market ministries and agencies often set the country's labour policy, regulate industrial relations and provide public employment services to individuals. The governance of skills systems entails more collaboration across government departments, including investment bodies. Education ministries and agencies are often in charge of policies related to skills development, whereas labour market ministries and agencies devise policies that maximise the effective use of skills by promoting further training opportunities and labour market activation measures. Ministries of finance are responsible for ensuring that the resources exist and for aligning financial incentives to maximise the effectiveness of employment and skills policies (OECD, 2020[56]).[1]

Bodies mandated with investment policy often include departments in the ministry of economy or industry and investment promotion agencies (IPAs). They can play a key role by developing and promoting policies for regional, sectoral or broad economic development, in which employment and skills occupy a central place. Thus, while investment bodies may not be directly involved in employment or skills policies, they still actively shape impacts of FDI by promoting and facilitating investment in specific job-creating or skill-intensive sectors, granting tax incentives to firms investing in regions with low employment rates or influencing wider reforms through policy advocacy actions. Investment bodies can also be responsible of raising investors' awareness of labour and other sustainability standards. It is important to align allocated budgets with such responsibilities to ensure effective implementation.

The extent to which investment, employment and skills mandates can be integrated – or overlapping if not well-defined – depends on national context and is most likely greater in countries that receive significant FDI. In Rwanda's *2019 National Employment Strategy*, the Ministry of Trade and Industry and the Rwanda Development Board, the country's IPA, are assigned specific actions to improve the FDI contribution to job quality and skills (Table 3.2). In fact, one mandate of Rwanda's IPA is to align skills development with labour market demands, including by co-ordinating and funding training opportunities (Box 3.3). Likewise, the Costa Rican or Thai IPAs have widened their mandates to also support skills development (OECD, 2021[57]). These cases are likely to be the exception rather than the norm, however, and they are not necessarily governance models for other countries with different contexts and priorities. But they illustrate how mandates can be partly integrated to leverage FDI for more inclusive labour markets, as long as responsibilities are clear, mutually understood by all and grounded in sound and coherent strategies.

Box 3.3. Promoting FDI, employment and skills under one umbrella agency: The case of Rwanda

Rwanda Development Board (RDB) is a government institution whose mandate is to accelerate Rwanda's economic development by enabling private sector growth. It is principally responsible for promoting domestic and foreign investments, but other key services include skills development and improving workers' employability.

The *2019 National Employment Strategy* indicates that while promoting exports to regional and international markets of goods and services, the opportunities for labour mobility should also be given much consideration by RDB. In its mandate to provide guidelines, analyse project proposals and follow up on the implementation of Government decisions in line with public and private investment, RDB should mainstream employment opportunities in project proposals.

RDB vision is skilling Rwanda for economic transformation. The Chief Skills Office was established under the RDB in 2018 to align skills development with labour market demands. The Chief Skills Office, together with key stakeholders in the skills development and employment promotion ecosystem, developed the National Skills Development and Employment Promotion Strategy (NSDEPS).

The Chief Skills Office is composed of two departments: the strategic development capacity department and the targeted labour market interventions department. It is mandated to provide effective oversight and co-ordination in the skills development and employment promotion ecosystem. Goals include promoting and co-ordinating sector skills, capacity development strategies and actions to respond to private sector needs; conducting labour market analysis to identify current and future skills needs in priority sectors and for key investment projects; and facilitating labour market integration through innovative partnerships and interventions.

Source: OECD based on https://rdb.rw/.

Effective horizontal co-ordination also can help achieve a better alignment across investment, employment and skills policies. In general, governments have no committees (or similar structures) exclusively dedicated to co-ordination between ministries, agencies and social partners dealing with labour and skills development and those responsible for investment. If they are to be created, such inter-governmental committees need clear and strong internal governance structures, and decision-making processes should be agreed on to maximise the commitment and involvement of all stakeholders, including technical agencies, the private sector, social partners, and specific groups that are of potential relevance such as youth representations. Establishing such dedicated committees may not be necessary, however, and could be even counter-productive, if other, narrower, co-ordinating mechanisms that already exist could be realistically adapted to help ensure some alignment across investment, employment and skills policies.

On the investment side, existing co-ordinating committees such as boards of IPAs could consider involving the labour and skills communities to help them voice their concerns with regards to FDI, better co-ordinate on specific measures and build consensus around future reforms that are of relevance to them (e.g. to introduce tax incentives for firms that provide training). In Jordan, for instance, the Minister of Labour sits in the Investment Council, a high-level co-ordinating body headed by the Prime Minister that sets the country's investment strategy and oversees the work of the IPA (OECD, 2022[54]). In general, the presence of representatives from the labour or skills communities is not widespread across IPAs' boards (or similar structures). The status of such boards and the breadth of their co-ordinating role can strongly vary across agencies (OECD, 2018[58]). In many countries, boards of IPAs have solely an advisory role that is confined to investment promotion and facilitation activities.

It is equally relevant to envisage including representatives of investment bodies in committees co-ordinating employment or skills policies. They can, for instance, provide feedback on labour market reforms under discussion or voice the concerns of foreign investors in terms of training needs. In Ireland, the National Skills Council provides advice on skills needs and secures delivery of the identified needs, as well as bringing together a wide range of actors, including the CEO of IDA Ireland, the Irish IPA. The CEO is charged with providing regular updates on sectoral opportunities and potential target areas for increased FDI and advice on issues associated with the availability of skills to support employment. Respectively, the 2021-24 investment promotion strategy indicates that the IPA will collaborate with the Department of Education and Skills, the National Skills Council, or the Expert Group on Future Skills Needs.

FDI can be a forward-looking indicator of what jobs and skills will be in demand in the future and could therefore be integrated into skills anticipation systems

FDI is a key driver of GVCs and technological changes (e.g. automation and digitalisation) that influence the kind of jobs that are available, the skills needed to perform them and related working conditions (e.g. new working arrangements on teleworking). The costs and benefits of these megatrends are complex and increase the uncertainty surrounding the future of work. In this context, it is of paramount importance to build responsive skill assessment and anticipation systems that enable countries to react to changing labour market and skills demands (OECD, 2019[6]). FDI decisions can constitute a forward-looking indicator of what jobs and skills will be in demand in the near future, rather than trade flows that reflect past investment decisions (Hallward-Driemeier and Nayyar, 2019[59]). Collecting information on foreign firms' operations and skills needs will help governments developing adequate policies, such as training programmes, that can prevent skills mismatches and shortages as well as reduce retraining costs. For instance, ILO's "Skills for Trade and Economic Diversification" guide recommends disaggregating data between foreign and domestic businesses when FDI accounts for a significant part of a sector.

Many countries have put in place labour market information systems and tools for assessing and anticipating skills needs, but limited co-ordination between stakeholders is often a barrier preventing the information from being used further in policy making (OECD, 2016[60]). Ministries of Labour and Education, the statistical offices and employer organisations are the actors most frequently involved in skills assessment and foresight exercises. Involving the investment community, including the IPA and the foreign firms, in such foresight exercises could help reduce the gap between the information produced and the skills needs driven by FDI. IPAs have often access to unique information on MNEs' operations and run surveys to identify their challenges and skills needs (OECD, 2018[61]). Furthermore, IPAs are increasingly tracking FDI impact by setting key performance indicators (KPIs), including on employment, wages and skills (Sztajerowska and Martincus, 2021[62]). Such data could be shared or even automatically connected to skills assessment and anticipation systems to ensure that policy responses are timely, coherent and well-targeted.

3.3.2. Ensure that regulations support investment and labour market adjustments that create good job opportunities for all and are adapted to a changing world of work

Product and labour market regulations affect FDI location choice, characteristics and, in turn, labour market impacts. They also affect how labour markets adjust in response to FDI entry and spillovers – impact is likely to be greater in settings with more efficient resource reallocation. Solid collective bargaining institutions and high labour standards are however fundamental to ensure that FDI creates opportunities for all. Regulations also include internationally agreed principles that can be instigated by governments, such as by joining international conventions or including labour provisions in investment agreements. They can also consist of non-binding recommendations addressed directly to business, such as the OECD Guidelines for MNEs, or agreements between MNEs and global union federations to ensure common labour standards across an MNE global operation.

Openness to foreign investment and wider pro-competition policies can help ensure that expected labour market gains from FDI materialise and are fairly shared

Governments should periodically assess existing regulatory restrictions on FDI against evolving public policy objectives on job quality and skills development and, where relevant, consider streamlining or removing them. Discriminatory measures on foreign investors' entry and operations deter FDI and, in turn, potential labour market gains from higher investment. Forgone FDI benefits hinge on the labour or skill-intensity of restricted sectors as well as their propensity to increase labour supply – increased investment in higher education could support the growth of a skilled workforce. The type of discriminatory measure also matters. Joint venture requirements may push foreign investors to limit skills transfers while restrictions on the employment of foreign personnel in key management positions may limit the diffusion of managerial expertise (Moran, Graham and Blomström, 2005[63]). In Jordan, for instance, restrictions on full foreign ownership exist in business services, transport and tourism, while greenfield FDI has a strong job creation potential in these sectors, including for the many unemployed young graduates (Figure 3.4).

Figure 3.4. FDI regulatory restrictions and job-creating potential of greenfield FDI in Jordan

FDI restrictions: a value higher than zero indicates that restrictions in Jordan are higher than the OECD average

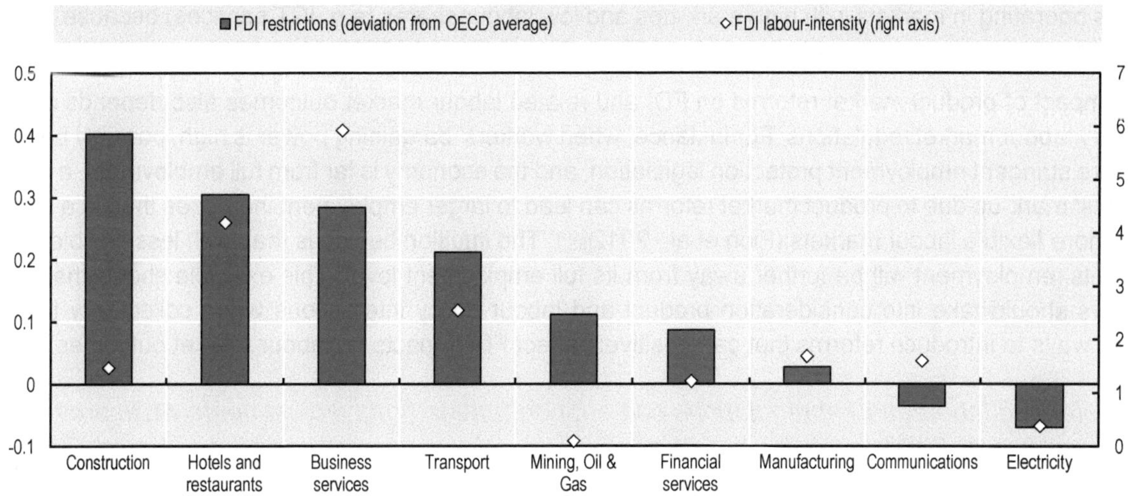

Source: OECD FDI Regulatory Restrictiveness Index and Financial Times fDi Markets; OECD (2022[54]), FDI Qualities Review of Jordan: Strengthening sustainable investment, https://doi.org/10.1787/736c77d2-en.

Governments often introduce FDI restrictions with the stated objective of protecting domestic firms (and their workers) from foreign competition or to ensure that FDI generates high development benefits, for instance when investor entry is conditional on mandatory job creation requirements. But these policies may not be optimal for tackling such concerns as they create uncertainty and negatively influence foreign investors' decisions (Mistura and Roulet, 2019[64]). By limiting competitive pressures, FDI restrictions also deter innovation and potential learning opportunities by domestic competitors, and related productivity spillovers that can help them retain their workers in better-paid jobs (Chapter 2). It is therefore essential to involve labour market bodies and social partners when assessing the costs and benefits of FDI restrictions as it can help promote collective solutions and build consensus around meaningful liberalisation reforms.

Whether openness leads to positive impacts of FDI on labour market outcomes also depends on the time horizon. For instance, liberalisation can crowd out domestic competitors and increase wage inequality in the short term, particularly in non-tradable services where foreign firms are more likely to capture market shares such as in the construction sector. Indeed, FDI in services is often associated with the largest increases in wage inequality because lower-skilled workers can be displaced in favour of higher-skilled workers. In the longer term, services liberalisation improves productivity in other sectors and can generate significant labour market gains, although not necessarily for all segments of the labour force. Governments could prioritise the tradable services sectors with solid comparative advantages to limit the transitory labour market losses from liberalising other services FDI (Steenbergen and Tran, 2020[16]).

Together with FDI restrictions, other regulations affect the degree of product market competition, including state control of business enterprises and barriers to trade, innovation and entrepreneurship. Product market competition can reduce foreign firms' entry and operation costs, increase their productivity and, in turn, job-creating potential (Fiori et al., 2012[65]; Gal and Theising, 2015[66]). For instance, research on the role of product market regulations for the employment dynamics of entering and incumbent firms suggests that, in sectors that are more risky or financially dependent, more stringent product market regulation is negatively associated with the net job contribution of firms (Calvino, Criscuolo and Menon, 2016[67]).

Pro-competitive product market reforms and competition policy enforcement can also help achieve fairer sharing of productivity gains by foreign firms. As restrictions on FDI decrease, countries need to adopt and enforce sound measures to control anti-competitive practices (OECD, 2018[68]). Enhanced competition can help reduce rents of firms active in highly concentrated markets, and to share more fairly these gains with workers. In particular, strengthened competition could contain rents in "superstar" or "winner-take-most" MNEs operating in markets with high mark-ups and low labour shares (e.g. ICT services) because of large product market concentration (Autor et al., 2020[69]; Criscuolo et al., 2020[70]).

The impact of product market reforms on FDI and related labour market outcomes also depends on host country labour market regulations. For instance, when workers' bargaining power is high, possibly because of more stringent employment protection legislation, and the economy is far from full employment, a decline in firms' mark-up due to product market reforms can lead to larger employment increases than in a context with more flexible labour markets (Fiori et al., 2012[65]). The intuition behind is that, with less flexible labour markets, employment will be further away from its full employment level. This example shows that policy makers should take into consideration product and labour policy interactions when collectively thinking about ways to introduce reforms that can positively affect FDI impacts on labour market outcomes.

Balanced labour market regulations can support foreign firms' adjustments while providing a level of employment stability that encourages learning in the workplace

Stringent employment protection can increase firms' labour adjustment costs but also improves job quality. Greater flexibility of the host country's labour market matters for the location choice of investors and affects FDI volumes – and thus job creation – as well as their skill intensity. For instance, stringent legislation can deter FDI in the services sector more than in manufacturing (Javorcik and Spatareanu, 2005[71]). It may also dissuade R&D firms from locating their core innovation projects, as these need drastic employment adjustment because many workers with new skills are needed (Griffith and Macartney, 2014[72]). Impact can differ across contracts and, for instance, stringent legislation on regular contracts may affect FDI-related employment more adversely than rules on temporary work (Gross and Ryan, 2008[73]). At the same time, job security protects workers from being fired in response to small business fluctuations, encourages them to invest in long-term training and is often associated with better (mental) health (OECD, 2018[5]).

Once established, foreign firms do not appear to be more constrained by labour regulations than domestic firms, although they can be in some countries – including those with high FDI stocks (Figure 3.5). Employment protection legislation may matter less for foreign firms that can move production across subsidiaries located in different countries or that are attracted by markets with low production costs (Leibrecht and Scharler, 2009[74]; Cuñat and Melitz, 2012[27]). These firms may be able to bargain from a privileged position with host governments and unions, thus obtaining exceptions on hiring and firing practices (Navaretti, Checchi and Turrini, 2003[75]). Notwithstanding the additional leeway MNEs may have over domestic companies, their divestment decisions might still be affected by regulations such as those on collective dismissals – which often cover large firms – particularly footloose large foreign firms.

Figure 3.5. Percent of firms identifying labour regulations as a major constraint, by ownership

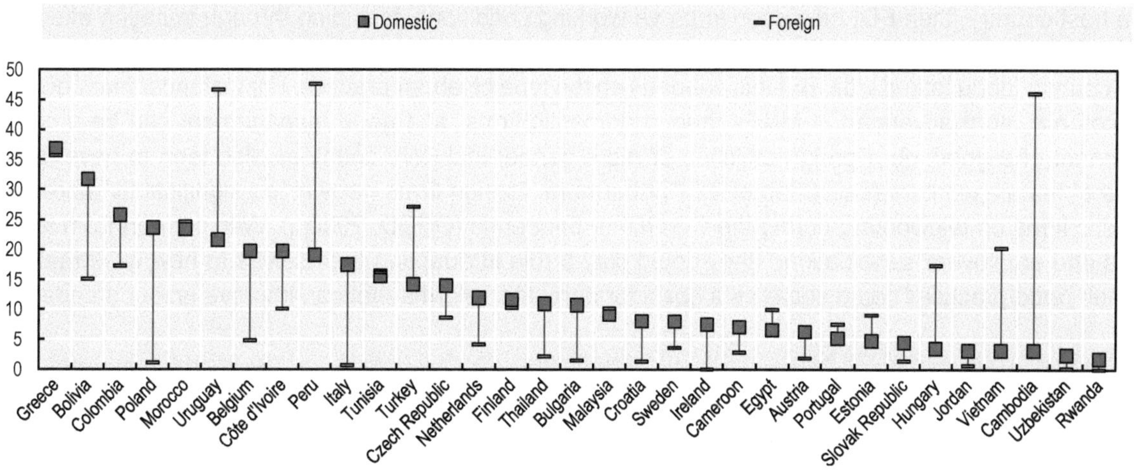

Note: The figure shows a group of selected OECD and non-OECD countries for which firm-level surveys were available from 2015 and beyond.
Source: OECD based on the World Bank Enterprise Surveys.

Employment protection legislation also affects how the wider labour market adjusts in response to FDI entry and spillovers. For instance, stricter employment protection can deter or delay labour mobility from domestic to foreign firms while it is typically via this channel that FDI enhances wages in host countries, at least in the short term (Hijzen et al., 2013[12]). However, it may protect vulnerable workers that otherwise would have been displaced and lose out via long unemployment spells or lower wages in post-displacement jobs, potentially in the informal economy. When local absorptive capacities are sufficiently high, i.e. when skills in demand by foreign firms are available, more flexible labour markets can host FDI without necessarily reducing employment or increasing wage disparities between foreign and domestic firms (Becker et al., 2020[52]).

Other regulations include working-time arrangements, minimum wages, occupational health and safety at work, legal guarantees of social insurance regimes or legislation on foreign workers – foreign firms tend to rely more often on foreign workers than their domestic peers do. Minimum labour standards ensure that those practiced by foreign firms are not less favourable than those by domestic firms. This helps to ensure that FDI is not worsening working conditions in the host country. Labour standards can be established through legislation, collective agreements or both. Core labour standards of the ILO aim to: 1) eliminate all forms of forced or compulsory labour; 2) effectively abolish child labour; 3) eliminate discrimination in respect of employment and occupation; and 4) ensure the freedom of association and the right to collective bargaining (see next sections). Labour market regulation must also enable companies to create formal jobs and avoid creating incentives for employers and workers alike to shift to, or remain in, the informal economy, where workers are not protected by labour laws and lack access to work-related measures of social protection. Specific strategies are needed to encourage workers to move into the formal economy and to address social protection for workers in the informal sectors (OECD, 2015[53]).

Countries may not want to raise or enforce labour standards because they fear this will deter foreign investors. But empirical evidence suggests that lowering labour standards does not facilitate, and may even discourage, FDI and might also change its composition and related societal benefits (Kucera, 2002[35]; OECD, 2008[20]). This holds equally in special economic zones, where governments should further harmonise labour standards, in particular minimum wages or restrictions to freedom of association, with those in the wider economy. Evidence shows that there is no strong link between higher formal labour standards and better actual labour practices, indicating that labour standards are not always properly enforced (OECD, 2008[20]). This is likely to reflect institutional weaknesses and insufficient resources.

When foreign firms export their home country labour standards practices, and these are higher than those of the host country, then FDI may even improve working conditions, including through imitation effects or through relationships with suppliers. There is, however, limited evidence that foreign firms export their home country labour standards. But this depends on the type of labour practice. For instance, management practices are more advanced in MNEs than in domestic firms, and good management can be a critical component of a good job. Foreign affiliates of more gender-inclusive countries also tend to have higher shares of female workers (see Chapter 4). Furthermore, foreign firms have relied significantly more than domestic firms on teleworking during the COVID-19 pandemic (OECD, 2020[1]). With support from labour unions and employers' associations, they could play a role in adapting themselves to new work realities, and their good practices could serve as a basis for domestic reforms that can improve labour standards.

The right to collectively bargain and workers' representations can support better working conditions in MNEs but they must be adapted to a changing world of work

FDI – combined with trade, innovation, climate change and other factors – transforms the world of work and creates uncertainties on related labour market gains and losses. Collective bargaining systems and workers' voice arrangements help ensure that all workers benefit from these transformations by supporting solutions to emerging issues (e.g. automation, digitalisation, teleworking, protecting biodiversity), complement policies to anticipate skills needs, or support to displaced workers in new forms of work (OECD, 2019[38]). Collective bargaining can also support a fairer sharing of productivity gains by influencing the wage formation process. This is relevant in the context of foreign firms that poorly translate productivity-related rents into wage benefits, particularly for less skilled workers with lower bargaining power (OECD, 2019[2]; Criscuolo et al., 2020[70]). Indeed, sector-level collective bargaining is associated with lower wage inequality while bargaining and workers' representation at the firm-level can increase wages, productivity and job satisfaction (OECD, 2019[38]; Blanchflower and Bryson, 2020[76]).

Collective bargaining systems are generally based on a complex set of rules and practices, partly written in national laws and partly based on longstanding traditions. They can strongly differ across both developing and developed countries (Lamarche, 2015[77]; OECD, 2019[38]). The main aspects of collective bargaining are the level at which bargaining occurs (national or multi-sector level, sectoral level, or firm level), the coverage rate, the degree of co-ordination between social partners and the effective enforcement of collective agreement (OECD, 2019[38]). Governments should ensure the freedom of association and the right to collective bargaining for all workers and across the country, including in free or special economic zones where foreign firms often operate. In some countries, specific sectors or geographical areas are excluded from the right to organise and bargain collectively. In some other countries, laws can prohibit union pluralism or prevent foreign workers from forming unions (OECD, 2022[54]). Governments and social partners may also want to embrace the diversity of existing and evolving models of collective bargaining and workers' voice and consider to make collective bargaining systems more flexible and more inclusive.

A challenge for collective bargaining is to remain relevant in a globalised and rapidly changing world of work (OECD, 2019[38]). Technological and organisational changes are encouraging new forms of employment, blurring traditional categories, such as 'employer', 'employee' and 'place of work'. Employers' organisations, which are part of the collective bargaining system, are also being put to the test by changes to the world of work. They have an interest in ensuring a level-playing field for their members in the face of new competitors, who may circumvent existing labour regulations – for instance, digital platforms often consider themselves as matchmakers rather than employers (OECD, 2019[38]). As to FDI, existing, albeit limited, evidence indicates that foreign firms in host countries may not have sufficient incentives to join collective bargaining agreements or employers' associations (Jirjahn, 2021[78]).

Collective bargaining coverage has declined in most OECD countries, a trend that may have been accelerated by outward FDI to countries where industrial relations and collective bargaining are weaker (OECD, 2018[68]; Duval and Loungani, 2019[79]) – the role of outsourcing in this decline is yet to be clarified and may not hold for all countries. In the absence of broad membership, one way to maintain high coverage is to extend the coverage of collective agreements beyond the signatory unions and employer organisations to all workers and firms in a sector (OECD, 2018[68]). In some countries, extensions are issued to ensure the same treatment and standards to all workers in the same sector, in particular for workers of foreign firms (Hayter and Visser, 2018[80]). Extensions may have a negative impact when the terms set in the agreement do not consider the economic situation of a majority of firms in the sector. In order to alleviate these concerns, extension requests could be subjected to reasonable representativeness criteria, in line with the ILO Recommendation on collective agreements No. 91 (OECD, 2019[38]).

It is an open question how the decentralisation of collective bargaining affects MNEs' industrial relations. In practice, even when there is a right to collectively bargain in the host country, foreign firms' negotiation power may still differ from that of domestic firms, possibly reflecting union fears that wage demands (or negative shocks) may lead to the relocation of production (OECD, 2008[20]). Their higher propensity to bypass collective employee representation when going abroad could adversely affect rent-sharing with workers. It may also weaken MNEs' compliance with labour standards in GVCs. The OECD Guidelines for MNEs (OECD Guidelines) indicate that, in the context of negotiations with workers' representatives, or while workers are exercising a right to organise, MNEs should not threaten to transfer activity to other countries in order to influence unfairly negotiations or to hinder the exercise of a right to organise (Box 3.4).

One concrete consequence of the bargaining imbalance in foreign firms at the national level has been the development of transnational workers' representations to better co-ordinate workers' bargaining policies. Innovative cross-border mechanisms such as Global Framework Agreements (GFAs) have emerged to spread workers' rights, including the right to unionise and bargain collectively, within MNEs (Helfen, Schüßler and Stevis, 2016[81]). GFAs are non-binding agreements negotiated between a MNE and global union federations. They are instruments for regulating labour conditions and employment relations within MNEs and throughout their global value chains. As such, they can help protect the interests of workers and support transnational co-ordination of collective bargaining.

More than 300 GFAs have been signed by 2019, according to the ILO and the European Commission. In the EU, for instance, European Works Councils are consulted by MNE management on decisions at European level that affect workers' employment or working conditions. They can be established, as per EU directives, in companies or groups of companies with at least 1 000 employees in the EU and the other countries of the European Economic Area, when there are at least 150 employees in each of two Member States. The large majority of GFAs make reference to ILO Conventions – most often to ILO fundamental Conventions, and an increasing number are also referring to the OECD Guidelines for MNEs and the ILO MNE Declaration. Furthermore, most GFAs make reference to supply chain due diligence, even if supplier companies are not parties to them (ILO, 2016[82]). Evidence suggests that GFAs do have the capacity to improve fundamental rights at work such as freedom of association and the rights to organise and bargain collectively, although this also depend on the MNE home country labour practices (Bourque, 2008[83]; Papadakis, 2011[84]; Helfen, Schüßler and Stevis, 2016[81]).

GFAs can also benefit MNEs by helping them standardise their behaviour across the operations of subsidiaries and raise levels of trust in labour – management relations. Unlike domestic firms, MNEs must consider how different approaches to industrial relations can be implemented in the various countries in which they operate. This can be challenging for MNEs that wish to implement uniform global practices and standards, but that may be prevented from doing so due to varying policies across countries. With the engagement of global union federations, GFAs could potentially help address such challenges by serving as a basis for MNEs to promote global standards across their subsidiaries. This could also explain why foreign firms can be less interested in joining national employers' associations than in interacting with other subsidiaries of the parent company (Jirjahn, 2021[78]).

ILO's labour conventions and OECD's Guidelines for Multinational Enterprises can help raise labour standards of MNEs and their domestic partners along the supply chain

International labour standards are an essential component in the international framework for ensuring that the global economy, including FDI, provides benefits to all. The ILO Declaration on Fundamental Principles and Rights at Work (1998) represents the most widely accepted effort to define a set of core labour standards that may be considered universal. It covers eight fundamental conventions, namely the: Freedom of Association and Protection of the Right to Organise Convention; Right to Organise and Collective Bargaining Convention; Forced Labour Convention; Abolition of Forced Labour Convention; Minimum Age Convention; Worst Forms of Child Labour Convention; Equal Remuneration Convention; and Discrimination (Employment and Occupation) Convention.

The large majority of countries has formally subscribed to some or all parts of the ILO Declaration, with important implications at the national level, as ratification of ILO conventions is strongly correlated with changes in national labour laws. Indeed, many developing countries where poor labour practices in the operations of foreign firms have been a concern tend to have reasonable de jure labour standards, in some cases comparable to those in developed countries. Poor labour practices in the operations of businesses can reflect weak enforcement of national and international labour provisions. Indeed, non-compliance with international labour provisions continues to be a concern in many countries with weak rule of law.

The OECD Guidelines and ILO's Tripartite Declaration of Principles Concerning Multinational Enterprises and Social Policy are international instruments rooted in the ILO Declaration on Fundamental Principles and Rights at Work. They are voluntary recommendations by adhering governments, supported by employer and worker organisations, which are directly addressed to MNEs. The OECD Guidelines come with binding commitments and have a unique implementation mechanism called National Contact Points (NCPs), which are agencies established by governments to promote the Guidelines and related due diligence guidance, and to handle cases (referred to as "specific instances") as a non-judicial grievance mechanism. The Employment and Industrial Relations chapter of the OECD Guidelines covers the fields of employment, training, working conditions, and industrial relations (Box 3.4).

The OECD Guidelines recommend MNEs to carry out due diligence through their value chain relationships to address existing or potential adverse impacts on various aspects related to labour. Overall, countries are increasingly adopting due diligence legislation that covers various labour standards and that applies to MNEs supply chain operations. To support the implementation of the Guidelines, the OECD Due Diligence Guidance for RBC provides practical support to firms on implementation (OECD, 2018[85]). Implementing these recommendations can help companies avoid and address adverse impacts related to labour, industrial relations and human rights that may be associated with their operations, supply chains and other business relationships. The OECD has also developed practical actions in specific sectors. For instance, the due diligence guidance on child labour in minerals supply chains helps companies identify, mitigate and account for the risks of child labour in their mineral supply chains (OECD, 2017[86]).

Box 3.4. OECD Guidelines for Multinational Enterprises: Employment and Industrial Relations

MNEs should, within the framework of applicable law, regulations and prevailing labour relations and employment practices and applicable international labour standards:

- Respect the right of workers employed by the MNE to establish or join trade unions and representative organisations of their own choosing.
- Observe standards of employment and industrial relations not less favourable than those observed by comparable employers in the host country. Where comparable employers may not exist, provide the best possible wages and conditions of work, within the framework of government policies.
- To the greatest extent practicable, employ local workers and provide training, in co-operation with worker representatives and, where appropriate, relevant governmental authorities.
- Take adequate steps to ensure occupational health and safety in their operations.
- In considering changes in their operations which would have major employment effects, provide reasonable notice of such changes to representatives of the workers, and, where appropriate, to the relevant governmental authorities, and co-operate to mitigate practicable adverse effects.
- In the context of bona fide negotiations with workers' representatives on conditions of employment, or while workers are exercising a right to organise, not threaten to transfer activity in order to influence unfairly those negotiations or to hinder the exercise of a right to organise.

Source: OECD (2011[87]), OECD Guidelines for Multinational Enterprises, http://dx.doi.org/10.1787/9789264115415-en.

International trade and investment agreements can seek to raise labour standards and support monitoring of commitments

Trade and investment agreements can promote and facilitate FDI that positively influences host countries' labour market outcomes, including working conditions. Comprehensive free trade agreements (FTAs), including agreements with investment provisions, have been increasingly incorporating provisions on labour issues in one or several parts of the agreement. Some FTAs include references to labour or sustainable development in the preamble or in co-operation chapters while others have dedicated chapters or side agreements on labour.

Trade agreements can promote better labour practices by strengthening the incentives of governments to transpose international labour standards into national law. Some agreements contain government commitments to maintain, implement or strive to implement internationally recognised labour standards, most prominently ILO's 1998 Declaration and related Conventions (ILO, 2016[88]; Gaukrodger, 2021[89]). Labour provisions can also refer to government commitments on minimum wages, working hours or occupational safety and health. Some agreements include non-binding language, often in the preamble of the treaty, on the importance of sustainable development and the implementation of the treaty in a way that is consistent with national and international commitments on labour. Others explicitly require treaty parties not to lower labour standards.

A few treaties contain more specific commitments – often, albeit not always, in labour chapters of FTAs – to achieve better labour practices. For example, the labour chapter of the United States – Mexico – Canada Agreement (USMCA) requires Mexico to strengthen protection for collective bargaining and related enforcement tools. Another example is the ASEAN Economic Community Agreement, which includes provisions to facilitate labour mobility in specific high-skilled occupations.

Furthermore, the USMCA includes a provision in its dedicated chapter on labour issues requiring that a certain percentage of a car manufactured in North America be built by workers earning at least USD 16 per hour in order to qualify for preferential trade market access treatment. The chapter on labour issues also includes a provision on promoting information sharing and dialogue related to conditions of employment by enterprises operating in two or more parties – the provision explicitly refers to MNEs – with representative worker organisations in each of the co-operating parties.

Most agreements containing provisions on labour standards target government commitments to better practices. While this may help to strengthen incentives to protect basic labour rights and reduce the temptation of poor labour practices in order to gain a competitive advantage, they are likely to be less effective when poor practices reflect institutional weaknesses (OECD, 2008[20]). Agreements can also prompt workplace placement and skills development exchange programmes in parallel to the primary agreement, such as with the Australia-Indonesia CEPA (2019).

International investment agreements (IIAs) can be defined as standalone investment treaties (e.g. BITs) and investment chapters of FTAs. They thus overlap in part with FTAs and the provisions in FTAs referred above often apply to or affect both trade and investment. However, stand-alone IIAs rarely, albeit increasingly, contain provisions on labour issues. They are generally focused primarily on the protection of investors and investment.

The nature, design, context and interpretation of substantive investment treaty protection provisions and dispute settlement arrangements can be of key importance for investment impacts on labour market outcomes. The scope of absolute protections and government action with regard to their interpretation are key factors affecting policy space for non-discriminatory regulation. For example, investment protection obligations, if not carefully drafted and interpreted, may come into conflict with principles and labour standards included or promoted in ILO conventions. A number of recent treaties limit protection to discrimination or to direct expropriation and discrimination. Other treaties provide for state-state dispute settlement (SSDS) rather than investor-state dispute settlement (ISDS) for investment protection claims which tends to reduce both expansive interpretations and claims.

Some IIA provisions aim at preserving domestic policy space for governments to enact or update labour laws. They affirm governments' right to regulate to achieve legitimate policy objectives including in relation to labour standards. Treaty-based litigation between investors and governments often raise questions about the appropriate balance between protecting investments by covered investors and preserving the policy space of the host country.

Careful drafting of exceptions to IIA protections that give more room for governments to enact labour measures can be one way for treaty parties to preserve their right to regulate. Some agreements seek to exclude certain non-discriminatory measures or subject matters from ISDS claims in order to allow the state to meet public policy goals. These may cover the protection or promotion of workers' rights but the interpretation and effectiveness of clauses of this type in ISDS remains uncertain.

Some treaties prohibit governments from imposing performance requirements on covered investors to meet certain quotas of local employees or managers. Exceptions to these rules in some agreements can allow governments to require investors to employ or train local workers under certain conditions.

IIAs may also directly influence business conduct and impacts on labour market outcomes. A few agreements include provisions that encourage or require investors to observe RBC standards, contribute to skills development, or commit to pay a certain minimum wage. For example, the Brazil-Malawi BIT (2015) requires investors to make best efforts to strengthen local capacities, especially by creating employment opportunities and facilitating access of workers to training. More recently, the USMCA chapter on investment encourages enterprises to voluntarily incorporate into their internal policies those internationally recognised standards, guidelines, and principles of responsible business conduct addressing areas such as labour and human rights, including the OECD Guidelines for MNEs.

Table 3.3 describes a range of different types of explicit references to labour issues in trade and investment agreements (Table 3.3).

Table 3.3. Illustration of how FTAs and IIAs explicitly refer to labour issues

Policy objective	Type of reference	Examples of treaties
Encourage international co-operation	General promotion of progress in labour standards and co-operation	Armenia-EU Comprehensive and Enhanced Partnership Agreement (2017), Chapter 85-86.
	Commitment to co-operate on labour matters	EC-Uzbekistan Co-operation Agreement (1996), Art. 43.
Reinforce domestic law	Explicit safeguards or enhancements of labour standards	US-Mexico-Canada FTA (USMCA) (2019), Chapter 23 on labour
	Prohibitions on lowering of labour standards for the purpose of attracting investment	Japan-Jordan BIT (2018), Chapter 20; Japan-Switzerland FTA, Chapter 9 on investment, Art. 101; CARIFORUM-EU FTA (2008), Art 73
Preserve domestic policy space	Explicit affirmation of labour regulatory power of host state	Canada-EU Comprehensive Economic and Trade Agreement (CETA), Chapter 23
	Carve-out clauses for labour measures with respect to certain treaty provisions	US-Rwanda BIT (2008), Art. 13.
	Exclusion of non-discriminatory labour measures from ISDS	Canada – Mongolia BIT (2016), Art. 20
Influence investor conduct	Investor obligations or responsibilities related to labour standards	CARIFORUM-EU FTA (2008), Art 72; US-Mexico-Canada FTA (USMCA) (2019), Chapter 14 on investment, Art. 14.17, and Chapter 23 on labour, Art. 23.12

Source: This table contains selected examples of FTA and IIA provisions, based on the OECD FDI Qualities Mapping. The impact of these references is uncertain and is likely to depend on factors like treaty design, context and interpretation.

A significant challenge is to ensure implementation of provisions on labour issues for those Parties that do not enforce them. Overall, there is mixed evidence that such provisions can lead to a tangible improvement of working conditions in the domestic economies of the treaty parties. Some agreements follow a sanction-based approach to promote compliance with labour standards. For example, they condition market access on commitments relating to labour standards, allowing a treaty party to deny market access to products from a country where labour standards are routinely violated. By contrast, some trade agreements seek to use positive incentives. This is the case of the Cambodia – US Bilateral Textile Agreement (CUSBTA) made the extension of quota limits conditional on compliance with international and national labour laws, which induced Cambodia to accept ILO's support to enhance compliance, leading to a substantial increase in the possibility of forming trade unions (OECD, 2008[20]; 2018[90]). The EU's Generalised Scheme of Preferences Plus (GSP+) also makes use of positive incentives by granting special preferences to countries that have ratified and effectively implemented core labour and human-rights conventions.

More commonly, however, SSDS or softer forms of implementation like government consultations or third-party expert procedures are available for disputes about implementation of government commitments. Trade unions often express concerns that workers and unions do not have direct access to dispute settlement under agreements containing labour commitments, unlike covered investors under IIAs. Some recent agreements commit the treaty parties to establish inter-governmental committees or other bodies tasked with co-operation, dialogue and monitoring implementation of labour commitments; some envisage greater roles for NGOs and other stakeholders in these processes. Such frameworks could help address implementation gaps for institutions at the domestic level (ILO, 2016[88]). The USMCA establishes a committee to monitor Mexico's labour reforms and enforce USMCA labour provisions. The USMCA also establishes a company-specific labour enforcement system under Chapter 31 on dispute settlement, namely the "Rapid Response Labour Mechanism" that allows the US to take trade measures against factories that fail to comply with domestic freedom of association and collective bargaining laws including those adopted in connection with the treaty. The EU Chief Trade Enforcement Officer (CTEO) aims at ensuring effective enforcement of treaty commitments on workers' rights, among others. It manages a single entry point where EU companies, trade organisations or non-governmental organisations can submit complaints about non-EU countries not meeting commitments made on workers' rights.

3.3.3. Stimulate labour demand and develop workers' skills through targeted investment and active labour market policies and programmes

Active policies and programmes can help governments act on desired labour market outcomes of FDI, including by influencing specific transmission channels of FDI spillovers. Some policies aim at stimulating labour demand by attracting FDI in specific sectors or locations. Other policies aim at increasing the supply of adequate skills or mitigate potential adverse effects of FDI by supporting displaced or vulnerable workers. Such mutually reinforcing policy interventions are warranted as FDI effects on the labour market are externalities that can be both positive and negative. They are also crucial to meet the challenges that automation, digitalisation and low-carbon transition – all accelerated by FDI – impose on the labour market.

Qualified tax incentives, based on the labour market outcomes of firms, can help address specific market failures but they need to be targeted and properly evaluated

Governments use a wide range of financial support instruments that may induce directly or indirectly firms to create jobs, raise wages and train workers. Incentives usually do not differentiate between foreign and domestic investors but some tend to target implicitly foreign firms – for instance through eligibility conditions on the minimum number of jobs. Incentives can distort competition, however, and are not always cost-effective in inducing firms to create quality jobs, although this can depend on the instrument and the targeting strategy. Governments should ensure that incentives address a well-identified labour market failure such as the existence of skills gaps or labour immobility (i.e. labour does not move to where it is in demand). Their appropriateness should be evaluated periodically to ensure that benefits materialise and outweigh the costs, and developed through concerted efforts across relevant ministries and agencies (such incentives could be as much seen as investment policies as active labour market policies).

There are a variety of tax and financial incentives, each targeting directly or indirectly a specific labour outcome and influencing a specific transmission channel of FDI. Some incentives – often tax holidays – do not explicitly target labour market outcomes but can be conceived with the goal of attracting investment that stimulates labour demand in labour or skill-intensive sectors or in regions with low employment shares. Governments also often design incentives that target explicitly specific labour market outcomes. For instance 12 of the 36 countries included in the OECD Investment Tax Incentive Database use incentives to promote job creation and quality while 6 countries grant incentives to support skills (Celani, Dressler and Wermelinger, 2022[91]). These incentives are based on eligibility conditions that define *who* qualifies for tax relief (e.g. a firm that creates a minimum number of workers) and can include design features that describe *how* relief from taxation applies (e.g. tax relief related to training expenditures) (Table 3.4).

Tax exemptions or reductions are typical instruments governments use to attract FDI that directly relates to specific labour market outcomes (OECD, 2022[92]). For instance, Jordan provides CIT reduction to manufacturing firms that raise the employment of Jordanian citizens from a pre-defined threshold (OECD, 2022[54]). Such eligibility conditions related to outcome require careful monitoring to ensure that the outcome has been met and to avoid fraudulent behaviour; for example, to ensure that a required number of jobs were effectively created. Such monitoring requires resources and administrative capacity, which may be scarce in developing countries. In some countries, the IPA can access social security data to calculate the number of jobs created or wages in foreign firms and whether they deliver on their promises. However, even if it is technically feasible to measure the number of new jobs in firms that benefit from an incentive, this does not necessarily mean that these jobs have been created thanks to the incentive. This raises difficulties when attempting to evaluate whether the benefits materialise and outweigh the costs.

Table 3.4. Targeting specific labour market outcomes through investment tax incentives

Type of target	Examples of criteria	Country examples
Eligibility conditions related to outcomes	• Employ a minimum number of workers • Create a minimum number of new jobs • Pay an average wage at a certain level • Reach a minimum level of spending on training	• Jordan provides CIT reduction to manufacturers that raise employment from a defined baseline. • Viet Nam provides reduced CIT rate for 10 years if the project has more than 3 000 employees
Design Features	• Wages of newly created employment • Wages of trainees and apprentices • Expenditure on training and education of employees • Expenditures related to building training facilities	• Thailand allows expenditures on employee training to be deducted at 200% of the actual cost for tax purposes. • Armenia provides enhanced deductions for new jobs created within the business plan.

Source: OECD based on Celani, Dressler and Wermelinger, M. (2022), Building an Investment Tax Incentives database: Methodology and initial findings for 36 developing countries, https://doi.org/10.1787/62e075a9-en.

Subsidies and tax incentives such as allowances or credits are other instruments that can be directly tied to the performance of firms in terms of employment, the wage bill, or trained workers. They can target specific groups that the government supports as part of a national plan, such as R&D workers, youth transitioning from school to work or women (see Chapter 4). They can also influence transmission channels of FDI spillovers, such as support to firms that train workers of their domestic suppliers. Likewise, subsidies and tax incentives such as allowances or credits may benefit domestic firms that want to upgrade their workers' skills in response to foreign competitive pressure. Evidence on the effectiveness of incentives that are directly tied to objectives such as increasing employment or wages is mixed in both developed and developing countries (McKenzie, 2017[93]; Bown and Freund, 2019[94]). When they are not well targeted, incentives might benefit firms that did not need support to hire or train workers in the first place. Some evidence shows that interventions targeting geographical or sectoral labour mobility may work better than others (Duval and Loungani, 2019[79]).

Some governments, including local authorities, make special deals (or mega deals) with large companies, typically MNEs, operating in innovative or strategic sectors, and offer them upfront discretionary incentives packages against commitments to create a certain number of jobs. Such packages are not always cost effective and, while they may improve direct and indirect labour market outcomes, their impact from both a local or national welfare perspective is uncertain (Bartik, 2018[95]; Slattery and Zidar, 2020[96]). Furthermore, firms receiving upfront tax incentives could fail to fulfil employment requirements predicated on ex-ante contractibility because of rapidly changing or uncertain environments (Rodrik and Sabel, 2020[97]). In the United States, such discretionary deals are negotiated at the local level, more often in declining regions, and one-quarter of them go to large foreign firms (Setzler and Tintelnot, 2021[15]). If they are to be negotiated, firm-specific deals may be more effective if they include design features that describe how tax relief can apply ex post, i.e. depending on the actual performance of the firm.

Some incentives have a countercyclical nature and can mitigate the adverse effects of downturns on labour market by supporting firms, including foreign business. For instance, during the COVID-19 pandemic, many governments provided wage subsidies to employers to prevent layoffs and compensate for wage reductions. Foreign firms relied more than other firms on these subsidies, possibly because they tend to adjust labour by decreasing the number of hours worked, and thus lowering wages, more than through layoffs (Figure 3.6). This corroborates the possibility that foreign firms find it costly to reduce their workforce during a crisis: higher skilled staff are typically harder to find (OECD, 2020[1]). They may also be more resilient to crises due to their ability to shift temporarily production to other subsidiaries.

Figure 3.6. COVID-19 pandemic: Foreign firms relied more on active labour market policies

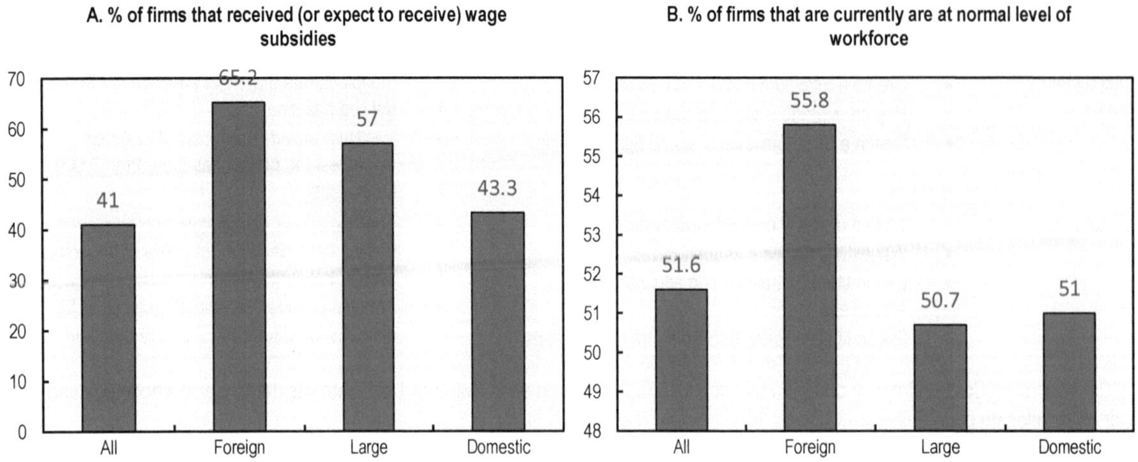

Note: Each indicator is an average of 19 countries covered by the World Bank Enterprise Survey "COVID-19: Impacts on Firms".
Source: Author's calculations based on the World Bank Enterprise Surveys "COVID-19: Impacts on Firms, Round 1".

Skills programmes that are adapted to MNEs' changing skills needs support workers' mobility towards better-paid jobs while retraining those adversely affected

Skills development features prominently among the active labour market policies affecting a country's enabling environment for investment and inclusive growth (OECD, 2015[53]). Skills imbalances lead to higher risk of unemployment, lower wages and lower job satisfaction. They are also associated with lower labour productivity through a misallocation of workers to jobs (Adalet McGowan and Andrews, 2015[98]). By reducing skills mismatches and shortages, training programmes can help increase labour mobility and raise the share of skilled workers following a surge in labour demand from FDI entry, including in domestic firms that will be more able to absorb potential spillover benefits (Becker et al., 2020[52]).

Vocational training programmes can be very different in nature and may differ in their cost and duration, in their curricular content, and in whether or not, and how, the private sector participates, and may address a diverse public, from engineers in the ICT sector to disadvantaged youth in poor regions. Effectiveness largely depends on how these programmes are designed, on the quality of implementation, on the context in which they were developed, and on target population (Levy-Yeyati, Montané and Sartorio, 2019[99]). It is therefore crucial that skills development programmes are developed in line with national economic and investment plans, in consultation with workers, the private sector and relevant investment bodies.

Existing variations in skills shortages and training provision by firms across countries and between foreign and domestic firms suggest that there is ample room for policy intervention. Four patterns can be identified based on the World Bank Enterprise Survey. First, levels of skills inadequacy and training provision of foreign and domestic firms are largely driven by national factors, although ownership matters (Figure 3.7). Second, skills inadequacy is a major constraint for firms in the OECD area more than in developing economies. This could reflect more severe skills shortages in OECD countries, even if this observation may be driven by better business climates – corruption is more likely to be a major constraint in developing economies. Third, foreign firms in the OECD area suffer from skills inadequacy less than domestic business while the reverse is often observed in non-OECD countries. Different sectoral concentrations of the two groups of firms and higher cross-border labour mobility in OECD countries could explain such pattern. Fourth, foreign firms systematically provide more training than domestic firms, including in countries where they report being relatively less constrained by skills availability. This reflects MNEs' permanent need to adapt to competitive international pressure through reskilling and upskilling.

Figure 3.7. The extent of skills shortages and training provisions by foreign and domestic firms

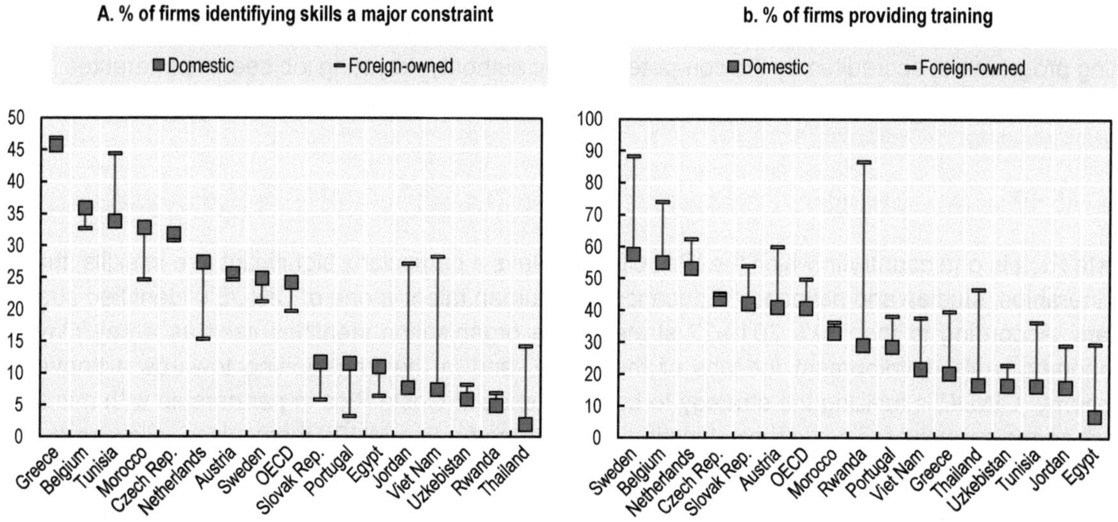

Note: The figure shows a group of selected OECD and non-OECD countries for which firm-level surveys were available from 2015 and beyond.
Source: OECD based on the World Bank Enterprise Surveys.

Firms may provide training on their own costs but skills policies targeted at employers can also be covered by government subsidies (see previous section). In general, training support provided or subsidised by government agencies, though costly, have shown some success when well-designed and targeting the right beneficiaries (Bown and Freund, 2019[94]). For instance, sectoral training or re-training programmes in transferable and certifiable skills can facilitate labour mobility and help workers move to better-paid jobs (Katz et al., 2020[100]). They can reduce skills shortages in high-growth sectors where FDI may crowd out competitors unable to retain their talented staff. Sectoral training could be equally helpful to help mitigate the potential adverse impacts of FDI by retraining displaced or vulnerable workers affected by rapidly changing labour markets due to, inter alia, evolving needs of MNEs or because of the low-carbon transition (see also Chapter 5). On-the-job training support contribute to a more flexible workforce and, in turn, to higher wages; and foreign firms tend to strongly rely on them (Almeida and Faria, 2014[101]; Konings and Vanormelingen, 2015[102]). Providing all firms with financial support for training can, however, lead to deadweight losses. Companies that compete in high-productivity environments, such as foreign firms, need to provide training in any case because it is critical to their productivity and survival (Saraf, 2017[103]).

While reskilling and upskilling support is essential, pre-employment training programmes can help host countries prepare future workers, particularly youth transitioning from school to work, with relevant skills. In countries or regions that are large recipient of FDI, pre-employment training programmes could be even designed specifically to quickly respond to the needs of foreign firms considering to invest. One example is Assured Skills, a state programme in Northern Ireland, introduced by the Department for the Economy and Northern Ireland's investment promotion agency Invest NI, that prepares and trains workers for guaranteed jobs in new foreign firms (OECD, 2020[104]). Overall, governments must ensure that, in light of the different training programmes (sectoral, on-the-job, pre-employment trainings) and providers (public, private, NGOs) that could exist, that there is a solid accreditation and skills certification system.

The investment community can play an important role by participating in skills development initiatives. As illustrated by the example of Assured skills, training programmes are sometimes developed and implemented by IPAs in co-operation with relevant partners. For instance, the Costa Rican IPA established the Skills4Life Program, in partnership with the Ministry of Labour and the Ministry of Education, and as part of the National Employment Programme, to retrain students and provide an accompaniment plan to help recipients find work afterwards (Box 3.5). IPAs could also co-operate with the relevant agencies to identify and support existing or potential local suppliers of foreign firms with relevant training options (see also Chapter 2). Sometimes, the foreign firms create their own training centres that serve beyond the company's needs. IPAs could support them in such undertakings and ensure that trainings are recognised by the relevant authority. In Jordan, for instance, Orange established a Coding Academy that offers a free training programme, accredited by the competent public authority, to young job seekers interested in digital technology who were unable to complete their university education (OECD, 2022[54]).

Box 3.5. IPAs as key partners in skills development: The case of CINDE in Costa Rica

Costa Rica is one country in which the IPA, CINDE, plays a particularly significant role in skills, through partnerships, studies and advocacy. Education and human talent is one of CINDE's identified strategic pillars. According to the IPA's 2019-22 strategy, the organisation identifies itself as a key player in supporting skills development for jobs of the future, and in the transitioning towards a knowledge economy. CINDE is fulfilling the strategy to boosting skills in Costa Rica in partnership with ministries, other agencies, universities, technical institutions and the foreign MNEs themselves, allowing the IPA to closely track patterns in emerging human talent.

In 2018, CINDE launched a partnership with the Ministry of Labour and the Ministry of Education, to create the Skills4Life Program, as part of the National Employment Program. Skills4Life retrains over 2 000 students per year in the English language, social skills in the workplace and also provides an accompaniment plan to help recipients find work afterwards. A 2020 initiative saw CINDE, in collaboration with Coursera, an online education platform, along with the Ministry of Labour, come together to launch an industry 4.0 train programme designed to benefit 50 000 recipients. CINDE is also part of a strategic partnership to boost education and skills development, with two key Costa Rican sustainable development NGOs, Crusa and Aliarse, as well as the Inter-American Development Bank.

CINDE also contributes to an overall understanding of the labour market and education outlook of Costa Rica, including skills needs, which encourages programmes that further boost the country's attractiveness as an FDI destination. One of these programs was launched in September 2021, Technological Seedlings, in which CINDE has partnered with Microsoft to boost the talent pool in certain high-tech sectors identified in CINDE's studies as needing the most new entrants. The training of these students has been relegated to the INA, Costa Rica's primary agency for learning and skills development, showing a strategic positioning of an IPA to actively shape skills development at home.

CINDE also incorporates digital tools in their talent development initiatives, such as their *Crystal Ball* programme that is directed at matching the supply of knowledge economy jobs with the demand. The programme uses an AI-based digital employment orientation platform that predicts and recommends learning paths to ensure users' employability opportunities, personalised based on experience, capabilities and interests, with the aim of impacting over 30'000 people.

Source: OECD (2022[92]), FDI Qualities mapping: A survey of policies and institutions that can strengthen sustainable investment; CINDE 2019-22 Strategy.

3.3.4. Align investment opportunities with labour market needs by addressing information failures on the product and labour markets and reducing administrative barriers

Together with financial and technical support, information and facilitation services can help address market failures that are preventing FDI from realising its labour market potential. Some policies such as linkages programmes can help connect foreign firms with the relevant skills while job search programmes help match job seekers with existing opportunities in MNEs. Other policies aim at raising awareness about labour standards and helping companies disclose their compliance with them. This increases suppliers' prospects to engage with foreign buyers that conduct due diligence checks in their supply chain.

Investment promotion and facilitation activities that reduce information barriers for foreign investors must be based on the existing skill base and labour market potential

Through their activities, IPAs can help address specific market failure (e.g. low labour mobility) by reducing information barriers for foreign investors (e.g. existing skill base) and, thus, improve labour outcomes of FDI. In coherence with existing strategies, IPAs could adopt activities and tools providing information on the national skill base or on local labour market conditions. They can also ensure that material on labour regulations, skills support programmes or employment incentives are visible and easily accessible online. Importantly, IPAs can provide targeted facilitation and aftercare services, such as guiding existing foreign investors that are looking to hire workers with specific skills or in identifying domestic suppliers disclosing high labour standards, and thereby also incentivise other firms to raise theirs.

The relevance of IPAs is stronger when information asymmetries are more severe, markets less transparent and institutional conditions generally weaker. They can be particularly effective if governments' efforts also include attracting FDI to regions with low employment rates. Co-operation between the national IPA and regional development agencies or the existence of regional IPAs can contribute to higher inflows of FDI at the local level and to increased number of jobs directly created by the foreign firm (Crescenzi, Di Cataldo and Giua, 2021[105]). IPAs' activities in the region can cut operational or search costs of foreign investors (for example when setting up a training centre or contributing to its creation), reducing transaction costs when interacting with local actors. This can ensure that the distribution of FDI across regions is also governed by local labour market potential and not information asymmetries or transaction costs.

Another, albeit related, way through which IPA influence the impact of FDI on quality job creation and skills is through prioritisation – IPAs can prioritise FDI in labour- or skill-intensive sectors, target countries with better records of human rights or RBC or focus on foreign investors' size. An increasing number of IPAs are using project evaluation and prioritisation tools that allow them to focus their limited resources on the most valuable deals. For instance, the Lithuanian IPA only treats potential projects that are expected to create a minimum number of jobs – five for an R&D project and 20 for other projects. It also scores projects based on the expected wage firms' will pay to workers. Overall, job quality and skills are important goals for IPAs when setting their prioritisation strategy, although there can be large differences across agencies (Sztajerowska and Martincus, 2021[62]). IPAs set key KPIs to help them identify investments of higher job quality and that can contribute to upskilling. Targets and promotion activities should be coherent with national strategies and reasonably reflect the country's skill base and labour market conditions.

IPAs are also increasingly taking into consideration the global race for attracting talent into their activities. The mobility of human resources has become a central aspect of globalisation, alongside FDI, trade and R&D internationalisation (OECD, 2008[106]). Attracting talent, including foreign, and facilitating workers' entry and establishment is becoming intrinsically connected with FDI attraction, and thus becoming an activity of some IPAs. Agencies can help ensure transparency and consistency of procedures and requirements for obtaining permits from labour authorities, including permits for foreign workers. Notwithstanding the relevance or not of regulating the entry of foreign workers, it is crucial to simplify their entry procedures. Countries like Thailand, for instance, impose restrictions on the entry of foreign workers. To remain attractive to investors, the government established a Strategic Talent Centre to facilitate the admission of skilled foreign workers. The Centre provides a mechanism that recognises the qualifications of foreign experts interested to work in Thailand. Once their qualifications are recognised, the Centre, together with the national IPA, assist foreign job seekers with their visas and work permits (OECD, 2021[57]).

Public employment services can assist vulnerable communities adversely affected by FDI by reducing job search costs and stimulating labour mobility near MNE activity

While investment promotion and facilitation activities lower information barriers for investors, public or private employment services reduce search costs in the labour market for job seekers. Such support is particularly important to mitigate possible adverse effects of FDI on vulnerable communities such as the less educated, youth and women (Steenbergen and Tran, 2020[16])(Chapter 4). Indeed, some workers can lose out following FDI entry and spillovers via long unemployment durations or displacement to lower-paid jobs. Supporting job seekers or low-wage workers with job search assistance, certification of their skills, matchmaking services (e.g. MNEs secondment programmes), and advice on available training support can help them adjust to changes in the marketplace and find better job opportunities. Overall, active labour market policies have a stronger impact when they are offered in an integrated manner – for example, when employment services are combined with training support (Angel-Urdinola, Kuddo and Semlali, 2013[107]).

Search and matching programmes to stimulate internal labour mobility could particularly help job seekers from areas with lower employment rates. The largest market failures in labour markets occur geographically, with very different employment opportunities for the same skills depending on where individuals are located (McKenzie, 2017[93]). As FDI often creates more jobs in urban areas, governments could help nearby communities by lowering search costs and offering public information about available jobs (Steenbergen and Tran, 2020[16]). Programmes providing information about job opportunities in a different location or subsidising job search in different parts of the city by covering transportation costs has been found to be effective (Jensen, 2012[108]; Abebe et al., 2016[109]; Franklin, 2018[110]). In Jordan, for instance, the IPA itself, in partnership with the Industrial Estate Company, recently launched an initiative – the Gold Professions Initiative – to rehabilitate the skills of the local communities surrounding the industrial estates and match them with job opportunities at employers operating there (OECD, 2022[54]).

Raising awareness on labour standards and supporting companies disclose their compliance with them can facilitate MNEs' due diligence checks and responsible sourcing

Policies supporting supply chain linkages between foreign and domestic firms typically aim at upgrading local suppliers' capabilities, but those helping companies improve and disclose their labour standards compliance can be equally relevant. Effective corporate disclosure, both by foreign and domestic firms, is crucial in integrating them into more inclusive, albeit complex, supply chains. Businesses have a responsibility to prevent and address negative impacts of their actions on the labour market, including by conducting due diligence checks. Policies that raise awareness on labour standards and encourage corporate disclosure can act as an incentive for firms to improve working conditions. In particular, transparency on labour standards of suppliers reduce information costs for foreign investors, encouraging them to pursue partnerships, thus boosting the standing of these companies and their suppliers.

Initiatives aiming at raising awareness of labour standards and helping companies disclose compliance are diverse and implemented by a variety of actors, including IPAs and civil society. In some OECD countries, corporate disclosure is a requirement; such as in France, where very large companies must establish, implement and publish their due diligence plans to prevent human rights' abuses in supply chains, or in the UK, where companies with a turnover of over GBP 36 million annually must disclose their approach in preventing modern slavery in their supply chains. In most countries, however, initiatives to raise awareness on labour standards and supporting companies disclose their compliance with them often rely on international donors' support. One relevant initiative is ILO's Better Work (BW) programme, which engages MNEs, local governments, business, and labour in social dialogue around compliance and competitiveness (Box 3.6). BW created a transparency portal which discloses the names of registered businesses and their compliance with key labour standards, such as payment for overtime work, the conditions of migrant workers, implementation of collective agreements, and health and safety conditions.

Box 3.6. Better Work: An initiative that supports corporate disclosure and due diligence

Better Work (BW) is a partnership between the ILO and the International Finance Corporation (IFC), as an initiative to improve labour standards and competitiveness in the garment sector across developing economies. One of their motivations comes from a noticed correlation between compliance with labour laws and increased productivity, profitability and resilience for enterprises. Workers in factories who enjoy a clean, safe and equitable working environment are also more motivated and less likely to leave their jobs – all of which can improve business performance. BW is an example of the benefits of co-operative initiatives to boost corporate disclosure and compliance, which has the potential to create a more competitive environment that not only strives to meet international labour standards, but also one which has an increased ability to attract MNEs and seek deeper linkages with the supply chain.

BW includes labour actors at all levels of programme design, adoption, implementation, monitoring, and evaluation. This includes global union federations in the global advisory committee, trade unions at the national level, and the provision of an institutionalised form of collective worker voice at the factory level. This approach holds the prospect of better enforcement outcomes by bringing labour to the table in an active role and by fostering worker voice through interpersonal interactions between workers and managers.

In Jordan, for instance, the BW programme has been active since 2008, in co-ordination with the Ministry of Labour, where it works to improve working conditions and competitiveness in the garment industry and other exporting sectors. It is active on both the factory-level and institutional-level, and not only provides frequent reporting and advice on conditions in factories, but also encourages a dialogue between industry, government and international stakeholders, and also participates in the training of trainers, in order to create a more safe and productive Jordanian workforce.

BW includes a Transparency Portal which "discloses the names of the apparel factories registered with Better Work country programmes and their compliance with key national and international labour standards," which according BW, "transparency has the potential to stimulate factory progress, improve working conditions, bolster the competitiveness of the sector and encourage ethical sourcing." For example, in the case of Jordan, publicly reported issues have included those such as payment for overtime, the conditions of migrant workers, implementation issues of collective agreements, and health and safety resources and infrastructure. Importantly, BW's direct advisory role provides resources for these same factories, such as a Compliance Assessment Tool, to ensure that once disclosure comes, the garment sector, and often other sectors such as chemicals and light manufacturing are in compliance with Jordanian laws and international labour standards as much as possible.

Source: OECD (2022[92]), FDI Qualities mapping: A survey of policies and institutions that can strengthen sustainable investment; Pike (2020[111]), Voice in Supply Chains: Does the Better Work Program Lead to Improvements in Labor Standards Compliance?, https://doi.org/10.1177%2F0019793920911905

The OECD Due Diligence Guidance for RBC is another relevant tool for governments and enterprises seeking to implement the OECD Guidelines. The NCPs operating under the OECD Guidelines – sometimes hosted by the IPA – are requested to promote the Guidelines and related due diligence guidance. The OECD Due Diligence Guidance helps companies implement the due diligence recommendations for risk areas such as child and forced labour, working time, occupational health and safety, trade union and collective bargaining, wages and informality. Conducting due diligence not only with respect to foreign firm's own activities but also to their supply chains and business relationships is particularly important when these relationships include informal firms. Formal companies' leverage on informal firms may help prevent and address adverse impacts on labour rights or working conditions in the supply chain, or even incentivise informal firms to transition toward the formal economy (OECD, 2020[112]).

While it is central for firms to assess due diligence risks from an issue-specific perspective (e.g. labour), risk assessment across sustainability areas can be equally important. For instance, companies' taking action to reduce carbon emissions in order to address and adapt to the transition risks of climate change on their direct operations and supply chains should also consider potential adverse impacts on workers and local communities to ensure a just transition (see Chapter 5). In some countries, the NCP has been largely inactive due to limited financial resources and institutional clarity about their role (OECD, 2021[113]).

References

Abebe, G. et al. (2016), "Anonymity or Distance? Experimental Evidence on Obstacles to Youth Employment Opportunities", *Working Paper*. [109]

Adalet McGowan, M. and D. Andrews (2015), "Labour Market Mismatch and Labour Productivity: Evidence from PIAAC Data", *OECD Economics Department Working Papers*, No. 1209, OECD Publishing, Paris, https://doi.org/10.1787/5js1pzx1r2kb-en. [98]

Almeida, R. and M. Faria (2014), "The wage returns to on-the-job training: evidence from matched employer-employee data", *IZA Journal of Labor and Development*, Vol. 3/1, https://doi.org/10.1186/2193-9020-3-19. [101]

Almond, P. and A. Ferner (2007), *American Multinationals in Europe: Managing Employment Relations Across National Borders*, https://doi.org/10.1093/acprof:oso/9780199274635.001.0001. [26]

Alsan, M., D. Bloom and D. Canning (2006), "The effect of population health on foreign direct investment inflows to low- and middle-income countries", *World Development*, Vol. 34/4, https://doi.org/10.1016/j.worlddev.2005.09.006. [33]

Angel-Urdinola, D., A. Kuddo and A. Semlali (2013), "Building Effective Employment Programs for Unemployed Youth in the Middle East and North Africa", *Building Effective Employment Programs for Unemployed Youth in the Middle East and North Africa*, https://doi.org/10.1596/978-0-8213-9904-0. [107]

Autor, D. et al. (2020), *The fall of the labor share and the rise of superstar firms*, https://doi.org/10.1093/qje/qjaa004. [69]

Autor, D., F. Levy and R. Murnane (2003), "The skill content of recent technological change: An empirical exploration", *Quarterly Journal of Economics*, Vol. 118/4, https://doi.org/10.1162/003355303322552801. [49]

Bandick, R. and P. Karpaty (2011), "Employment effects of foreign acquisition", *International Review of Economics and Finance*, Vol. 20/2, https://doi.org/10.1016/j.iref.2010.06.001. [11]

Bandick, R. and P. Karpaty (2011), "Employment effects of foreign acquisition", *International Review of Economics & Finance*, Vol. 20/2, pp. 211-224, https://doi.org/10.1016/j.iref.2010.06.001. [47]

Bartik, T. (2018), *What Works to Help Manufacturing-Intensive Local Economies?*, W.E. Upjohn Institute, https://doi.org/10.17848/tr18-035. [95]

Becker, B. et al. (2020), "FDI in hot labour markets: The implications of the war for talent", *Journal of International Business Policy*, Vol. 3/2, pp. 107-133, https://doi.org/10.1057/s42214-020-00052-y. [52]

Beladi, H., M. Dutta and S. Kar (2016), "FDI and Business Internationalization of the Unorganized Sector: Evidence from Indian Manufacturing", *World Development*, Vol. 83, pp. 340-349, https://doi.org/10.1016/j.worlddev.2016.01.006. [43]

Bernard, A. and J. Bradford Jensen (2007), *Firm structure, multinationals, and manufacturing plant deaths*, https://doi.org/10.1162/rest.89.2.193. [29]

Bernard, A. and F. Sjoholm (2005), "Foreign Owners and Plant Survival", *SSRN Electronic Journal*, https://doi.org/10.2139/ssrn.455280. [28]

Biglaiser, G. and H. Lee (2019), "The effects of different entry modes of foreign direct investment on labor rights in the developing world", *Journal of Human Rights*, Vol. 18/2, https://doi.org/10.1080/14754835.2019.1599833. [37]

Blanas, S., A. Seric and C. Viegelahn (2019), "Job Quality, FDI and Institutions in Sub-Saharan Africa: Evidence from Firm-Level Data", *The European Journal of Development Research 2019 31:5*, Vol. 31/5, pp. 1287-1317, https://doi.org/10.1057/S41287-019-00211-9. [19]

Blanchflower, D. and A. Bryson (2020), "Now Unions Increase Job Satisfaction and Well-Being", *SSRN*, https://doi.org/10.3386/W27720. [76]

Blanton, R. and S. Blanton (2012), "Labor Rights and Foreign Direct Investment: Is There a Race to the Bottom?", *International Interactions*, Vol. 38/3, https://doi.org/10.1080/03050629.2012.676496. [36]

Blomström, M. and A. Kokko (2002), "FDI AND HUMAN CAPITAL: A RESEARCH AGENDA", *OECD DEVELOPMENT CENTREWorking Paper No. 195*, Vol. 195/195. [51]

Bloom, N. and J. Van Reenen (2016), "Management as a Technology?", *SSRN Electronic Journal*, https://doi.org/10.2139/ssrn.2788794. [25]

Borga, M., P. Ibarlucea Flores and M. Sztajerowska (2020), "Drivers of Divestment Decisions of Multinational Enterprises - A Cross-country Firm-level Perspective", *OECD Working Papers on International Investment*. [9]

Bourque, R. (2008), "International Framework Agreements and the Future of Collective Bargaining in Multinational Companies", *Just Labour*, https://doi.org/10.25071/1705-1436.78. [83]

Bown, C. and C. Freund (2019), "Active Labor Market Policies: Lessons from Other Countries for the United States", *SSRN Electronic Journal*, https://doi.org/10.2139/ssrn.3324615. [94]

Calvino, F., C. Criscuolo and C. Menon (2016), "No Country for Young Firms? Start-up dynamics and national policies", *OECD Science, Technology and Industry Policy Papers*. [67]

Cao, D. (2020), *Three Essays on International Trade and Informal Employment*, University of Tennessee, https://trace.tennessee.edu/utk_graddiss/6792. [42]

Cazes, S., A. Hijzen and A. Saint-Martin (2015), "Measuring and Assessing Job Quality: THE OECD JOB QUALITY FRAMEWORK", *OECD Social, Employment and Migration Working Papers No.174* 174. [4]

Celani, A., L. Dressler and M. Wermelinger (2022), "Building an Investment Tax Incentives database: Methodology and initial findings for 36 developing countries", *OECD Working Papers on International Investment*, No. 2022/01, OECD Publishing, Paris, https://doi.org/10.1787/62e075a9-en. [91]

Coniglio, N., F. Prota and A. Seric (2015), "Foreign Direct Investment, Employment and Wages in Sub-Saharan Africa", *Journal of International Development*, Vol. 27/7, https://doi.org/10.1002/jid.3044. [7]

Crescenzi, R., M. Di Cataldo and M. Giua (2021), "FDI inflows in Europe. Does investment promotion work?", *Journal of International Economics*, Vol. 132, p. 103497, https://doi.org/10.1016/j.jinteco.2021.103497. [105]

Crespo, N. and M. Fontoura (2007), "Determinant Factors of FDI Spillovers - What Do We Really Know?", *World Development*, Vol. 35/3, https://doi.org/10.1016/j.worlddev.2006.04.001. [50]

Criscuolo, C. et al. (2020), "Workforce composition, productivity and pay: the role of firms in wage inequality", *OECD Economics Department Working Papers*, No. 1603, OECD Publishing, Paris, https://doi.org/10.1787/52ab4e26-en. [70]

Criscuolo, C. et al. (2020), "Workforce composition, productivity and pay: The role of firms in wage inequality", *OECD Social, Employment and Migration Working Papers*, No. 241, OECD Publishing, Paris, https://doi.org/10.1787/0830227e-en. [18]

Cuñat, A. and M. Melitz (2012), "Volatility, labor market flexibility, and the pattern of comparative advantage", *Journal of the European Economic Association*, Vol. 10/2, https://doi.org/10.1111/j.1542-4774.2011.01038.x. [27]

Duval, R. and P. Loungani (2019), "Designing Labor Market Institutions in Emerging and Developing Economies", *Staff Discussion Notes*, Vol. 19/04, https://doi.org/10.5089/9781498313261.006. [79]

Escobar, O. and S. Dougherty (2013), "The determinants of informality in mexico's states", *OECD Economics Department Working Papers,*. [41]

Feenstra, R. and G. Hanson (1997), "Foreign direct investment and relative wages: Evidence from Mexico's maquiladoras", *Journal of International Economics*, Vol. 42/3-4, https://doi.org/10.1016/S0022-1996(96)01475-4. [46]

Fiori, G. et al. (2012), "Employment effects of product and labour market reforms: Are there synergies?", *Economic Journal*, Vol. 122/558, https://doi.org/10.1111/j.1468-0297.2011.02494.x. [65]

Franklin, S. (2018), "Location , search costs and youth unemployment : A randomized trial of transport subsidies in Ethiopia", *Economic Journal*, Vol. 128/614. [110]

Gal, P. and A. Theising (2015), "The macroeconomic impact of structural policies on labour market outcomes in OECD countries: A reassessment", *OECD Economics Department Working Papers*, No. 1271, OECD Publishing, Paris, https://doi.org/10.1787/5jrqc6t8ktjf-en. [66]

Gaukrodger, D. (2021), "Business responsibilities and investment treaties", *OECD Working Papers on International Investment*, No. 2021/02, OECD Publishing, Paris, https://doi.org/10.1787/4a6f4f17-en. [89]

Griffith, R. and G. Macartney (2014), "Employment protection legislation, multinational firms, and innovation", *Review of Economics and Statistics*, Vol. 96/1, https://doi.org/10.1162/REST_a_00348. [72]

Gross, D. and M. Ryan (2008), "FDI location and size: Does employment protection legislation matter?", *Regional Science and Urban Economics*, Vol. 38/6, https://doi.org/10.1016/j.regsciurbeco.2008.05.012. [73]

Hale, G. and M. Xu (2020), "FDI Effects on the Labor Market of Host Countries", in *Encyclopedia of International Economics and Global Trade*, https://doi.org/10.1142/9789811200595_0013. [22]

Hallward-Driemeier, M. and G. Nayyar (2019), "Have Robots Grounded the Flying Geese? : Evidence from Greenfield FDI in Manufacturing", *Policy Research Working Paper*, World Bank, Washington, DC. [59]

Hayter, S. and J. Visser (2018), *Collective Agreements: Extending Labour Protection*. [80]

Helfen, M., E. Schüßler and D. Stevis (2016), *Translating European labor relations practices to the United States through global framework agreements? German and swedish multinationals compared*, https://doi.org/10.1177/0019793915624090. [81]

Herzer, D. and P. Nunnenkamp (2012), "FDI and Health in Developed Economies: An Empirical Analysis", *Empirical Economics Letters*, Vol. 12/7. [34]

Hijzen, A. et al. (2013), "Foreign-owned firms around the world: A comparative analysis of wages and employment at the micro-level", *European Economic Review*, Vol. 60, https://doi.org/10.1016/j.euroecorev.2013.02.001. [12]

Hijzen, A. et al. (2013), "Foreign-owned firms around the world: A comparative analysis of wages and employment at the micro-level", *European Economic Review*, Vol. 60, pp. 170-188, https://doi.org/10.1016/j.euroecorev.2013.02.001. [30]

ILO (2016), *Assessment of Labour Provisions in Trade and Investment Agreements*, International Labour Office, ILO Publications, Geneva. [88]

ILO (2016), *Global Framework Agreements: achieving decent work in global supply chains*, Geneva, ILO, https://www.ilo.org/wcmsp5/groups/public/---ed_dialogue/---actrav/documents/publication/wcms_759477.pdf. [82]

Javorcik, B. (2015), "Does FDI Bring Good Jobs to Host Countries?", *The World Bank Research Observer*, Vol. 30/1, https://doi.org/10.1093/wbro/lku010. [31]

Javorcik, B. and S. Poelhekke (2017), "Former foreign affiliates: Cast out and outperformed?", *Journal of the European Economic Association*, Vol. 15/3, https://doi.org/10.1093/jeea/jvw010. [10]

Javorcik, B. and M. Spatareanu (2005), "Do foreign investors care about labor market regulations?", *Review of World Economics*, Vol. 141/3, https://doi.org/10.1007/s10290-005-0035-7. [71]

Jensen, R. (2012), "Do labor market opportunities affect young women's work and family decisions? Experimental evidence from India", *Quarterly Journal of Economics*, Vol. 127/2, pp. 753-792, https://doi.org/10.1093/qje/qjs002. [108]

Jirjahn, U. (2021), "Membership in Employers' Associations and Collective Bargaining Coverage in Germany", *GLO Discussion Paper*, No. 954, Global Labor Organisation (GLO), Essen, https://www.econstor.eu/bitstream/10419/243141/1/GLO-DP-0954.pdf (accessed on 23 October 2021). [78]

Jude, C. and M. Silaghi (2016), "Employment effects of foreign direct investment: New evidence from Central and Eastern European countries", *International Economics*, Vol. 145, https://doi.org/10.1016/j.inteco.2015.02.003. [13]

Katz, L. et al. (2020), *Why Do Sectoral Employment Programs Work? Lessons from WorkAdvance*, National Bureau of Economic Research, Cambridge, MA, https://doi.org/10.3386/w28248. [100]

Konings, J. and S. Vanormelingen (2015), "The impact of training on productivity and wages: Firm-level evidence", *Review of Economics and Statistics*, Vol. 97/2, pp. 485-497, https://doi.org/10.1162/REST_a_00460. [102]

Kucera, D. (2002), "Core labour standards and foreign direct investment", *International Labour Review*, Vol. 141/1-2, https://doi.org/10.1111/j.1564-913x.2002.tb00230.x. [35]

La Porta, R. and A. Shleifer (2014), "Informality and development", *Journal of Economic Perspectives*, Vol. 28/3, https://doi.org/10.1257/jep.28.3.109. [39]

Lamarche, C. (2015), "Collective bargaining in developing countries", *IZA World of Labor*, https://doi.org/10.15185/izawol.183. [77]

Lee, H. and D. Park (2020), "Effects of Inward and Outward Greenfield FDI on Employment by Domestic Firms: The Korean Experience", *Korea and the World Economy*, Vol. 21/1, https://doi.org/10.46665/kwe.2020.04.21.1.1. [14]

Leibrecht, M. and J. Scharler (2009), "How important is employment protection legislation for Foreign Direct Investment flows in Central and Eastern European countries?", *Economics of Transition*, Vol. 17/2, https://doi.org/10.1111/j.1468-0351.2009.00353.x. [74]

Lembcke, A. and L. Wildnerova (2020), "Does FDI benefit incumbent SMEs?: FDI spillovers and competition effects at the local level", *OECD Regional Development Working Papers*, No. 2020/02, OECD Publishing, Paris, https://doi.org/10.1787/47763241-en. [17]

Levy-Yeyati, E., M. Montané and L. Sartorio (2019), "What Works for Active Labor Market Policies?", Center for International Development at Harvard University. [99]

Lin, S., D. Kim and Y. Wu (2013), "Foreign direct investment and income inequality: Human capital matters", *Journal of Regional Science*, Vol. 53/5, https://doi.org/10.1111/jors.12077. [24]

Lu, Y., Z. Tao and L. Zhu (2017), "Identifying FDI spillovers", *Journal of International Economics*, Vol. 107, https://doi.org/10.1016/j.jinteco.2017.01.006. [21]

McCaig, B. and N. Pavcnik (2015), *Informal employment in a growing and globalizing low income country*, https://doi.org/10.1257/aer.p20151051. [40]

McKenzie, D. (2017), "How effective are active labor market policies in developing countries? A critical review of recent evidence", *World Bank Research Observer*, Vol. 32/2, https://doi.org/10.1093/wbro/lkx001. [93]

Mistura, F. and C. Roulet (2019), "The determinants of Foreign Direct Investment: Do statutory restrictions matter?", *OECD Working Papers on International Investment*, No. 2019/01, OECD Publishing, Paris, https://doi.org/10.1787/641507ce-en. [64]

Moran, T., E. Graham and M. Blomström (2005), "Conclusions and implications for FDI policy in developing countries, new methods of research, and a future research agenda", *... Foreign Direct Investment ...*, Vol. c. [63]

Narula, R. (2020), *Policy opportunities and challenges from the COVID-19 pandemic for economies with large informal sectors*, https://doi.org/10.1057/s42214-020-00059-5. [45]

Narula, R. (2019), "Enforcing higher labor standards within developing country value chains: Consequences for MNEs and informal actors in a dual economy", *Journal of International Business Studies*, Vol. 50/9, https://doi.org/10.1057/s41267-019-00265-1. [44]

Navaretti, G., D. Checchi and A. Turrini (2003), "Adjusting labor demand: Multinational versus national firms: A cross-european analysis", *Journal of the European Economic Association*, Vol. 1/2-3, https://doi.org/10.1162/154247603322391332. [75]

OECD (2022), *FDI Qualities Indicators: 2022.* [3]

OECD (2022), *FDI Qualities mapping: A survey of policies and institutions that can strengthen sustainable investment.* [92]

OECD (2022), *FDI Qualities Review of Jordan: Strengthening Sustainable Investment*, OECD Publishing, Paris, https://doi.org/10.1787/736c77d2-en. [54]

OECD (2021), *Middle East and North Africa Investment Policy Perspectives*, OECD Publishing, Paris, https://doi.org/10.1787/6d84ee94-en. [113]

OECD (2021), *OECD Investment Policy Reviews: Thailand*, OECD Investment Policy Reviews, OECD Publishing, Paris, https://doi.org/10.1787/c4eeee1c-en. [57]

OECD (2020), *FDI Qualities Assessment of Ireland*, http://www.oecd.org/investment/FDI-Qualities-Assessmentof-Ireland.pdf. [55]

OECD (2020), *Investment and sustainable development: Between risk of collapse and opportunity to build back better, Discussion paper for the joint IC-DAC session at the 2020 Roundtable on Investment and Sustainable Development*, OECD, Paris, https://www.oecd.org/investment/investment-policy/Between-risk-of-collapse-and-opportunity-to-build-back-better.pdf. [1]

OECD (2020), *OECD Responsible Business Conduct Policy Reviews: Peru*, OECD, Paris, https://mneguidelines.oecd.org/OECD-Responsible-Business-Conduct-Policy-Review-Peru.pdf. [112]

OECD (2020), *OECD Skills Strategy Northern Ireland (United Kingdom): Assessment and Recommendations*, OECD Skills Studies, OECD Publishing, Paris, https://doi.org/10.1787/1857c8af-en. [104]

OECD (2020), *Strengthening the Governance of Skills Systems: Self-Assessment Tool*, OECD Publishing, Paris, https://doi.org/10.1787/3d59bed4-en. [56]

OECD (2019), *FDI Qualities Indicators: Measuring the sustainable development impacts of investment*, http://www.oecd.org/fr/investissement/fdi-qualities-indicators.htm. [2]

OECD (2019), *Negotiating Our Way Up: Collective Bargaining in a Changing World of Work*, OECD Publishing, Paris, https://doi.org/10.1787/1fd2da34-en. [38]

OECD (2019), *OECD Skills Strategy 2019: Skills to Shape a Better Future*, OECD Publishing, Paris, https://doi.org/10.1787/9789264313835-en. [6]

OECD (2018), *Good Jobs for All in a Changing World of Work: The OECD Jobs Strategy*, OECD Publishing, Paris, https://doi.org/10.1787/9789264308817-en. [5]

OECD (2018), *Mapping of Investment Promotion Agencies in OECD Countries*, https://www.oecd.org/investment/investment-policy/mapping-of-investment-promotion-agencies-in-OECD-countries.pdf. [61]

OECD (2018), *Mapping of investment promotion agencies in OECD countries - OECD*, OECD, Paris, http://www.oecd.org/investment/Mapping-of-Investment-Promotion-Agencies-in-OECD-Countries.htm (accessed on 27 February 2021). [58]

OECD (2018), *OECD Due Diligence Guidance for Responsible Business Conduct*, http://mneguidelines.oecd.org/OECD-Due-Diligence-Guidance-for-Responsible-Business-Conduct.pdf. [85]

OECD (2018), *OECD Investment Policy Reviews: Cambodia 2018*, OECD Investment Policy Reviews, OECD Publishing, Paris, https://doi.org/10.1787/9789264309074-en. [90]

OECD (2018), *Opportunities for All: A Framework for Policy Action on Inclusive Growth*, OECD Publishing, Paris, https://doi.org/10.1787/9789264301665-en. [68]

OECD (2017), *OECD Guidelines on Measuring the Quality of the Working Environment*, OECD Publishing, Paris, https://doi.org/10.1787/9789264278240-en. [32]

OECD (2017), *Practical actions for companies to identify and address the worst*, http://mneguidelines.oecd.org/Practical-actions-for-worst-forms-of-child-labour-mining-sector.pdf. [86]

OECD (2016), *Getting Skills Right: Assessing and Anticipating Changing Skill Needs*, Getting Skills Right, OECD Publishing, Paris, https://doi.org/10.1787/9789264252073-en. [60]

OECD (2015), *Policy Framework for Investment, 2015 Edition*, OECD Publishing, Paris, https://doi.org/10.1787/9789264208667-en. [53]

OECD (2011), *OECD Guidelines for Multinational Enterprises, 2011 Edition*, OECD Publishing, Paris, https://doi.org/10.1787/9789264115415-en. [87]

OECD (2008), *OECD Employment Outlook 2008*, OECD Publishing, Paris, https://doi.org/10.1787/empl_outlook-2008-en. [20]

OECD (2008), *The Global Competition for Talent: Mobility of the Highly Skilled*, OECD Publishing, Paris, https://doi.org/10.1787/9789264047754-en. [106]

Papadakis, K. (ed.) (2011), *Shaping Global Industrial Relations*, Palgrave Macmillan UK, London, https://doi.org/10.1057/9780230319448. [84]

Peluffo, A. (2014), "Foreign Direct Investment, Productivity, Demand for Skilled Labour and Wage Inequality: An Analysis of Uruguay", *The World Economy*, Vol. 38/6, pp. 962-983, https://doi.org/10.1111/twec.12180. [48]

Pike, K. (2020), "Voice in Supply Chains: Does the Better Work Program Lead to Improvements in Labor Standards Compliance?", *ILR Review*, Vol. 73/4, pp. 913-938, https://doi.org/10.1177/0019793920911905. [111]

Ragoussis, A. (2020), "How Beneficial Are Foreign Acquisitions of Firms in Developing Countries?: Evidence from Six Countries", in *Global Investment Competitiveness Report 2019/2020: Rebuilding Investor Confidence in Times of Uncertainty*, https://doi.org/10.1596/978-1-4648-1536-2_ch2. [8]

Rodrik, D. and C. Sabel (2020), *Building a Good Jobs Economy.* [97]

Saraf, P. (2017), *On-the-Job Training: Returns, Barriers to Provision, and Policy Implications*, World Bank, Washington, DC, https://doi.org/10.1596/27290. [103]

Setzler, B. and F. Tintelnot (2021), "The Effects of Foreign Multinationals on Workers and Firms in the United States", *The Quarterly Journal of Economics*, Vol. 136/3, pp. 1943-1991, https://doi.org/10.1093/QJE/QJAB015. [15]

Slattery, C. and O. Zidar (2020), "Evaluating State and Local Business Incentives", *Journal of Economic Perspectives*, Vol. 34/2, pp. 90-118, https://doi.org/10.1257/jep.34.2.90. [96]

Steenbergen, V. and G. Tran (2020), "The Distributional Effects of FDI: Evidence from Ethiopia, Vietnam, and Turkey", in *Global Investment Competitiveness Report 2019/2020: Rebuilding Investor Confidence in Times of Uncertainty*, https://doi.org/10.1596/978-1-4648-1536-2_ch3. [16]

Sztajerowska, M. and C. Martincus (2021), *Together or apart: Investment Promotion Agencies' prioritisation and monitoring and evaluation for sustainable investment promotion across the OECD countries*, https://www.oecd.org/daf/inv/investment-policy/Investment-Insights-Investment-Promotion-Prioritisation-OECD.pdf. [62]

Wu, J. and C. Hsu (2012), "Foreign direct investment and income inequality: Does the relationship vary with absorptive capacity?", *Economic Modelling*, Vol. 29/6, https://doi.org/10.1016/j.econmod.2012.06.013. [23]

Annex 3.A. Assessing the impact of FDI on job and quality skills

Annex Table 3.A.1. Core questions to assess the impact of FDI on job quality and skills

Dimension	Questions	Potential data sources
Structure of the economy	Which sectors and activities drive most labour market outcomes?	OECD and ILO statistics
	Does the country have a comparative advantage in labour-intensive sectors?	UN Comtrade Database
	Is there a productivity/skills gap between domestic and foreign firms?	OECD FDI Qualities Indicators
	Are observed regional disparities high in comparison with other countries?	OECD Regional Database
Labour market characteristics	What are the rates of employment and unemployment in the economy?	OECD and ILO statistics
	What is the percentage of child and forced labour?	ILO statistics
	What is the percentage of informal employment in the economy?	ILO statistics
	What is the percentage of skilled workers in the economy?	OECD and ILO statistics
	What is the extent of labour mobility in the economy?	National statistics and empirical research
	What is the extent of skills imbalances in the economy?	National statistics and empirical research
	What is the percentage of workers with the right to bargain? What is the trade union density?	OECD and ILO statistics
FDI characteristics	What types (greenfield vs. M&A) and motives of FDI are more conducive to positive labour outcomes in the economy?	Refinitiv; Financial Times' fDi Markets; World Bank Enterprise Surveys
	Is FDI concentrated in sectors with higher labour- or skill-intensity?	OECD FDI Qualities Indicators
	Is FDI concentrated in sectors with lower occupational injuries?	OECD FDI Qualities Indicators
	What is the share of FDI from countries that have adhered to the OECD Guidelines?	National statistics and empirical research
FDI transmission channels	Are average wages higher in foreign firms relative to domestic firms?	OECD FDI Qualities Indicators
	Do foreign firms train more theirs workers than domestic firms do? To which extent foreign they also train workers of their suppliers?	OECD FDI Qualities Indicators; National statistics and empirical research
	Is job security higher in foreign firms relative to domestic firms?	OECD FDI Qualities Indicators
	Is labour mobility between foreign and domestic firms happening and does it contribute to skills transfers and wage growth?	National statistics and empirical research
	Is FDI associated with positive/negative competition effects and imitation?	National statistics and empirical research

Annex Table 3.A.2. Core questions to assess policies that influence the impact of FDI on job quality and skills

Dimension	Instrument	Policy questions
Governance	National strategies and plans	Are the country's priorities in terms of labour market outcomes (e.g. create more jobs, increase the share of skilled workers, etc.) clearly defined? Is the country's FDI attraction strategy aligned with strategies related to employment, job quality and skills? Are these strategies aligned with broader development objectives?
		Do national development or economic plans provide coherent and strategic directions on investment, employment and skills development objectives? Are investment considerations integrated in employment and skills strategies and vice versa?
		Is there a dedicated strategy that articulates the government's vision on the contribution of investment to job quality and skills development? If yes, does the strategy sets the goals, identifies priority policy actions and clarifies responsibilities of institutions and co-ordinating bodies?
	Policy coherence and co-ordination	Are responsibilities across government ministries and agencies on investment, employment and skills development clearly defined, balanced, sufficiently funded, mutually understood by all actors and grounded in sound and coherent strategies?

Dimension	Instrument	Policy questions
		Is there a centralised mapping of all institutions involved in developing and delivering policies at the intersection of investment, employment and skills development? Do actors involved in governance decisions know about it and use it as a point of reference?
		Is there horizontal co-ordination between stakeholders at the same level of governance, i.e. strategic co-ordination between different ministries via inter-ministerial bodies and operational co-ordination between implementing agencies via working groups (e.g. skills councils), boards of directors (IPA's boards), etc.? Are the mandates and internal governance structures of the co-ordinating bodies clearly defined?
		Are there formal co-ordination mechanisms with social partners to receive feedback and build consensus around reforms at the intersection of investment, employment and skills development?
	Labour market information and skills assessment and anticipation systems	Do relevant institutions systematically undertake labour market impact assessment of their policies and programmes? Do they run skills assessment and anticipation exercises?
		Are investment bodies such as IPAs involved in labour market information and skills assessment and anticipation exercises? Are information on inward FDI characteristics and MNEs' activity used as forward-looking indicators of what jobs and skills will be in demand in the future in skills anticipation systems?
International agreements & standards	International labour standards	Has the country signed and ratified the fundamental ILO conventions related to core labour standards? Does the government comply with these conventions in practice, regardless of whether they have been ratified Are there measures are in place to ensure and promote the effective implementation of these conventions?
	OECD Guidelines for MNEs	Has the country adhered to the OECD Guidelines for MNEs and related OECD Due Diligence Guidance for RBC? If yes, to what extent do governments align their laws, regulations and labour relations with the Employment and Industrial Relations chapter of the Guidelines?
	International investment and trade agreements	Does the country promote the inclusion of provisions in international investment and trade agreements that raise labour standards, including by referring to ILO's conventions and the OECD Guidelines? Do agreements allow for sufficient domestic policy space and commit the parties to establish institutional mechanisms to monitor implementation of labour commitments?
Domestic regulations	FDI restrictions and wider product market regulations	Are existing regulatory restrictions on FDI periodically reassessed against evolving public policy objectives on job creation and skills development and, where relevant, streamlined or removed? Are relevant labour bodies and social partners involved in such assessments, and are potential liberalisation reforms designed in co-operation with them?
		Does the government ensure that wider product market regulations and competition policy are adapted to foreign investors' entry and operations and that they promote a fair sharing of benefits between firms and workers through fostered competition?
	Labour market regulations and informality	Does the employment protection legislation provide a level of employment stability that encourages learning in the workplace while allowing for enhanced labour mobility? Does the government take into account how labour market regulations affect foreign firms' entry and operations? Are labour market reforms discussed with public and private bodies in charge of investment?
		Is the right to collective bargaining ensured by the law and workers' voice arrangements promoted by the government? Does the right to collective bargaining exclude specific sectors or workers (e.g. foreign workers)? Are existing collective bargaining systems are adapted to a changing world of work and to MNEs' supranational activities? Does the government support global framework agreements between MNEs and global union federations?
		Are other labour regulations (e.g. minimum wage, temporary work, occupational health and safety, child and forced labour, etc.) aligned with international standards? Does the government ensure nation-wide implementation of these regulations, including in special economic zones?
		What measures are in place to protect workers at the margin of the labour force, including in the informal sector and migrant workers, if owing to their situation they are not covered by labour laws or social protection schemes? Does policy have a discouraging effect on employment in the formal sector? Do taxes and social security contributions excessively penalise those in the formal sector relative to the informal? Do regulations discourage operating in the formal economy?
Financial & technical support	Investment and employment incentives	If provided, is financial support, particularly corporate tax relief, which aims at attracting FDI in job-creating or skill-intensive sectors or in regions with low employment rates time-limited and subject to regular impact assessments?
		If provided, do incentives tied to the performance of firms in terms of jobs created, wages or trained workers, including workers of suppliers, aim at addressing specific market failures (e.g. labour immobility)? Are they developed through concerted efforts with all relevant bodies?
	Training and skills development	Are vocational training and skills development programmes developed in line with national development and investment strategies and in partnership with businesses and workers? Is there a unified accreditation system that certifies all programmes? Are training centres established by foreign firms regularly subject to accreditation? Do IPAs work with skills development agencies to identify and support

Dimension	Instrument	Policy questions
		local suppliers of foreign firms with relevant training options?
		Are vocational training and skills development programmes adapted to MNEs' changing skills needs and to rapidly evolving labour markets (e.g. green transition)? Do sectoral training programmes provide transferable and certifiable skills? Are there retraining programmes for displaced workers adversely affected by FDI? If they exist, do pre-employment training programmes help prepare future workers, particularly youth transitioning from school to work, with relevant skills?
Information & facilitation services	Investment promotion and facilitation services	Do investment promotion and facilitation activities information barriers for foreign investors based on the country's skill base and labour market potential? Do they support investors in identifying suppliers with high labour standards? Do they ensure transparency and consistency of procedures for obtaining permits from labour authorities, including permits for foreign workers?
	Public employment services	Do job search programmes and matching services reduce information gaps and lower search costs in labour markets and stimulate labour mobility, particularly of job seekers or workers in communities near foreign firms' activities? Do they support job seekers or workers in vulnerable communities such as lower-skilled workers or youth? Are there mechanisms to support co-ordination between investment and public employment services?
	Awareness raising and corporate disclosure of labour standards	If the country is an adherent to the OECD Guidelines, does the government raise awareness on the recommendations of the Employment and Industrial Relations chapter and is the National Contact Point sufficiently active and adequately staffed? Does the country raise awareness about the content of the ILO's Tripartite Declaration of Principles Concerning MNEs and Social Policy?
		Does the government incentivise companies to disclose their compliance with labour standards, including local suppliers, to facilitate due diligence checks and assess labour risks in supply chain? Does the government also encourages companies to assess risks not only from an issue-specific perspective (e.g. labour), but also across sustainability areas (for instance, do companies' that reducing carbon emissions in order to address the transition risks of climate change also consider potential impacts on workers and local communities to ensure a just transition?).

Note

[1] See OECD's self-assessment tool to help governments strengthen governance of skills systems (OECD, 2020[56]).

4 Policies for improving the impacts of FDI on gender equality

This chapter presents a Policy Toolkit that can help countries improve the impacts of FDI on gender equality. It describes the channels through which FDI can affect gender and shows what policies and institutional arrangements can enhance its contribution to SDG 5. It builds on existing OECD instruments related to investment and gender equality, notably the Policy Framework for Investment, the Guidelines for Multinational Enterprises, and the Council Recommendations on Gender Equality in Education, Employment and Entrepreneurship, and on Gender Equality in Public Life.

Main policy principles

1. Provide coherent strategic direction on investment and gender equality and ensure policy co-ordination and effective implementation

- Align strategic objectives in the areas of investment, gender equality, labour markets, small and medium enterprises (SMEs), entrepreneurship and human resource development. Develop a national strategy for gender equality, clearly defining priorities, actors involved and budget.
- Improve policy coherence and co-ordination between actors responsible for gender and investment policies, as well as other relevant policies, through existing or new co-ordination mechanisms, including by establishing a focal point for responsible business conduct (RBC) (i.e. a National Contact Point for RBC) for countries adhering to the OECD Guidelines for MNEs.
- Conduct regular gender impact assessment of investment and relevant policies to improve policy design and implementation. Systematically collect gender-disaggregated data in areas such as investment, labour markets, entrepreneurship and human resource development.

2. Ensure that domestic regulation is aligned with international standards and supports the positive impact of FDI on gender equality

- Adhere to key international agreements that promote gender equality and integrate a gender perspective to identify and assess risks in supply chains and ensure that access to remedy considers a gendered perspective, as highlighted in the OECD Guidelines for Multinational Enterprises and the OECD Due Diligence Guidance for Responsible Business Conduct. Consider including gender provisions in regional trade agreements and bilateral investment treaties and provide mechanisms for their implementation.
- Remove regulatory restrictions on FDI and trade in sectors that employ or have the potential to employ many women, such as the service sectors.
- Ensure that internal regulations on employment (e.g. minimum wage), social protection, and the workplace (e.g. sexual harassment) support the creation of good quality jobs for women by MNEs.
- Remove regulatory barriers that hold back women entrepreneurs and prevent them from taking advantage of the presence of foreign MNEs, such as businesses opportunities generated along MNE value chains and technology and productivity spillovers.
- Ensure equal access for women and men to a gender-equitable education system and to quality and affordable health care.

3. Stimulate investment, particularly international investment, that promotes gender equality, and strengthen the capacities of female entrepreneurs and the skills of female workers

- Design transparent investment incentive systems that promote gender equality, or that do not exacerbate existing gender inequalities, and regularly assess the benefits and costs of such schemes.
- Provide financial and technical support to help women entrepreneurs access the capital and skills they need to develop business linkages with foreign MNEs and benefit from foreign spillovers.

  Offer training and skills development programmes to women, particularly those at the bottom of the productivity ladder and those returning to the workforce, to prepare them to work for foreign MNEs and for their local suppliers.

4. Eliminate information barriers and gender stereotypes that penalise women in the labour market; and provide social support services to enable women to work

- Help women entrepreneurs overcome information asymmetries caused by gender stereotypes and connect with foreign investors and business partners.
- Eliminate gender stereotypes on traditional gender roles that inhibit women's participation in the labour force and prevent them from taking advantage of jobs created by MNEs.
- Provide good quality social support services such as childcare and elderly care services and safe transport to enable women to work, including for foreign MNEs.

4.1. Continued pressures on gender equality at the workplace

Achieving gender equality in the labour market can bring significant benefits to countries. Greater inclusion and empowerment of women in the labour market is related to lower income inequality and greater economic diversification (Kazandjian et al., 2016[1]), and contributes to more resilient economies (OECD, 2017[2]) (Box 4.1). OECD estimates suggest that reducing the gender gap in labour force participation by 25% by 2025 could increase GDP per capita growth by 24% in Mexico, 23% in Turkey, 19% in South Korea and 10% in the United States (OECD, 2017[2]). In the Nordics, increasing employment of women accounted for 3-20% of per capita GDP growth over the past 50 years (OECD, 2018[3]).

Participation of women in the labour market remains low in many countries, however, with a global average at less than 50% in 2019, compared to 75% for men (ILO, 2019[4]). In some regions such as the Middle East and North Africa and Central and South Asia, women's participation rates are even lower, at below 30%. In OECD countries, female labour force participation is higher, at around 65%, but the gap with men is still significant (OECD, 2019[5]). Women are also more likely to work part-time, in lower paid, less secure jobs and in the informal sector. Gender inequalities also persist with regard to wages. Globally, women earn, on average, 20% less than men (ILO, 2018[6]). A lower gender wage gap is observed in the OECD area, at around 13%, but with a large variation between countries (OECD, 2019[5]).

Women are also less likely to reach the highest levels of management, in both the private and public sectors. In the OECD area, only about one-third of managers are women. Women are also much less likely than men to become Chief Executive Officers (CEOs), sit on the boards of private companies or hold public leadership positions (OECD, 2020[7]). Similarly, in developing countries few women reach high-level, well-paid positions such as legislators, senior officials and managers (ILO, 2016[8]). In both developed and developing countries, women are also underrepresented as entrepreneurs. Women-owned businesses are generally smaller, tend to operate in low-productivity sectors and, especially in developing countries, in the informal economy (OECD, 2017[2]).

Persistent gender inequalities in the labour market are likely to make women more vulnerable than men during periods of economic turbulence, such as those caused by the COVID-19 pandemic. A recent OECD analysis indicates that the impact of the COVID-19 outbreak has been particularly hard on women (OECD, 2020[9]). This is because women are over-represented in the health care system, do most of the unpaid care work in households, face high risks of economic insecurity and are more at risk of violence, abuse or harassment during quarantine periods. The OECD analysis also shows that, so far, the economic crisis linked to the COVID-19 pandemic has hit hardest the sectors of the economy that are the main employers of women. These include many services sectors such as air travel, tourism, retail, accommodation services (e.g. hotels), but also manufacturing industries such as clothing.

Box 4.1. Key gender terms and concepts

Gender: According to the World Health Organization (WHO), 'gender is used to describe the socially constructed characteristics of women and men'. It refers to "roles, behaviours, activities, attributes and opportunities that each society considers appropriate for girls and boys, women and men". These vary across societies and cultures and change over time. Gender often aligns, but is different from biological sex. The different gender roles of women and men are at the root of inequalities, including those in the labour market.

Gender equality: UN Women states that "gender equality refers to the equal rights, responsibilities and opportunities between women and men, girls and boys. Equality means that the rights, responsibilities and opportunities of women and men do not depend on whether they were born or identify as male or female. Equality between women and men is seen as a precondition and indicator of sustainable and inclusive development". In this chapter, gender equality is mainly discussed in relation to labour market outcomes (e.g. gender equality in employment).

Gender gap: refers to the difference between women and men in relation to a given economic, political or social outcome (e.g. the gender wage gap is the difference between the remuneration of women and men). Gender gap and gender inequality, the opposite of gender equality, are often used interchangeably in gender studies.

Gender empowerment: according to UN Women, 'the empowerment of women concerns women gaining power and control over their own lives. It involves awareness-raising, building self-confidence, expansion of choices, increased access to and control over resources and actions to transform the structures and institutions which reinforce and perpetuate gender discrimination and inequality'. Gender empowerment is closely related to, but goes beyond, gender equality. This chapter focuses on gender empowerment in the labour market, which is defined as the possibility for women to develop new skills and access better employment opportunities, including executive and leadership positions.

Gender mainstreaming: The conclusions agreed in 1997 by the UN Economic and Social Council define gender mainstreaming as "the process of assessing the implications for women and men of any planned action, including legislation, policies or programmes, in all areas and at all levels. The ultimate goal is to achieve gender equality". Gender mainstreaming is not a substitute for gender policies. On the contrary, gender policies and gender mainstreaming complement each other.

4.2. The impact of FDI on gender equality

4.2.1. FDI can affect gender equality in the labour market through several channels

FDI generates multiple gender-specific effects in the labour market of host countries. It influences the relative demand and prices of factors of production, including labour. Since women and men have different preferences and skillsets due to policy and non-policy factors (taxation, social and cultural norms, etc.), and employment intensities of female and male labour varies across industries, FDI generates shifts in the relative demand for labour by gender and affects the employment and wages of women and men differently. FDI can also influence other dimensions of gender equality and the empowerment of women in the labour market, such as women's non-wage working conditions (job security, occupational health, etc.) and prospects for skills development and career advancement (e.g. training and promotion) (Chapter 3). The operations of affiliates of foreign multinational enterprises (MNEs) (hereafter referred to as foreign MNEs or foreign firms) can also have significant implications for local women entrepreneurs (Figure 4.1, green box).

Figure 4.1. Conceptual framework: FDI impacts on gender equality in the labour market

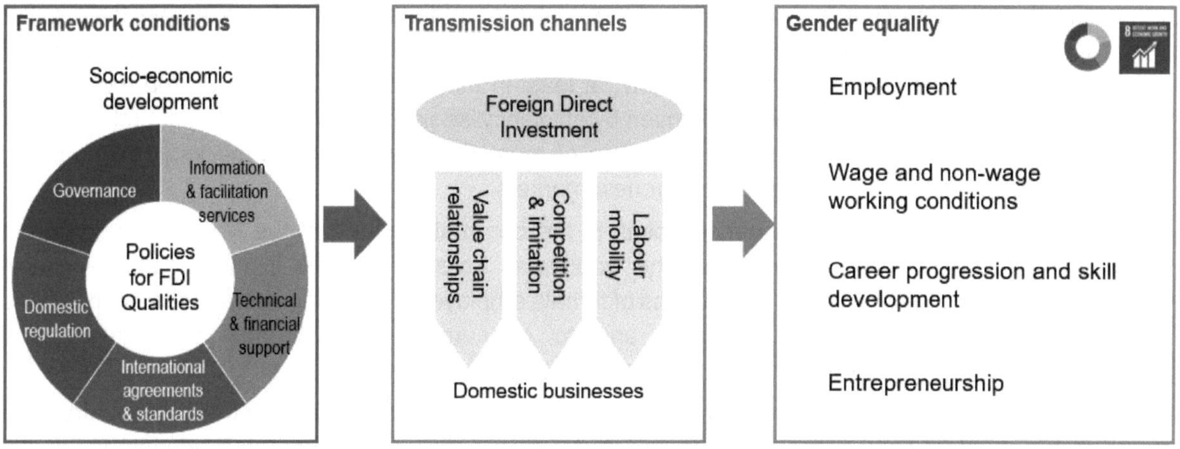

FDI can influence gender outcomes through the direct operations of foreign MNEs or indirectly through business linkages and other market interactions with domestic firms (Figure 4.1, yellow box):

- **Activities of MNEs**: FDI affects women in host countries mainly through the direct employment activities and practices of foreign affiliates of MNEs (e.g. recruitment, remuneration, training, promotion, benefits). These, in turn, are influenced by the MNE corporate culture,[1] which is highly dependent on the country of origin.
- **Value chain relationships**: FDI can create jobs for local women not only in affiliates of foreign MNEs, but also in domestic companies through value chain relationships with local suppliers and buyers. Value chain relationships can be a channel for the transfer of gender practices and values from foreign MNEs to domestic companies (UNCTAD, 2021[10]). Through value chain relationships, FDI can also support local women entrepreneurs.
- **Competition and imitation effects**: Foreign MNEs compete with local firms in both product markets (i.e. crowding-out) and labour markets for local talent. Especially in female-dominated sectors, competitive pressures from foreign MNEs can lead to job losses for women if domestic firms downsize or close down. As women-owned firms are generally smaller and less productive than those owned by men (OECD, 2017[2]; OECD/European Union, 2019[11]) they are also more likely to be negatively affected by foreign competition. At the same time, higher wages and better job opportunities brought by foreign firms may force local competition to respond by improving wages and working conditions of women (Aguayo-Tellez, 2012[12]). Imitation effects occur when domestic firms imitate the business practices of the multinational firm, including human resources management (HRM) activities related to gender. Through imitation, foreign MNEs can have an impact on women in domestic firms or on women-owned businesses.
- **Labour mobility**: This channel concerns the movement of women workers from foreign MNEs to domestic enterprises or the start-up of enterprises by women previously employed by foreign MNEs. Previous work experience with the MNE can help women get better jobs in domestic enterprises. While working for the MNE, women can acquire new skills through on-the-job training and learning, which can give them better prospects for career development in future jobs. Labour mobility can also contribute to the transfer of information on gender practices from foreign to domestic companies (UNCTAD, 2021[10]; Davis A., 2020[13]). Women can also use the knowledge gained at the foreign MNE to set up their own company.

The direction and magnitude of gender-specific impacts of FDI depend on several policy and non-policy factors (Figure 4.1, blue box). Policy framework conditions include a broad set of policies that will be discussed in Section 4.3. Non-policy factors comprise:

- **Sector, entry mode, and motive of FDI**: In general, the impacts on gender equality are expected to be greater when investment takes place in sectors with higher proportions of women than men. The choice of entry mode by foreign investors is also an important factor. For example, the creation of a new affiliate (greenfield FDI) is likely to have a greater effect on employment than a merger or acquisition (M&A) of an existing company, at least in the short term. Moreover, the motives that drive investors can vary widely. FDI driven by efficiency-seeking motives (e.g. the search for cheap labour and inputs) may lead to the creation of more (low-wage) jobs in the local economy, as opposed to FDI driven by the search for new markets.
- **MNE corporate culture:** Evidence points to the corporate culture of the MNE as an important factor governing gender equality in the workplace. Foreign affiliates in more gender-inclusive countries tend to have higher proportions of female employees, including in management positions, to have smaller gender pay gaps and to offer more family-friendly ways of working (e.g. teleworking) (Kodama, Javorcik and Abe, 2018[14]; Tang, 2017[15]).
- **Socio-economic development of the host country:** The characteristics of the host country, such as the structure of its economy, endowment of natural resources, comparative advantage, level of specialisation, explain the types of FDI attracted. Different types of FDI, in turn, are likely to have differentiated impacts on gender outcomes in the local economy. Social and cultural norms also play a crucial role as they influence women and men's roles in society and at work and affects women's decisions, aspirations and opportunities in relation to job opportunities.

An extensive review of the literature about the channels and non-policy determinants of gender-specific FDI impacts is discussed in Montinari and Wermelinger (2020[16]). Annex 4.A provides detailed questions for governments to self-assess the impact of FDI on gender equality.

4.2.2. The impact of FDI on gender equality varies greatly

FDI has varying effects on the employment and wage dimensions of gender equality. For example, in less developed countries, FDI in labour-intensive industries (e.g. clothing, electronics, toys, tourism) generates significant employment for women. However, these are generally low-skilled and low-paying jobs and offer limited career prospects (UNACTD, 2014[17]; Chen and Carr, 2004[18]). In countries with a more advanced industrial structure, the inverse relationship tends to be observed: FDI is directed towards more productive and technology-intensive sectors (Benfratello and Sembenelli, 2006[19]; Criscuolo and Martin, 2003[20]), which on average have smaller shares of women, but with jobs that are on average well paid, and with a smaller wage gap compared to men (OECD, 2019[21]; 2022[22]) (Figure 4.2).

Figure 4.2. Contribution of FDI to gender equality in wages and employment

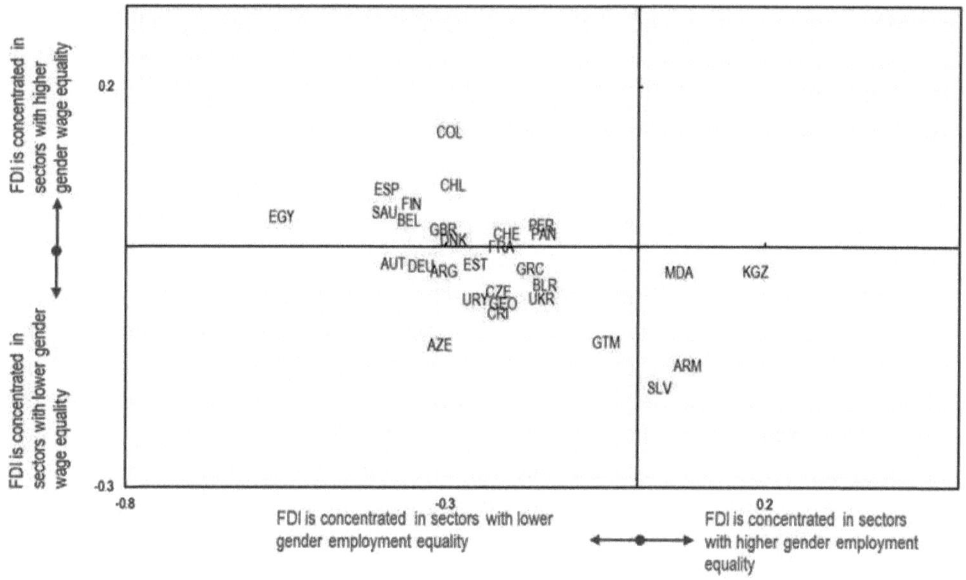

Note: See OECD (2019[21]) for a description of the methodology and data.
Source: OECD based on Financial Times' fDi Markets database, ILO and UN National Accounts.

There is limited evidence on the contribution of FDI to non-wage working conditions of women due to the lack of comparable data on issues such as job security, safety, and benefits. Some studies suggest that the working conditions offered by foreign MNEs tend to be better than the alternatives available in the domestic economy because MNEs are more resilient to adverse economic cycles, offer better job security and greater protection of labour rights (Davin, 2004[23]; Ver Beek, 2001[24]). On the other hand, other studies indicate that women working for MNEs are more likely to have precarious contracts than their male co-workers (Chen and Carr, 2004[18]; Ghosh, 2002[25]). Regarding practices that empower women in the workplace and allow them to grow professionally, evidence for some countries indicates that foreign firms offer better opportunities for career advancement than domestic firms, as evidenced by their higher shares of women in top-management positions (Kodama, Javorcik and Abe, 2018[14]; Olcott, 2014[26]; Ono, 2004[27]). Yet, even if employed by foreign MNEs, women are not immune to the discriminatory barriers that prevent them from advancing in their professional career. Women remain largely under-represented in the top management and boards of MNEs (UNCTAD, 2020[28]).

Corporate culture is a key factor governing the gender employment practices of MNEs, and is strongly influenced by the values and norms in place in the country of origin. Affiliates of MNEs from more gender-equal countries tend to be more gender-inclusive than domestic firms: they have higher female employment shares, show a smaller gender pay gap and are more likely to offer family-friendly working arrangements (Kodama, Javorcik and Abe, 2018[14]; Tang, 2017[15]). With respect to entrepreneurship, some evidence points to a negative competition effect of foreign firms on women-owned businesses, possibly due to the fact that women-owned businesses tend to be smaller and less productive than men-owned businesses (OECD, 2017[2]). At the same time, the FDI Qualities Indicators show that, in countries with a less developed industrial structure, FDI tends to prevail in sectors with larger shares of businesses owned by women. These are typically female-dominated industries, which are labour-intensive and low-skilled (e.g. garment) (OECD, 2019[21]).

Economic and other disruptions can further affect the impact of FDI on gender equality, as the recent COVID-19 pandemic and related economic crisis has shown. Measures introduced by governments to contain the pandemic have generated significant disruptions in MNE activities and their value chains, and has put employment of women at risk, particularly in sectors where women are over-represented such as health care, tourism, accommodation, but also in manufacturing sectors like apparel and food. Longer-term changes in MNE investment decisions and business strategies in response to the crisis are likely to have important implications for women workers, especially in female-dominated sectors and in low-cost countries. Similar disruptions in MNE activities could also be caused by environmental disasters (e.g. floods, wild fires) and other events (e.g. economic and financial crisis).

4.3. Policies that influence FDI impacts on gender equality

Policies that influence the impact of FDI on gender equality pertain to different areas, from investment to labour markets, small and medium sized enterprises (SMEs), entrepreneurship and human resource development. This Policy Toolkit aims to provide a comprehensive policy framework for countries to maximise positive impacts of FDI on gender equality. It builds on existing OECD instruments related to investment and gender equality, notably the Policy Framework for Investment, the Guidelines for Multinational Enterprises, and the Council Recommendations on Gender Equality in Education, Employment and Entrepreneurship, and on Gender Equality in Public Life. It complements these instruments by offering a comprehensive mapping of policies and institutional settings that influence the impacts of FDI on gender equality across selected OECD and developing countries (Chapter 1). The Policy Toolkit is structured around four principles and the policy instruments that support these principles (Table 4.1). Annex Table 4.A.2 provides detailed questions for governments to self-assess policies influencing the impacts of FDI on gender equality, while Annex Table 4.A.3 classifies policy instruments by policy area.

Table 4.1. Overview of FDI Qualities Policy Toolkit for enhancing FDI impact on gender equality

Principle 1: Provide coherent strategic direction on investment and gender equality and ensure policy coordination and effective implementation	Governance	National strategies and plans on gender equality
		Policy coherence and coordination
		Gender impact assessment and data collection
Principle 2: Ensure that domestic regulation is aligned with international standards and supports the positive impact of FDI on gender equality	International agreements & standards	International agreements on gender equality
		OECD Guidelines for MNEs and sectoral Guidance for RBC
		Gender provisions in RTAs and BITs
	Domestic regulations	Regulatory restrictions on FDI and trade in female-dominated sectors
		Labour market regulations, social protection, labour income taxation
		Regulatory barriers to women entrepreneurship
		Education and health care systems
Principles 3: Stimulate investment, particularly international investment, that promotes gender equality, and strengthen the capacities of female entrepreneurs and the skills of female workers	Financial and technical support	Investment incentives to attract FDI in female-dominated sectors and to promote gender equality
		Financial and technical assistance to women entrepreneurs
		Training and skills development programmes for women
Principle 4: Eliminate information barriers and gender stereotypes that penalise women in the labour market; and provide social support services to enable women to work	Information & facilitation services	Information services and matchmaking programmes to link women entrepreneurs with foreign MNEs
		Public information campaigns to eliminate gender stereotypes
		Social support services (e.g. childcare services, safe transport)

4.3.1. Provide coherent strategic direction on investment and gender equality and ensuring policy co-ordination and effective implementation

Align strategic objectives in the areas of investment, particularly foreign investment, gender equality, labour market, entrepreneurship/SMEs and human resources development

Policy priorities and objectives in the area of investment and gender equality can vary considerably depending on a country's stage of socio-economic development. At the same time, the institutional framework governing the policy areas of investment and gender equality may also differ from country to country. For example, some countries may have a more centralised policy system, while others may give more power and responsibility to sub-national levels of government. Regardless of the institutional set-up, it is important that different institutions and levels of government have clear responsibilities and that their actions are aligned. National strategies and plans are an important tool for ensuring policy coherence between relevant institutions, as they can help identify potential trade-offs between different strategic development objectives and encourage co-ordinated policy responses between the actors involved. The alignment of national strategies and plans implies that they are made available to all stakeholders, including international donors, and that they are regularly updated.

Maximising the impact of FDI on gender equality requires coherence between policy objectives and actions in several policy areas, including investment, gender equality, labour markets, entrepreneurship and SMEs, and human resource development. Establishing a comprehensive policy framework for investment promotion with a clear link to sustainable development goals, including in the area of gender equality, is important to raise awareness of the impact of FDI and sustainable development and to encourage targeted and co-ordinated policy actions. This would ensure that attracting FDI to specific sectors or regions does not exacerbate existing gender inequalities, but rather supports gender equality goals. At the same time, gender equality priorities, as well as the actors and budget needed to achieve them, should be clearly defined in the national gender equality strategy. The 2015 OECD Recommendation on Gender Equality in Public Life provides guidelines for the development of an effective gender equality strategy. According to the guidelines, the gender equality strategy should follow a whole-of-government approach to ensure co-ordination and coherence between relevant actors and gender initiatives.

Promote policy co-ordination among relevant actors

The governance framework for gender and investment policies can vary considerably from one country to another. Especially in developed countries, gender policies are highly integrated into the activities of all government ministries and agencies, which ensures a more comprehensive approach. In less developed countries, which rely more on private investment, there is often more limited government intervention and gender equality initiatives depend largely on dedicated ministries and institutions supporting women and gender equality, including private actors and the donor community. Nonetheless, institutional arrangements and programmes can change significantly even among countries with similar levels of development and gender equality performance (Box 4.2). Improving policy coherence and co-ordination among actors responsible for gender and investment policies, as well as other relevant policies, is key to improving the impact of FDI. Co-ordination mechanisms can take different forms, from gender focal points in relevant ministries and agencies to inter-ministerial committees. In countries that have adhered to the OECD Guidelines, an important role can be played by the National Contact Point for Responsible Business Conduct (NCP for RBC), which provides an important link between investment and other sustainable development areas, including gender equality.

Box 4.2. Institutional approaches to gender mainstreaming in investment, labour markets and SME/entrepreneurship policies: a comparison between Canada and Sweden

Canada and Sweden have made extensive efforts to incorporate gender equality into their policy frameworks. In Canada, there is a dedicated ministry called Women and Gender Equality Canada, while in Sweden there is a Minister of Women who is part of the cabinet. Sweden has implemented a formal gender mainstreaming programme and formally defines itself as a 'feminist government'. Canada depends on a diverse set of gender initiatives taken at both the federal and provincial levels.

The Programme for Gender Mainstreaming in Government Agencies was implemented in Sweden over 2013-19, as a way to increase awareness in over 60 government agencies. In Canada, initiatives are more fragmented and are largely taken by individual ministries, or within an individual province. There is also a greater focus on encouraging women's entrepreneurship and economic leadership, whereas in Sweden the aim is more to encourage women's welfare and participation and socio-economic life.

When it comes to policy areas that are crucial for improving the impact of FDI on gender equality, namely labour markets, entrepreneurship, and skills, there are no specific programmes for women in either Invest in Sweden or Sweden's innovation agency, Vinnova, but rather gender equality considerations are based on organisational governance approaches and strategies. Vinnova, for example, has a gendered perspective, especially through the inclusion of female staff, in the assessment of its funding allocations to company innovation and development projects. Business Sweden, the parent organisation of Invest in Sweden, also takes a similar approach in aiming to ensure that women make up 40-60% of all activities in the organisation.

Meanwhile in Canada, there are numerous programmes dedicated to women in both ministries and agencies such as Business Development Canada; Canadian Trade Commission; and Innovation, Sciences and Research Development Canada. Innovation Science and Economic Development Canada spearheads the Women Entrepreneurship Strategy, which provides both funding and networking opportunities for female entrepreneurs. Business Development Canada also provides two unique programmes that target women business owners and entrepreneurs. With regard to export development, the Canadian Trade Commissioner Service has its own Business Women in International Trade Initiative, which even organises women-led trade missions and provides mentorship and capacity building for women-led businesses that want to engage in foreign markets.

In terms of FDI, Invest in Canada does not have a formal programme or initiative to support gender equality. However, FinDev Canada, an arm of the Canadian Government that deals with outbound investment in supporting the private sector in developing countries, has a gender-focused investment strategy, which is dedicated to directing investment towards women's economic empowerment and entrepreneurship, and helps corporate clients to do the same. In contrast, Sweden's provisions in the relevant fields of investment are more symbolic in nature and designed to support equality between men and women by leveraging the gender perspective in business activity.

Source: OECD (2022[29]), FDI Qualities Policy Mapping (database).

Conduct systematic gender impact assessments of investment and relevant polices; and collect data disaggregated by gender

Determining the impact of FDI on gender equality outcomes is important to identify areas where policy intervention might be most needed. The first part of this chapter provides a conceptual framework for analysing the impact of FDI on gender equality by identifying the main transmission channels. Moreover, Annex 4.A offers a set of questions and indicators that can guide policy makers in assessing the link between FDI and gender equality in their country. In addition to evaluating the impact of FDI on gender equality, assessing the impact of policies, including investment policies, on gender equality is important for improving policy design and implementation. On the one hand, this helps to ensure that policies are effective in promoting gender equality. On the other hand, policy evaluation helps prevent unintended negative impacts of policies on women more generally.

Gender impact assessment, however, is not possible without adequate data. The FDI Qualities Indicators (OECD, 2019[21]; OECD, 2022[22]) are an important effort insofar as they shed light on the link between FDI and gender equality in the labour market and allow for comparative analysis across countries and over time. In an effort to improve the measurement of gender impacts and policies, the government should also prioritise the collection of timely and internationally comparable data and indicators disaggregated by gender in areas such as investment, entrepreneurship and SMEs, labour markets and human resource development. The use of quantitative methodologies (e.g. analysis of data collected through surveys) should be accompanied by the use of qualitative tools (e.g. interviews or consultations). For example, consultations with foreign investors can help to improve the completeness and reliability of the data collected. In addition, collaboration between institutions responsible for investment promotion, gender equality, labour markets, entrepreneurship and SMEs, including the department of statistics, can facilitate the exchange of information, experience and expertise.

4.3.2. Ensure that domestic regulation is aligned with international standards and supports the positive impact of FDI on gender equality

Join and implement major international agreements on gender equality

Gender equality and non-discrimination based on sex are fundamental rights enshrined in numerous international human rights instruments (Table 4.2). Although not all of these agreements are legally binding, they are important insofar as they contribute to the integration of gender equality principles into national law. The UN Charter of 1945 is the first international instrument binding on signatory countries to establish the principle of equality between men and women. Since then, numerous international instruments have promoted women's rights. After the UN Charter, an important milestone is the UN Convention on the Elimination of All Forms of Discrimination against Women (CEDAW) in 1979. The CEDAW Convention defines gender discrimination for the first time and provides the basis for achieving gender equality in many areas. Countries that have ratified the convention are legally bound by its provisions and must report regularly on the measures they take. Other key treaties are the Beijing Declaration and Platform for Action, adopted in 1995, and a number of ILO conventions dealing with gender-specific issues such as the Equal Remuneration Convention, the Discrimination (Employment and Occupation) Convention, the Workers with Family Responsibilities Convention and the Maternity Protection Convention. The adoption of the 2030 Agenda for Sustainable Development and the 17 Sustainable Development Goals (SDGs) by UN members in 2015 is another important step towards achieving gender equality. Gender equality and women's empowerment are reflected in SDG 5 and integrated into many of the other SDGs (e.g. good health and well-being, quality education, decent work and economic growth). Although the 2030 Agenda for Sustainable Development is not in itself a legally binding international agreement, it has the merit of having increased the transparency and measurability of countries' efforts in the area of gender equality. Companies operating in countries adhering to and implementing these international agreements must take these standards into account in their operations.

Table 4.2. Major international agreements on women's human rights and gender equality

International agreement	Year	Legally binding on signatory countries	Number of countries that have joined
UN Charter	1945	yes	193
UN Convention on the Elimination of All Forms of Discrimination against Women (CEDAW)	1979	yes	189
Beijing Declaration and Platform for Action	1995	no	189
ILO's Equal Remuneration Convention (n100)	1951	yes	173
ILO's Discrimination (Employment and. Occupation) Convention (n 111)	1958	yes	175
ILO's Workers with Family Responsibilities Convention (n 156)	1981	yes	44
ILO's Maternity Protection Convention (n 183)	2000	yes	38
2030 Agenda for Sustainable Development and the 17 Sustainable Development Goals	2012	no	193
Buenos Aires Declaration on Women and Trade	2017	no	118

Adhering to the OECD Guidelines for Multinational Enterprises

The OECD Guidelines for Multinational Enterprises are recommendations made by governments to companies to prevent and address the negative impacts of business operations on the economy, society, and the environment (OECD, 2011[30]). The Guidelines provide non-binding principles and standards for responsible business conduct, which signatory governments commit to promoting. Coverage of gender issues in the Guidelines is limited though (Box 4.3). Only chapter V on "Employment and Industrial Relations" contains an explicit reference to gender, particularly to the principle of equal treatment in employment and non-discrimination on the grounds of sex. Other explicit references can be found in the commentaries of chapters V and IV on "Human Rights". The OECD Due Diligence Guidance for Responsible Business Conduct (RBC) (OECD, 2018[31]) and Sectoral Guidance provide additional tools to help companies identify and address potential negative impacts on women in their operations and value chains. Other multilateral instruments that promote responsible business practices contain references to gender equality, such as the ILO Tripartite Declaration of Principles on Multinational Enterprises (ILO, 2017[32]) and the United Nations Norms on the Responsibilities of Transnational Corporations. Like the OECD Guidelines for MNEs, these instruments do not impose any legal obligations on companies.

Box 4.3. Gender issues in the OECD Guidelines for MNEs

Two chapters of the OECD Guidelines for MNEs are more closely related to gender issues: chapter IV on 'Human Rights' and chapter V on "Employment and Industrial Relationships". Commentary 40 of chapter IV on 'Human Rights' states that enterprises should pay particular attention to the human rights of individuals belonging to vulnerable groups such as women. Chapter V on "Employment and Industrial Relationships" refers to principles of equal treatment in employment and non-discrimination on grounds of sex. Commentary 54 of chapter V further stresses the importance of equal criteria for selection, pay and promotion and of preventing discrimination or dismissals based on marriage, pregnancy and maternity, whereas Commentary 58 states that equal opportunities should also be ensured in training.

Practical guidance for companies on how to identify and address potential negative impacts on women in their own operations and value chains is further provided in the OECD Due Diligence Guidance for Responsible Business Conduct. The OECD Due Diligence Guidance helps companies to become aware of actual and potential risks across GVCs in situations where women may be disproportionately impacted, for instance in certain sectors or geographical areas. It also provides guidance on how to ensure that actions taken to prevent and mitigate negative impacts on women are effective and appropriate. In addition to the OECD's general guidance on due diligence, other OECD sectoral guidance instruments help companies operating in specific sectors to identify how their actions may disproportionately affect women. For example, the OECD Due Diligence Guidance for "Responsible Supply Chains in the Garment and Footwear Sector" explains how companies along these value chains can identify and address gender-specific risks, such as sexual harassment and discrimination. Similarly, the OECD-FAO Due Diligence Guidance for Responsible Agricultural Supply Chains integrates gender as a cross-cutting theme in supply chain due diligence to support companies in taking a proactive and systematic approach to risk management while ensuring that actions do not undermine gender equality.

Mainstream gender in international trade and investment agreements

The inclusion of gender provisions in regional trade agreements (RTAs) and bilateral investment treaties (BITs) has increasingly been seen as a means to make trade and investment more gender inclusive. Nonetheless, there is still a lack of evidence on the impact of these provisions and it is unclear whether they contribute to improving gender equality outcomes in signatory countries. Currently, 80 out of 350 regional trade agreements, 69 of which are in force and notified to the WTO, contain specific gender provisions. While gender provisions have evolved over time, they remain general in nature. Korinek, Moïsé and Tange (2021[33]) classifies them into three main categories, ordered from most to least ambitious: (i) provisions that reaffirm parties' existing commitments to gender equality; (ii) "safeguard" provisions designed to ensure that the RTA will not adversely affect gender equality; and (iii) provisions that actively promote gender equality and women's economic empowerment by incorporating gender-sensitive policies or co-operation on gender equality issues between countries. The provisions in these three categories rarely contain binding obligations.

Mechanisms to implement gender provisions are also important, e.g. budgetary commitments for implementation or provisions for consequences of non-compliance. The most detailed and comprehensive gender chapters and provisions are those included in the RTAs to which Chile is a party with Argentina and Uruguay and the amended RTAs negotiated by Canada with Chile and Israel (Monteiro, 2018[34]). An interesting example is also the modernised Canada-EU RTA for which organisations representing women entrepreneurs were consulted and engaged both in the design phase of the agreement and during implementation and monitoring (Korinek, Moïsé and Tange, 2021[33]). Gender provisions are generally absent from bilateral investment treaties (BITs). One notable exception is provided by the 2019 model BIT of the Netherlands, which contains an explicit provision on gender equality. In particular, the provision recognises the relevant contribution of women to economic growth and emphasises the importance of 'incorporating a gender perspective' to promote inclusive growth and support the economic integration of women. Although this provision is excluded from investor-state dispute settlement, as it is aimed at inter-state relations rather than investor-state relations, it has an important policy and programmatic function (De Brabandere, 2021[35])).

Eliminate regulatory restrictions on FDI and trade in sectors that employ or have the potential to employ many women

Restrictions on FDI inflows can take different forms. Some restrictions directly affect FDI flows, such as limits on foreign ownership, a screening and approval process, and constraints on foreign personnel. These restrictions tend to be justified by national policy objectives, such as the desire to protect domestic firms and workers from foreign competition. Other impediments stem from national policies regulating product and labour markets (e.g. competition policy), intellectual property rights, infrastructure, state-owned enterprises (SOEs), and public procurement and tend to have a negative impact not only on foreign but also on domestic firms.

These restrictions and barriers increase uncertainty for investors and may divert investment to less risky locations, and thus undermine the potential benefits associated with FDI, such as job creation, productivity spillovers and the transfer of skills and technology (Chapters 2 and 3). These restrictions also have implications on gender equality when they affect sectors where many women work or have the potential to work (e.g. services sectors). Trade restrictions both at the border (e.g. tariffs and quotas) and behind the border (e.g. technical and sanitary barriers, migration barriers) also reduce the expected returns on investment projects and limit the positive spillover effects of FDI on women, especially when they concern female-dominated sectors. Furthermore, trade barriers tend to have a negative impact especially on women-owned/led businesses due to their more limited financial, managerial and time resources (Korinek, Moïsé and Tange, 2021[33]).

Ensure that domestic regulation supports the creation of good quality jobs for women by foreign MNEs

Foreign MNEs can create employment opportunities for women in host countries, both within their affiliates and in domestic companies through supply chain relationships. The 'quality' of these jobs, as well as the ability of women to take advantage of these opportunities, is influenced by domestic regulation related to employment (e.g. minimum wage, employment protection, Chapter 3), social protection (e.g. length of maternity leave), the workplace (e.g. sexual harassment law, flexible working arrangements), and taxation of labour income (e.g. taxation of secondary workers) (Thomas and O'Reilly, 2016[36]). Employment and social protection policies are found to be more impactful in countries with less advanced legal and regulatory frameworks and tend to be more effective when negotiated with trade unions and workers' representatives (Chapter 3). On the other hand, policies that address gender inequalities in the workplace, such as policies in favour of teleworking, are found to be more effective in developed countries (IMF, 2018[37]).

While labour market regulations are important for setting minimum standards and protecting women from gender discrimination and life cycle risks, they can also perpetuate patterns of gender inequality. For example, regulations prohibiting women from working in certain sectors, which are not imposed on men, can reinforce gender inequality gaps. Similarly, taxation of labour income that disproportionately penalises secondary income earners, who are often women, is likely to discourage female labour participation. These regulatory barriers are likely to prevent women from benefiting from the employment opportunities created by foreign multinationals or to make such opportunities more attractive to men than to women.

Remove regulatory barriers that prevent women entrepreneurs from taking advantage of the business opportunities created by FDI

FDI can have a beneficial effect on local women's entrepreneurship. For example, linkages with foreign MNEs can help women-owned enterprises become more productive and expand their business in domestic and international markets (Chapter 2). Regulatory barriers, however, can hold back women entrepreneurs and reduce their ability to profit from the presence of foreign MNEs. Regulatory procedures such as business registration and licensing, worker registration, and reporting requirements can be more burdensome for women entrepreneurs, especially when they are complex and non-transparent. This is due to the fact that female entrepreneurs tend to have fewer resources, time and skills to deal with these complex procedures than male entrepreneurs (OECD/European Union, 2019[11]).

In addition, in some countries, regulations and laws may explicitly prevent women from registering a business, signing contracts, owning a bank account and using formal credit services. In several countries, women also face discrimination in relation to property and inheritance rights (World Bank, 2021[38]). This makes starting and running a business even more difficult, as property can be sold and used as collateral for loans that finance the start-up and growth of the business. Furthermore, if women do not have equal inheritance rights, they are less able than men to accumulate property and wealth that could be used for the enterprise.

Improve women's access to quality education and health systems

A well-educated and productive female workforce is an important prerequisite for improving the impact of FDI on gender equality. It can attract technology-intensive FDI, which creates better jobs for women. In countries with a comparative advantage in low-value-added production, it can help women move to alternative or better job opportunities when technology improves and wages rise. In some developing countries, women do not have the same access to education as men. Even in advanced countries, stereotypes about gender roles underlie inequalities between girls and boys in performance and career choices (OECD, 2018[39]).

The 2013 OECD Council Recommendation on Gender Equality in Education, Employment and Entrepreneurship provides principles for a gender-equal education system (OECD, 2017[40]). These include ensuring equal access to quality education for both boys and girls, eliminating gender discrimination and stereotypes in curricula and teaching practices, making science, technology, engineering and mathematics (STEM) subjects as well as financial and entrepreneurial issues more attractive to girls, and raising awareness among parents and teachers about gender stereotypical attitudes on school performance. In some countries, women also have limited access to health services due to their more precarious economic status and various cultural and social barriers. This can have a negative impact on their health and further hinder their participation in the labour market (OECD, 2017[2]). A universally accessible health care system is an important condition for developing a productive workforce and enabling women to benefit from economic prospects brought by FDI.

4.3.3. Stimulate investment, particularly foreign investment, that promotes gender equality, and strengthen the capacities of female entrepreneurs and the skills of female workers

Design investment incentive systems that promote gender equality

Investment incentives can support gender equality objectives. Incentives used to attract FDI in specific sectors can boost women's employment and wages when used in sectors that employ many women. They can also be used to directly promote gender equality goals. For example, tax incentives can be given to companies that encourage the hiring of women or their training, or that provide services such as childcare. Similarly, subsidies and grants can be given to companies to help offset the higher costs they may face in hiring, promoting and training women. Currently, the use of investment incentives to promote gender inclusive practices in the workplace remains limited (Kronfol, Nichols and Thu Tran, 2019[41]). An interesting example is Jordan, which provides incentives to companies that hire a certain proportion of women in specific sectors (Box 4.4).

Incentives, however, have distorting effects as they can divert resources from more efficient to less efficient activities and entail an economic cost both in terms of expenditure and revenue forgone (OECD, 2021[42]). The use of investment incentives may therefore reduce the fiscal space for other policies that are important for achieving gender equality. For this reason, it is important that investment incentive schemes are designed in a transparent way and regularly assessed.

Box 4.4. Investment incentives and gender equality in Jordan

There are several investment incentives in Jordan that can have a positive effect on gender equality, including a direct tax incentive for employing Jordanian women, as well as incentives in special economic zones (SEZs) and satellite production units that employ many women:

Corporate tax incentive to hire women: In 2020, the Government of Jordan adopted Regulation No. 18, introducing corporate income tax (CIT) incentives. According to this regulation, companies receive a reduced CIT rate if the share of Jordanian women and workers with disabilities is not less than 15% of the total workforce, with the exception of companies in the textile and garment sector that are located in QIZs, for which the share must not be less than 25%. Although this is a low percentage, it is a rare example of a corporate tax incentive directly linked to the achievement of a gender equality objective. The tax incentive, however, discriminates against foreign women, who represent an important share of workers especially in industries such as textiles and clothing.

Investment incentives in SEZs: Jordan has numerous SEZs that enjoy investment incentives, including a series of exemptions from income tax, export taxes and customs duties. These incentives have attracted many foreign companies since the 1990s. As many of these zones are dominated by female-intensive sectors, especially textiles and garments (73% women in 2021), these incentives have significant potential to boost local women's employment and wages, although they do not ensure that jobs created are 'good' jobs.

Investment incentives in satellite production units: As of 2017, incentives for satellite production units, outside the defined SEZs, have also encouraged the integration of women into the workforce. Satellite production units, created to stimulate female employment in rural areas, provide a range of incentives to companies in terms of land, rent exemptions and subsidised wages, transport, social security and utilities for companies. Currently about 85% of the workforce in satellite units are women.

Sources: OECD (2022[29]), OECD (2022[43])

Provide financial and technical assistance to women entrepreneurs

Due to various economic, social and cultural barriers, including the fact that women spend more time than men on family care and domestic work, women entrepreneurs tend to have fewer entrepreneurial and managerial skills and have more difficulty accessing formal credit than male entrepreneurs (OECD/European Union, 2019[11]). Lack of skills and capital can affect the capacity of women entrepreneurs to develop linkages with foreign firms and benefit from related technology and productivity spillovers. The 2013 OECD Council Recommendation on Gender Equality in Education, Employment and Entrepreneurship encourages countries to design policy instruments to help female entrepreneurs overcome barriers related to lack of skills and credit (OECD, 2017[40]). Financial support can take the form of soft loans or microcredit, or tax benefits. Technical support can help women entrepreneurs strengthen their skills and grow their business. This can include training programmes to develop skills in business, management and digitisation, professional advice on legal and tax issues and other business development services.

Offer training and skills development programmes to female workers

Skills development and upgrading is key to increasing women's employability and career prospects, including within foreign companies. This is particularly important for women at the bottom of the productivity ladder and those re-entering the workforce. Especially in developing countries, investing in women's skills minimises the risk of women remaining in low-skilled jobs or moving into informal employment when wages rise (Braunstein, 2009[44]). In addition to ensuring equal access to a quality education system, governments can support women's skills development through training programmes that take into account the needs of domestic and foreign companies (Chapters 2 and 3). These programmes can be organised in collaboration with companies, training centres or universities. Governments can also provide incentives to companies to train their female employees, for example through training grants. Offering training incentives to companies may be preferable when they have a better understanding of the skills that are lacking in the local labour market. In addition, governments can also provide certification and qualification programmes to help women obtain a standardised accreditation that they can use to signal their skills to companies (Kronfol, Nichols and Thu Tran, 2019[41]).

4.3.4. Eliminate information barriers and gender stereotypes that penalise women in the labour market; and providing social support services to enable women to work

Help women entrepreneurs overcome information barriers and develop linkages with foreign MNEs

Women entrepreneurs often have more limited access to information due to a lack of time and resources and their smaller professional networks (OECD, 2017[2]). In addition, gender stereotypes can influence potential business partners and investors' perceptions (Kronfol, Nichols and Thu Tran, 2019[41]). These information asymmetries hold back women entrepreneurs and can hinder the development of business linkages with foreign firms. Several information and facilitation measures can help women entrepreneurs overcome these information barriers. For example, programmes such as mentoring, coaching or trade fairs and events aimed primarily at women-owned businesses can help women entrepreneurs acquire relevant information about their business and expand their professional network. Matchmaking events, supplier diversity programmes and supplier databases identifying women-owned enterprises can enable women entrepreneurs to connect with potential business partners and investors (Box 4.5). In addition, especially in developing countries, women entrepreneurs tend to have limited access to the internet and digital platforms (OECD/European Union, 2019[11]). Improving women's access to affordable digital technologies, particularly mobile technology, could help them more easily obtain information and develop business connections.

Box 4.5. Programmes to link women entrepreneurs with foreign MNEs: Experiences from Canada, Rwanda and Morocco

Connecting women entrepreneurs to foreign multinationals, thus creating links for women in the global supply chain and increasing their capacity as suppliers, is another crucial policy approach taken by governments. Some notable examples are Supplier Diversity Canada and programmes implemented with the support of SheTrades Global in Rwanda and Morocco.

Supplier Diversity Canada is an initiative funded by Women and Gender Equality Canada, which aims to advance business diversity and inclusion in Canada by bringing women-owned, aboriginal-owned, minority-owned and LGB-owned businesses into corporate supply chains and government contracts. The initiative includes training procurement professionals on the advantages and tools available to broader their supplier network and connecting diversity suppliers with procurement opportunities. Numerous MNEs have engaged in supplier diversity programmes, including Marriott, Sodexo, IBM, Dell, and several others.

SheTrades Global is a programme of the Centre for International Trade that helps women-owned businesses expand their network, learn new skills and connect with business partners and investors. With the support of SheTrades Global, Rwanda and Morocco have developed similar programmes. In

Rwanda, where 98% of women-owned businesses are small or micro enterprises, these programmes focus on connecting different female suppliers with local and regional supply chains. The programme is especially adapted to the horticulture and coffee sectors, where women business owners dominate. In Morocco, the programme is geared more towards women in the agri-food sector, with an international focus on linking Moroccan suppliers with potential buyers in both Canada and Europe.

Source: OECD (2022[29])

Eliminate gender stereotypes that prevent women from participating in the labour market

Women in host countries may not be able to benefit from the job opportunities generated by foreign MNEs due to various social and cultural barriers. Social norms shape the acceptable roles for women and men in society and influence women's aspirations and opportunities. In most developed and developing countries, men are still seen as breadwinners, while unpaid care work is considered a women's prerogative (OECD, 2017[2]). Even at school age, girls have different aspirations from boys and show less interest in some professional careers (e.g. science, technology, engineering, mathematics: STEM) (Mostafa, 2019[45]). These gender stereotypes are at the root of patterns of gender inequality in the labour market, e.g. the fact that women tend to be concentrated in low-value-added sectors (e.g. labour intensive manufacturing, education, health, social services) and in part-time jobs. Because of these social barriers, women may not be able to take advantage of job opportunities brought by foreign multinationals. Transforming these social gender norms is therefore key to increasing female labour force participation and maximising the positive impact of FDI on employment. This can be achieved through social media, public information and awareness-raising campaigns that aim to change traditional gender roles and patterns in society and at work. In schools, programmes targeting female students and their teachers can eliminate differences in approaches to learning and teaching. For example, mentoring programmes can help girls expand their networks, influence their career aspirations, and raise awareness of different educational and professional careers.

Provide good quality social support services to enable women to work

The provision of public social support services such as childcare, elderly care and transport are crucial to enable women to benefit from the employment opportunities created by foreign MNEs. The opportunity cost of entering the labour market is higher for women than for men. This is due to an unequal distribution of unpaid care responsibilities between men and women (OECD, 2017[2]). The disproportionate share of care work for which women are responsible has a negative impact on their labour force participation and affects the types of job opportunities available to them (e.g. more women work part-time than men) (OECD, 2019[5]). The provision of public childcare and elderly care services is therefore important for increasing women's labour force participation. The ability of women to travel to work by safe and affordable means of transport is also an important factor influencing their decision to work and the quality of employment opportunities available to them (Livingston, 2004[46]; UNACTD, 2014[17]).

References

Aguayo-Tellez, E. (2012), "The Impact of Trade Liberalization Policies and FDI on Gender Inequalities: A Literature Review", *World Development Report Background Papers*, https://openknowledge.worldbank.org/handle/10986/9220. [12]

Benfratello, L. and A. Sembenelli (2006), "Foreign ownership and productivity: Is the direction of causality so obvious?", *International Journal of Industrial Organization*, Vol. 24/4, pp. 733-751. [19]

Braunstein, E. (2009), *Making policy work for women: gender, foreign direct investment and development.* [44]

Chen, M. and M. Carr (2004), "Globalization, social exclusion and gender", *International Labour Review*, Vol. 143/1-2. [18]

Criscuolo, C. and R. Martin (2003), "Multinationals, foreign ownership and US productivity leadership: Evidence from the UK", *Royal Economic Society Annual Conference 2003 50, Royal Economic Society*. [20]

Davin, D. (2004), "The Impact of Export-oriented Manufacturing on the Welfare Entitlements of Chinese Women Workers", *Globalization, Export-oriented Employment and Social Policy*, pp. 67–90. [23]

Davis A., P. (2020), "Can Multinational Firms Promote Gender Equality? The Role of Labour Mobility", *Transnational Corporations Journal*, Vol. 27/3. [13]

De Brabandere, E. (2021), "The 2019 Dutch Model Bilateral Investment Treaty: Navigating the Turbulent Ocean of Investment Treaty Reform", *ICSID Review - Foreign Investment Law Journal*, Vol. 36/2, pp. 319–338, https://doi.org/10.1093/icsidreview/siab014. [35]

Ghosh, J. (2002), "Globalization, Export-Oriented Employment for Women and Social Policy: A Case Study of India", *Social Scientist*, Vol. 30/11/12, pp. 17-60. [25]

ILO (2019), *ILO - modelled estimates – July 2019*, https://ilostat.ilo.org/resources/methods/ilo-modelled-estimates/. [4]

ILO (2018), *Global Wage Report 2018/19: What lies behind gender pay gaps*, https://www.ilo.org/wcmsp5/groups/public/---dgreports/---dcomm/---publ/documents/publication/wcms_650553.pdf. [6]

ILO (2017), *Tripartite Declaration of Principles concerning Multinational Enterprises and Social Policy*, https://www.ilo.org/wcmsp5/groups/public/---ed_emp/---emp_ent/---multi/documents/publication/wcms_094386.pdf. [32]

ILO (2016), *Women at Work: Trends 2016*, https://www.ilo.org/gender/Informationresources/Publications/WCMS_457317/lang--en/index.htm. [8]

IMF (2018), *Pursuing Women's Economic Empowerment*, https://www.imf.org/en/Publications/Policy-Papers/Issues/2018/05/31/pp053118pursuing-womens-economic-empowerment#:~:text=Summary%3A,in%20turn%2C%20supports%20economic%20resilience. [37]

Kazandjian, R. et al. (2016), "Gender Equality and Economic Diversification", *IMF Working Paper*, https://www.imf.org/external/pubs/ft/wp/2016/wp16140.pdf. [1]

Kodama, N., B. Javorcik and Y. Abe (2018), "Transplanting corporate culture across international borders: Foreign direct investment and female employment in Japan", *The World Economy*, Vol. 41/1, pp. 1148–1165. [14]

Korinek, J., E. Moïsé and J. Tange (2021), "Trade and gender: A Framework of analysis", *OECD Trade Policy Papers*, https://doi.org/10.1787/6db59d80-en. [33]

Kronfol, H., A. Nichols and T. Thu Tran (2019), "Women at Work. How Can Investment Incentives Be Used to Enhance Economic Opportunities for Women?", *Policy Research Working Paper 8935, The World Bank Group*. [41]

Livingston, J. (2004), "Murder in Juárez: Gender, Sexual Violence, and the Global Assembly Line", *A Journal of Women Studies*, Vol. 25/1, pp. 59-76. [46]

Monteiro, J. (2018), "Gender-related provisions in regional trade agreements,", *WTO Staff Working Papers ERSD-2018-15, World Trade Organization (WTO), Economic Research and Statistics Division.*. [34]

Montinari, L. and M. Wermelinger (2020), "Enhancing the positive impact of FDI on gender equality: design of a Policy Toolkit", *DAF/INV/WD(2020)24*. [16]

Mostafa, T. (2019), "Why don't more girls choose to pursue a science career?", *PISA in Focus* 93, https://doi.org/10.1787/02bd2b68-en. [45]

OECD (2022), *FDI Qualities Indicators: 2022*. [22]

OECD (2022), *FDI Qualities mapping: A survey of policies and institutions that can strengthen sustainable investment.*. [29]

OECD (2022), *FDI Qualities Review of Jordan: Strengthening sustainable investment, OECD Publishing, Paris*, https://doi.org/10.1787/736c77d2-en. [43]

OECD (2021), "OECD Investment Tax Incentives Database: Enhancing transparency through comparable data in developing countries", *COM/DAF/INV/CTPA/CFA/WP2(2021)1.*. [42]

OECD (2020), *OECD Employment Database*, https://stats.oecd.org/index.aspx?queryid=54753. [7]

OECD (2020), *Women at the core of the fight against COVID-19 crisis*, OECD Publishing, Paris, https://doi.org/10.1787/553a8269-en. [9]

OECD (2019), *FDI Qualities Indicators: Measuring the sustainable development impacts of investment*, http://www.oecd.org/fr/investissement/fdi-qualities-indicators.htm. [21]

OECD (2019), *OECD Employment Outlook 2019: The Future of Work*, OECD Publishing, Paris, https://doi.org/10.1787/9ee00155-en. [5]

OECD (2018), *Is the Last Mile the Longest? Economic Gains from Gender Equality in Nordic Countries*, https://doi.org/10.1787/9789264300040-en. [3]

OECD (2018), *OECD Due Diligence Guidance for Responsible Business Conduct*, http://mneguidelines.oecd.org/OECD-Due-Diligence-Guidance-for-Responsible-Business-Conduct.pdf. [31]

OECD (2018), *Programme for International Student Assessment*, https://www.oecd.org/pisa/. [39]

OECD (2017), *2013 OECD Recommendation of the Council on Gender Equality in Education, Employment and Entrepreneurship*, https://doi.org/10.1787/9789264279391-en. [40]

OECD (2017), *The Pursuit of Gender Equality: An Uphill Battle*, OECD Publishing, Paris, https://doi.org/10.1787/9789264281318-en. [2]

OECD (2011), *OECD Guidelines for Multinational Enterprises, 2011 Edition*, OECD Publishing, Paris, https://doi.org/10.1787/9789264115415-en. [30]

OECD/European Union (2019), *The Missing Entrepreneurs 2019: Policies for Inclusive Entrepreneurship*, https://doi.org/10.1787/3ed84801-en. [11]

Olcott, G. (2014), "The impact of foreign ownership on gender and employment relations in large Japanese companies", *Work, Employment & Society, British Sociological Association*, Vol. 28/2, pp. 206-224. [26]

Ono, H. (2004), "Foreign ownership and the structure of wages in Japan", *Paper presented at the National Bureau of Economic Research Conference,*. [27]

Tang, H. (2017), "Do Multinationals Transfer Culture? Evidence on Female Employment in China", *CESifo Working Paper Series* 6295. [15]

Thomas, A. and P. O'Reilly (2016), "The Impact of Tax and Benefit Systems on the Workforce Participation Incentives of Women", *Documents de travail de l'OCDE sur la fiscalité*, Éditions OCDE, Paris, https://doi.org/10.1787/d950acfc-en. [36]

UNACTD (2014), *Investment by TNCs and Gender: Preliminary Assessment and Way Forward*, https://unctad.org/en/PublicationsLibrary/webdiaeia2014d4_en.pdf. [17]

UNCTAD (2021), *Multinational Enterprises and the International Transmission of Gender Policies and Practices*, https://unctad.org/system/files/official-document/diaeinf2021d1_en.pdf. [10]

UNCTAD (2020), *World Investment Report 2020*, https://unctad.org/en/PublicationsLibrary/wir2020_en.pdf. [28]

Ver Beek, K. (2001), "Maquiladoras: Exploitation or Emancipation? An Overview of the Situation of Maquiladora Workers in Honduras", *World Development*, Vol. 29/9, pp. 1553-1567. [24]

World Bank (2021), *Women, Business and the Law*, https://wbl.worldbank.org/en/wbl. [38]

Annex 4.A. Assessing the impact of FDI on gender equality

Annex Table 4.A.1. Core questions to assess the impact of FDI on gender equality

Dimension	Policy questions	Potential data source
Gender equality in the labour market	What is the gender employment gap in the country? How does it vary across sectors? Has it increased (or decreased) over time?	ILO's databases on labour market statistics
	What is the gender wage gap in the country? How does it vary across sectors? Has it increased (or decreased) over time?	OECD's Employment Outlook Equal Pay Legal Database – EPIC
	How many women reach the top levels of management in private and public companies? Has this share increased (or decreased) over time?	OECD's Employment Outlook
	What is the share of women-owned/led businesses and how does it vary across sectors? Has this share increased (or decreased) over time?	OECD Entrepreneurship Database Global Entrepreneurship Monitor
	What is the level of discrimination against women in social institutions (formal and informal laws, social norms, and practices)?	OECD SIGI
Structure of the economy	In which sectors and value chains do women work? Have these changed over time?	ILO's databases on labour market statistics
	In which sectors and value chains are women-owned/led businesses concentrated? Have these changed over time?	OECD's Employment Outlook WB's Doing Business
	Does the country have a comparative advantage in female-dominated sectors? How has this changed over time?	UN Comtrade Database
FDI characteristics	Is FDI concentrated in sectors that employ many women?	OECD FDI Qualities Indicators
	How has the gender employment gap shifted, if at all, in sectors that have seen FDI growth? How has the gender wage gap shifted, if at all, in sectors that have seen FDI growth?	OECD FDI Qualities Indicators
	What is the share of FDI coming from more gender-equal countries?	OECD FDI statistics OECD Development Centre
FDI transmission channels	What is the female employment share of affiliates of foreign MNEs? How does this compare to the labour force as a whole?	OECD FDI Qualities Indicators*
	Is the gender wage gap higher in foreign firms relative to domestic firms?	OECD FDI Qualities Indicators*
	What is the share of women in top levels of management /boards in foreign and domestic firms?	OECD FDI Qualities Indicators*
	What is the extent of linkages between foreign and domestic firms in female dominated sectors?	OECD extended TiVA database (based on AMNE data)
	To what do extent female workers move from foreign to domestic firms?	National Sources*

Annex Table 4.A.2. Core questions to assess policies that influence the impact of FDI on gender equality

Dimension	Instrument	Policy questions
Governance	National strategies and plans	What are the country's priorities in terms of gender equality and women empowerment in the labour market? Are these priorities aligned with broader development objectives?
		What is the country's FDI attraction strategy? Are gender equality objectives and gender considerations incorporated in the strategy?
	Policy coherence and co-ordination	What is the quality of the broader institutional framework that affects gender-specific impacts of FDI? Do relevant institutions have enough decisional power and financial resources?
		Do institutions co-ordinate their policies, activities and strategic priorities? Are these co-ordination mechanisms formal?

Dimension	Instrument	Policy questions
	Gender impact assessment and collection of data	Do relevant institutions systematically undertake gender impact assessment of their policies and programmes?
		Do institutions regularly collect gender-disaggregated data in areas such as investment/FDI, labour market, SMEs/entrepreneurship and human resource development? Are the data timely and internationally comparable?
International agreements	International standards on gender equality	Has the country ratified major international instruments promoting gender equality (e.g. CEDAW)? Has the country placed reservations on specific articles? Has the country adopted legislation to conform to such international obligations?
	OECD Guidelines on MNEs and Sectoral Guidance on RBC	Has the country adhered to the OECD Guidelines for MNEs and to any of the OECD Due Diligence Guidance for RBCs?
		Does the country allocate sufficient resources to the National Contact Point for RBC?
	RTAs and BITs	Is the country party of RTAs or BITs that incorporate gender provisions? How strong are the mechanisms to enforce these provisions?
		Is market access granted in partner countries in sectors where women work and own businesses?
Regulation	FDI and trade openness	Are there restrictions on FDI and trade in sectors that employ or have the potential to employ many women?
	Labour market regulations	Does the country have a law on minimum wage? Does the country have a law demanding equal pay between women and men?
		Does the country have a well-designed and implemented social protection system that addresses women's specific life-cycle transitions and risks? Does the government provide quality and affordable childcare services?
		Are there restrictions for women to work in certain jobs and/or sectors? Is there a legislation on sexual harassment in employment? Does the country have gender-neutral labour income taxation?
	Regulatory barriers to women entrepreneurship	Can a woman open a bank account, take out a loan, or assume a mortgage in the same way as a man? Can a woman sign a contract in the same way as a man? Can a women register a business in the same way as a man?
		Can a woman inherit property in the same way as a man?
	Education and health care systems	Is there universal access to education and health care in the country? Does the education system provide equal opportunities for girls and boys (e.g. what is the share of girls in STEM subjects)?
Financial & technical support	Investment incentives	Are there investment incentives in sectors where many women work? If so, are they designed in a transparent way and regularly assessed?
		Are there incentives for companies that promote gender-inclusive business practices (e.g. tax incentives to hire women; wage/training subsidies for women)? If so, are they designed in a transparent way and regularly assessed?
	Financial and technical support to women entrepreneurs	Are there financial programmes to support women entrepreneurs (e.g. soft loans, microcredit, tax incentives)?
		Are there training programmes and business support services (e.g. advice on legal and tax issues) for women entrepreneurs?
	Training and skills development programmes for women workers	Are there skill development programmes and/or certification and qualification programmes targeting women? Are they organised in collaboration with foreign MNEs?
Information & facilitation services	Information and facilitation services for women entrepreneurs	Are there programmes to help women overcome information barriers and link to foreign MNEs (e.g. matchmaking events, supplier diversity programmes)?
	Initiatives to eliminate gender bias and stereotypes	Are there initiatives in place to eliminate stereotypes about gender roles (e.g. public information campaign)?
	Social support services	Is safe public transport available to women, particularly in areas where foreign MNEs are located? Are there affordable and accessible childcare and elder care services for families?

Annex Table 4.A.3. Policies for positive FDI impacts on gender equality by policy area

Policy area	Policy dimension	Institutions and policies			
		Governance	Regulation	Financial and technical support & information and facilitation services	International agreements
Investment policy	FDI/trade openness	Gender equality strategy encompassing all relevant policy areas; Sectoral strategies incorporating gender equality objectives or considerations (e.g. investment promotion strategy); Systematic gender impact assessment; Collection of data for gender analysis; Gender mainstreaming & policy co-ordination and coherence in relevant policy areas	FDI and trade restrictions in female in sectors that employ or have the potential to employ many women		Gender provisions in BITs and RTAs WTO Joint Declaration on Trade and Women's Economic Empowerment
	Investment promotion & facilitation			Tax incentives to attract FDI in female-dominated sectors;	
	Business linkages			Information and facilitation programmes to link women-owned/led businesses to foreign MNEs;	
	Responsible business conduct				OECD MNE Guidelines for MNEs; OECD Due Diligence Sectoral Guidance on RBC;
Labour market policy	Employment and job quality		Labour market regulation (e.g. minimum wage, employment protection, sexual harassment)	Tax incentives to hire and train women; Information services to reduce gender bias in the workplace;	ILO Conventions on gender equality; Convention on the Elimination of All Forms of Discrimination against Women (CEDAW); Beijing Declaration and Platform for Action; 2030 Sustainable Development Goal Agenda (SDG 5: Achieve gender equality and empower all women and girls);
	Social protection		Social protection legislation (e.g. paid maternity leave; parental leave)	Affordable quality childcare and elderly care services	
	Taxes on labour income		Labour income taxes that affect male and female labour demand differently (e.g. taxation on secondary earners);		
	Transport to work			Safe public transport	
Private sector development	Entrepreneurship/SMEs		Regulation affecting women's ability to start and run a business	Subsidised loans or grants to support women entrepreneurs; Business development support for women entrepreneurs;	
	Property		Regulations affecting women's ability to own and inherit assets, including land;		
Human resources development	Education		Regulation on the education system	Training and skills development programmes for women; Information programmes to reduce gender stereotypes in teaching and learning;	
	Health		Regulation on the health system		

Note

[1] Evidence shows that the corporate culture of the MNE is influenced by the home country's policy context as well as its social and cultural norms (Kodama, Javorcik and Abe, 2018[14]; Tang, 2017[15]). While the Policy Toolkit focuses on host country policies, home country policies also play an important role through their effect on the MNE corporate culture.

5 Policies for improving FDI impacts on carbon emissions

This chapter presents a Policy Toolkit to help governments attract foreign direct investment (FDI) that contributes to decarbonisation, both by reducing the emissions associated with foreign investments and inducing low-carbon spillovers to domestic firms. The chapter describes the channels through which FDI affects carbon emissions and the contextual factors determining the magnitude and direction of such impacts. The objective of the Policy Toolkit is to provide an overview of the policy choices that can improve the impacts of FDI on decarbonisation.

Main policy principles

1. Provide strategic direction and promote policy coherence and co-ordination on investment and climate action

- Ensure a coherent, long-term strategic framework to mainstream decarbonisation across economic sectors that is linked to the national vision or goals for growth and development, with clear climate goals (e.g. emissions reductions, renewable energy) that are translated to science-based targets for the private sector.
- Develop a dedicated strategy that articulates the government's vision on the contribution of investment, including foreign direct investment, to decarbonisation. The strategy sets the goals, identifies priority policy actions and clarifies responsibilities of institutions and co-ordinating bodies.
- Strengthen co-ordination both at strategic and implementing levels by establishing appropriate co-ordinating bodies or by considering to expand the mandate and composition of existing ones, such as boards of investment promotion agencies and higher councils for green growth.
- Encourage public consultations and stakeholder engagement to receive feedback and build consensus around policy reforms and programmes to decarbonise investments.
- Design and implement effective monitoring and evaluation frameworks to assess the impact of FDI and related policies on decarbonisation, and to identify bottlenecks in policy implementation, including strategic environmental assessment (SEA) and environmental impact assessment (EIA) systems. Build capacity at national and subnational levels to review environmental assessments, reduce delays in the process, and improve transparency and information systems supporting the review process.

2. Ensure that domestic and international investment regulations are aligned with and reinforce national climate objectives, including commitments under the Paris Agreement.

- Endeavour to join major international agreements and conventions promoting decarbonisation and set domestic environmental standards for investments (e.g. on emissions, fuel economy, appliances) that are aligned with climate objectives and that support climate-friendly business conduct.
- Ensure that international investment and trade agreements are aligned with climate objectives and allow for sufficient domestic policy space to achieve these objectives.
- Develop laws and regulations that level the playing field for climate-friendly investment, including by ensuring an open and non-discriminatory environment for foreign investors in low-carbon technologies, strengthening competition in electricity markets, and ensuring intellectual property protection for low-carbon innovations.

3. Stimulate investment and build technical capabilities related to low-carbon technologies, services and infrastructure

- Phase out subsidies for investments that distort price signals and reduce the competitiveness of low-carbon technologies and consider introducing carbon pricing measures. Address any adverse effects on jobs with appropriate measures to compensate and retrain workers so as to ensure a just transition.
- Ensure that financial support to stimulate low-carbon investment addresses market failures that reduce the competitiveness of low-carbon investments, and is transparent, time-limited and subjective to regular reviews.

- Use financial and technical support to build domestic low-carbon capabilities, and to support the flow of knowledge and technology from foreign to domestic firms.

4. Address information failures and administrative barriers that reduce the competitiveness of low-carbon investments

- Raise public awareness on climate priorities and individual actions for investors and consumers to reduce carbon footprint.
- Encourage corporate disclosure of carbon emissions embodied in products and services (e.g. carbon labelling), and facilitate reporting of suspected violations of environmental regulations, or risks of violations, related to their business operations.
- Tailor investment promotion activities and tools raise visibility of low-carbon investment opportunities. Facilitate compliance with environmental permitting. Support foreign investors in identifying domestic suppliers and partners with complementary capabilities. Use IPAs as intermediaries to make policy makers aware of the regulatory needs of low-carbon investors.

5.1. The urgency of reducing CO_2 emissions

Adverse environmental developments are among the gravest global threats of current times. A global economy reliant on fossil fuels and the resulting rising greenhouse gas emissions, now 60% higher than their 1990 level (Figure 5.1), are creating drastic changes to the climate, including more frequent and extreme weather events, land degradation, ocean acidification, and biodiversity loss. Climate change and the resulting migration pressures and threats to food and health security are at the forefront of global efforts to sustain the planet (WEF, 2020[1]). To address these mounting challenges, on 12 December 2015, 190 countries signed the Paris Agreement to combat climate change, pledging to achieve carbon neutrality by 2050 (UNFCCC, 2015[2]). This landmark agreement was discussed at the 26st Conference of the Parties (COP26) of the United Nations Framework Convention on Climate Change (UNFCCC) with new impetus and more ambitious pledges to accelerate actions and investments needed for a sustainable low-carbon future.

Figure 5.1. Global annual CO_2 emissions

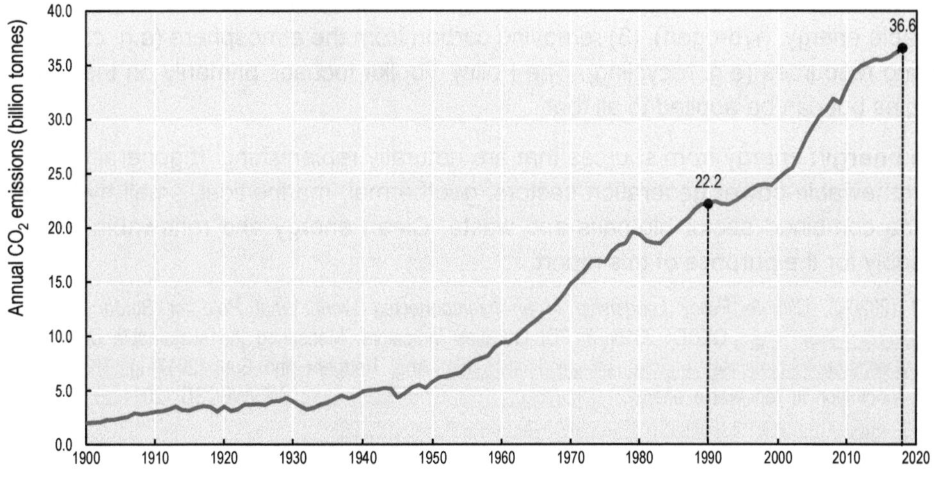

Source: International Energy Agency's World Energy Statistics.

The climate crisis has serious financial repercussions, including disaster-related damage costs that amount to hundreds of billions of dollars, annually (IPCC, 2018[3]); adaptation costs associated with protection and reinforcement; and mitigation costs associated with decarbonisation. Climate change mitigation and adaptation will require an estimated USD 7 trillion per year worth of public and private investments alone to meet global infrastructure development needs and climate objectives through 2030 (OECD, 2017[4]). Of these, USD 4 trillion per year are needed across emerging economies, and USD 1.7 trillion per year in emerging Asia (OECD, 2020[5]). In the wake of the COVID-19 pandemic, government efforts to support economic recovery are essential but should not undermine actions to limit the climate crisis. Stimulus measures and policy responses must be aligned with ambitions on climate change, biodiversity and wider environmental protection (OECD, 2020[6]; OECD, 2020[7]). The window of opportunity for climate action is closing fast and short-term economic measures will have a significant impact on the ability to meet global goals (United Nations, 2015[8]).This chapter focuses on the potential contribution of FDI to climate change mitigation.[1] Box 5.1 provides some definitions and clarifications for the following discussion.

Box 5.1. Key terms and concepts

CO_2 emissions: Carbon dioxide (CO_2) is the primary greenhouse gas (GHG) responsible for global warming. This Policy Toolkit focuses primarily on CO_2 because it is generated by all economic activities, but its implications can be extended to cover other GHGs. The GHG Protocol jointly developed by the World Resources Institute and the World Business Council for Sustainable Development uses a delineation that has become standard, dividing emissions into three types:

- *Scope 1:* Direct emissions generated by industrial processes and any other on-site activities.
- *Scope 2:* Indirect emissions associated with energy (i.e. electricity, heat or steam) imported from off-site.
- *Scope 3:* All other indirect emissions in the life cycle of the products produced, including those associated with any intermediate goods, transport of goods to market, emissions in end use and disposal of products produced. It includes also emissions associated with leased assets, franchises and investments.

Carbon intensity: the emission rate of CO_2 of a specific economic activity. A common measure used to compare emissions from different sources of electrical power is carbon intensity per kilowatt-hour.

Low-carbon technology: a technology that helps reduce CO_2 emissions by (1) reducing energy use (e.g. energy-saving); (2) reducing or eliminating carbon emissions from production or use (e.g. renewable energy, hydrogen); (3) removing carbon from the atmosphere (e.g. carbon capture); or (4) conserving resources (e.g. recycling). The Policy Toolkit focuses primarily on the first two classes of technologies but can be applied to all four.

Renewable energy: energy from sources that are naturally replenishing. It generally is considered to include six renewable-power generation sectors: geothermal, marine/tidal, small hydroelectric, solar, wind, and the combined sector biomass and waste. Clean energy and renewable energy are used interchangeably for the purpose of this report.

Source: OECD (2020[9]), *Climate Policy Leadership in an Interconnected World: What Role for Border Carbon Adjustments?*, https://doi.org/10.1787/8008e7f4-en; OECD (2019[10]), FDI Qualities Indicators: Measuring the sustainable development impacts of investment, www.oecd.org/fr/investissement/fdi-qualities-indicators.htm; Ang, Röttgers and Burli (2017[11]), The empirics of enabling investment and innovation in renewable energy, https://doi.org/10.1787/67d221b8-en; WRI/WBCSD (2004[12]), The Greenhouse Gas Protocol, https://ghgprotocol.org/sites/default/files/standards/ghg-protocol-revised.pdf.

5.2. The impact of FDI on carbon emissions

Evidence stemming from the traditional literature on the trade-FDI-environment nexus proposes that FDI affects the host country's carbon footprint in contending ways by expanding the scale of economic activity, changing the structural composition of economic activity and delivering new techniques of production (Grossman and Kruger, 1991[13]; Copeland and Taylor, 1994[14]; Porter and van der Linde, 1995[15]). In isolation, the *scale effect is* expected to increase carbon emissions, since an increase in the size of an economy implies more production and, in turn, more emissions. The *technique effect,* which refers to a change in production methods resulting from FDI inflows and the transfer of technology from foreign to domestic firms, is expected to reduce emissions by helping diffuse less emitting technologies (Pazienza, 2015[16]). The *composition effect* is associated with a change in industrial structure driven by FDI, and its impact on emissions will depend on the production specialisation of a country. An FDI-driven shift toward services would for instance be associated with a reduction in emissions, while a shift toward heavy manufacturing would deteriorate the host country's carbon footprint.

These various effects underpin the channels through which FDI influences carbon emissions (Figure 5.2, yellow box). Specifically, FDI generates emissions from production processes, energy use, product end use and product disposal that reflect investor characteristics (e.g. sector, technology, and motive). The supply chain relationships that foreign investors forge affect the emissions embodied in the intermediate goods they use, and the emissions generated from the distribution of goods to market. Market interaction with local firms can influence the emissions of domestic business through competition and imitation effects. Similarly, mobility of workers from foreign to domestic firms can influence the business practices and resulting emissions-intensity of domestic firms.

Figure 5.2. Conceptual framework: FDI impacts on carbon emissions

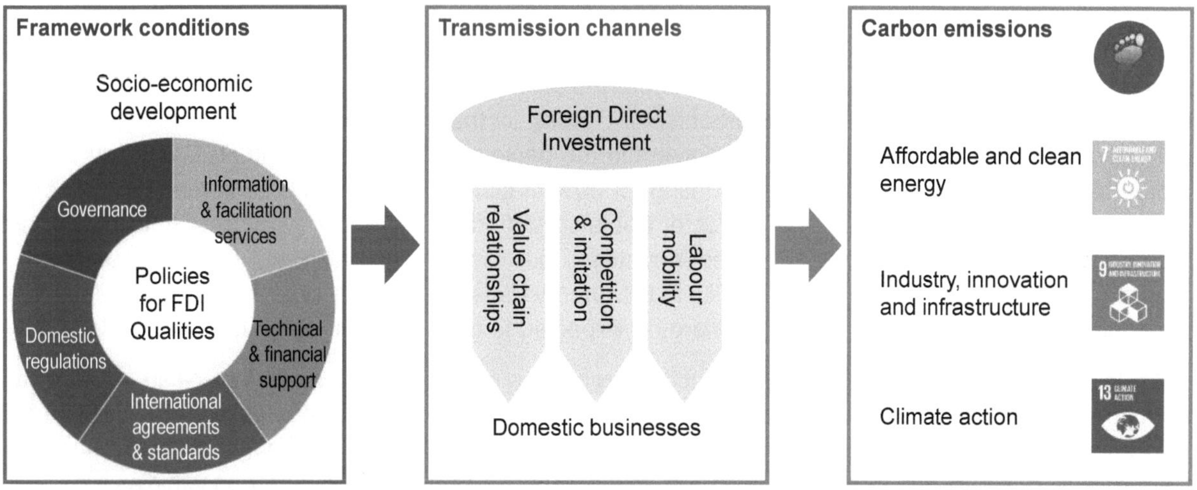

The motivation behind this Policy Toolkit is that, under certain circumstances, FDI can contribute the needed financial and technological resources to advance the low-carbon transition. Developing countries that face greater constraints both in mobilising finance and acquiring and disseminating technologies may draw particular benefits from FDI in their efforts to tackle climate change. Resulting benefits for host countries include (Figure 5.2, green box):

- improving energy security, diversifying energy sources, reducing reliance on energy imports and electrifying remote rural areas (SDG7);
- fostering innovation, creating new industries and jobs, and gaining an edge over competitors and attendant export opportunities in key industries (SDG9);

- and the localised benefits of mitigating climate change, reducing environmental degradation, and improving air quality and associated health impacts (SDG13).

The manner in which FDI affects carbon emissions and the extent to which it can contribute to decarbonisation depend on a number of contextual factors that are the focus of this chapter, including FDI characteristics and spillover potential, socio-economic factors, and the policy environments of home and host countries. Targeted policy interventions can level the playing field for more climate-friendly FDI, and influence spillovers to domestic firms. The next section will look closely at framework conditions and policies that affect the impact of FDI on emissions (Figure 5.2, blue box).

5.2.1. FDI characteristics and impacts on carbon emissions

The carbon intensity of foreign investments depends on a range of characteristics specific to investors, including the technologies they use, the energy they consume, the products and services they offer, their motives for investing internationally, and their corporate cultures and environmental policies. Annex Table 5.A.1 provides the core questions of the Policy Toolkit for governments to self-assess the impacts of FDI on decarbonisation, including through spillovers.

Low-carbon technologies

Low-carbon technologies, by definition, reduce the CO_2 emissions associated with economic activity in any sector and are therefore key attributes that determine the carbon intensity of FDI. Broadly speaking, low-carbon technologies reduce CO_2 emissions by (1) reducing energy use (e.g. energy-saving); (2) reducing or eliminating carbon emissions from production or use (e.g. renewable energy, hydrogen); (3) removing carbon from the atmosphere (e.g. carbon capture); or (4) conserving resources (e.g. recycling).

The energy sector, one of the largest contributors to CO_2 emissions, is a noteworthy example in which FDI can deliver innovations in energy generation, storage, and distribution (e.g. smart grids). Large-scale diffusion of these technologies is particularly important as it reduces the indirect emissions of all electricity-consuming activities. In fact, electrifying other sectors is an important avenue for decarbonisation provided that electricity generation itself is decarbonised. Thanks to their financial and technical advantages, multinational enterprises (MNEs) are key players in the deployment of capital- and R&D-intensive clean energy technologies across borders, accounting for 30% of global new investments in renewable energy (Figure 5.3, Panel A). FDI in the energy sector has also shifted considerably away from fossil fuels and into renewables, particularly in advanced countries, but increasingly also in developing countries (Figure 5.3, Panel B). The contribution of FDI to the energy transition may become increasingly relevant in developing countries, where demand for energy is expected to grow most rapidly in the coming decades.

In the industrial sector, decarbonising production processes requires switching to lower-carbon fuels for production and making more efficient use of materials. According to some studies, 20% of the energy consumed in industry is electricity, while it is already technologically possible to electrify up to half of the industrial fuel consumption (McKinsey, 2020[17]). In the transport sector, new low-carbon vehicles are being developed for road transport, rail, waterborne transport and aviation, including vehicles that run on electricity, hydrogen fuel cells, and compressed or liquefied natural gas. In the construction sector, advanced building materials and energy-efficient home appliances are being developed and existing technologies improved. As multinationals are key players in these emissions-intensive activities, they can make an important contribution to furthering electrification or developing altogether new breakthrough technologies for emissions reductions (e.g. hydrogen fuel cell, carbon capture utilisation and storage), as well as integrating climate action into their risk management processes, business models and supply chains.

Figure 5.3. Renewables as a share of total FDI in the energy sector

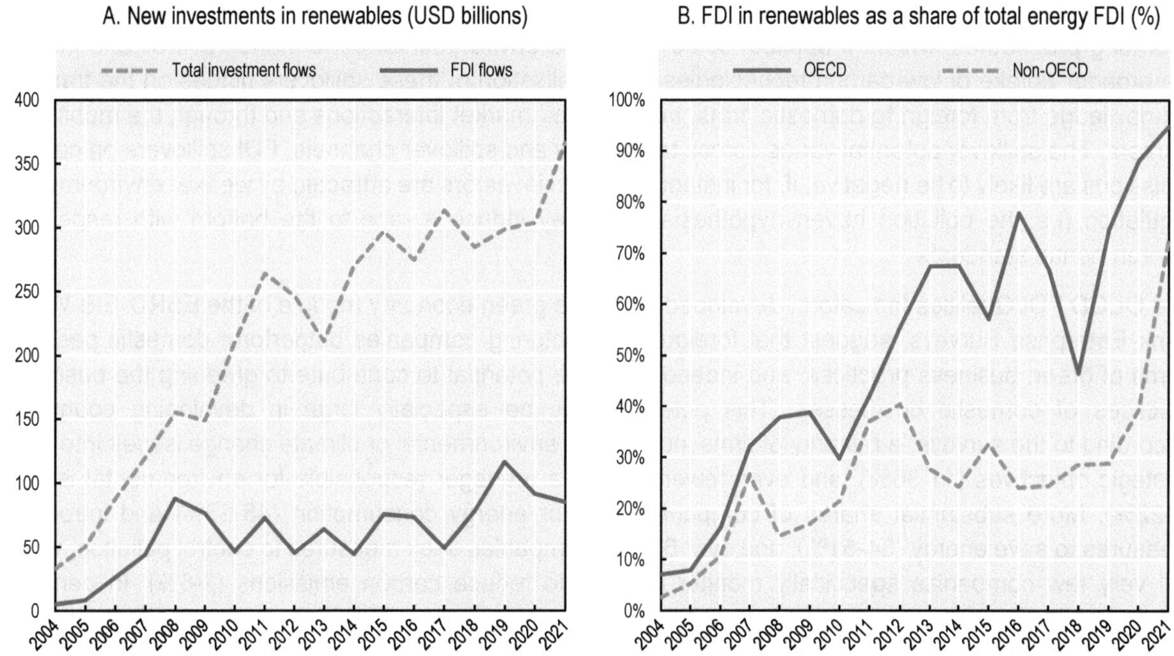

Source: OECD elaboration based on Financial Times (2022[18]), FDI Markets: the in-depth crossborder investment monitor from the Financial Times, https://www.fdimarkets.com/; and BloombergNEF (2022[19]), Energy Transition Investment Trends 2022, https://about.bnef.com/energy-transition-investment/.

Investor attributes

FDI motives are among the factors that push firms to invest abroad in low-carbon technologies, or alternatively to transfer high-carbon production to foreign locations. Foreign markets offer opportunities to sell new low-carbon products and services designed in relatively small or saturated home jurisdictions. Scarcity of production factors (e.g. labour), natural resources (e.g. wind power) or strategic assets (e.g. infrastructure) in home countries may also drive MNEs to seek cross-border opportunities for their low-carbon investments, while accumulated technical knowhow related to low-carbon technologies in home countries can give investors a competitive edge internationally.

Investor entry modes also have implications on the carbon intensity of FDI activities. Mergers and acquisitions entail changes in corporate ownership, structure and governance, which in turn can affect the environmental policies and implications of existing establishments in host countries, for better or worse. Yet, greenfield investments involve new economic activity or expansions of existing activities and will typically result in greater (positive or negative) impacts on host countries. From a climate perspective, the direction of the impact will depend on the carbon intensity of the new investments and the technologies they generate and deploy.

Home country consumer and shareholder expectations and pressures from civil society can further contribute to green branding strategies and drive MNEs to reconsider their foreign operations and supply chains, strengthen environmental reporting or adopt carbon labelling. These considerations are consistent with the 'Pollution Halo' hypothesis, whereby, MNEs apply a universal environmental standard across borders and, in so doing, tend to spread their greener technology to their affiliates in host countries (Porter and van der Linde, 1995[15]).

5.2.2. FDI spillovers on carbon emissions

The premise behind FDI spillovers is that multinational firms have access to innovative technologies and operating procedures, which, if applied, could help raise environmental performance overall and induce the broader uptake of low-carbon technologies. The realisation of these spillovers hinges on the transfer of knowledge from foreign to domestic firms, through their market interactions and through the mobility of workers. The spillover potential varies across technology and spillover channels. FDI spillovers on carbon emissions are likely to be negative, if, for instance, foreign investors are attracted by weaker environmental regulation (i.e. the pollution haven hypothesis) and they induce a race to the bottom with respect to environmental standards.

The OECD FDI Qualities Indicators, developed using the green economy module of the EBRD-EIB-World Bank Enterprise Surveys, suggest that foreign manufacturing companies outperform domestic peers in terms of green business practices, and indeed have the potential to contribute to greening the business practices of domestic businesses. This potential may be especially large in developing countries. According to the surveys, a minority of firms incorporate environmental or climate change issues into their strategic objectives (11-36%), and even fewer employ a manager responsible for environmental issues (5-22%). More substantial shares of companies monitor energy consumption (48-63%) and introduce measures to save energy (34-51%), and over 60% of companies seek measures to control pollution, while still very few companies specifically monitor or seek to reduce carbon emissions (2-6%). In general, companies in OECD countries tend to outperform companies in non-OECD countries, and foreign firms perform at least as well as domestic firms across all environmental dimensions (Figure 5.4). The gap between foreign and domestic firms is often wider in non-OECD countries than in OECD countries, particularly when it comes to addressing carbon emissions.

Figure 5.4. Green performance of foreign and domestic firms

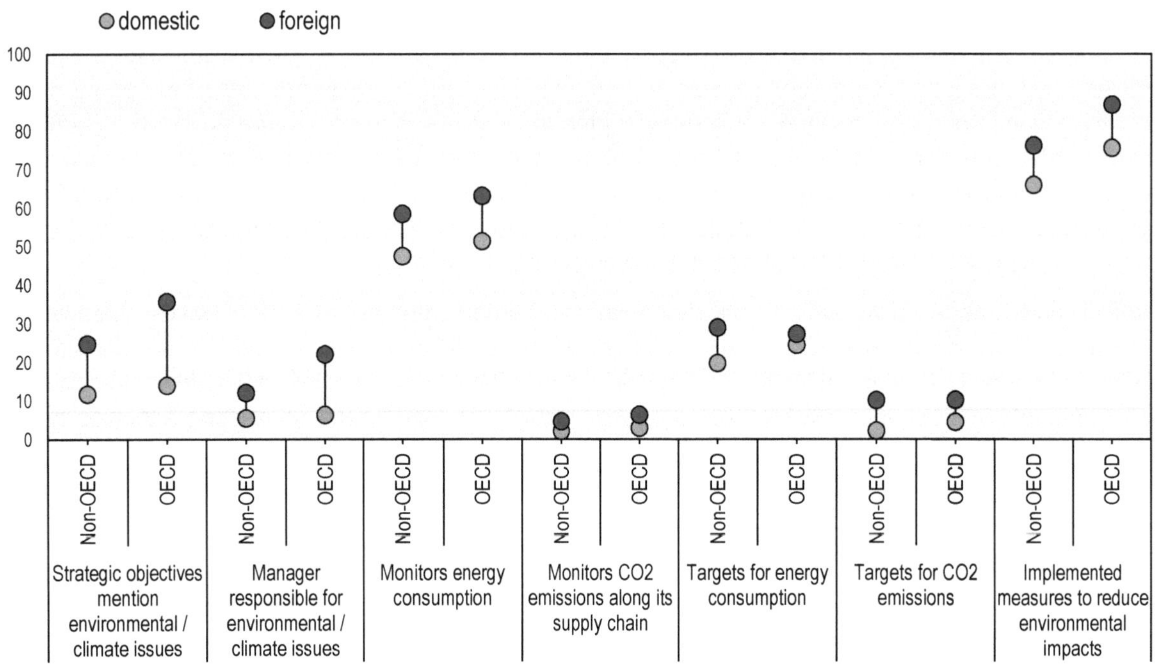

Note: The OECD and non-OECD averages are based on a subset of countries from Europe, Middle East, North Africa and Central Asia.
Source: OECD based on EBRD-EIB-WB (2022[20]), World Bank Enterprise Surveys, https://www.enterprisesurveys.org/en/enterprisesurveys.

Value chain spillovers

The supply chain decisions of foreign investors influence the emissions embodied in the intermediates they use in production; similarly, their choices of distributors will influence the emissions associated with the delivery of goods to market. In practice, there is evidence that very few firms monitor carbon emissions along their supply chains, even though the practice is more common among foreign firms, suggesting that these emissions are rarely internalised by investors (Figure 5.4). At the same time, the bulk of MNE impacts on emissions originates from their supply chains in many industries. For instance, in the garment industry the supply chains of global leaders in the garment industry account for 70% of emissions in the sector (McKinsey-GFA, 2020[21]). Encouraging foreign investors to engage with sustainable suppliers and partners, both locally and in their foreign operations, can further support emissions reductions objectives.

Moreover, advancing the low-carbon transition and maximising its contribution to employment generation depends on countries' abilities to build and strengthen domestic supply chains (IRENA, 2013[22]). Linkages with local suppliers and buyers are an important channel of knowledge and technology diffusion. In the context of the low-carbon agenda, these types of spillovers can take many forms, ranging from increased compliance with environmental regulations to innovations in energy use and industrial processes. Broadly speaking, these spillovers are more likely to occur in manufacturing industries and services sectors, as the opportunities for local linkages are greater than in the energy, building and transport sectors. A key requirement for these spillovers to materialise is that local businesses have sufficient absorptive capacity to meet the demands of foreign investors. This means that the realisation of FDI's low-carbon spillovers through value chain linkages requires a parallel evolution of skills and shifts in the labour force, which also helps ensure a just transition (OECD, 2015[23]).

In addition to supplier and buyer linkages, a key conduit for FDI's low-carbon spillovers is through local partnerships, strategic alliances and joint ventures. This may be the most important transmission channel of R&D-intensive investments in the development and commercialisation of breakthrough technologies, where research collaborations across a number of private and public sector actors are common.

Other spillover effects

The entry and establishment of foreign investors heightens the level of competitive pressure on domestic companies, inducing them to innovate or imitate in order to keep up and remain competitive. As noted previously, foreign multinationals may be particularly successful in catering to end users that are responsive to environmental performance and green branding. As companies compete to serve growing consumer demands for low-carbon products and services, foreign competition can catalyse low-carbon innovation across domestic businesses in their efforts to retain customers or tap into new markets. Thanks to these competitive pressures, low-carbon technologies and operating procedures can disseminate to the wider business sector and make a significant contribution to reducing its environmental and carbon footprint.

A special case in which monopolistic markets can inhibit decarbonisation is the energy sector, traditionally dominated by incumbent utilities that control power generation, transmission and distribution, and have little incentive to diversify energy sources. Unbundling the power sector by separating power generation, transmission and distribution functions can help create more space for foreign investment in renewable power, which in turn can exert competitive pressures toward conventional power generators, and spur the wider diffusion of renewable power investments across domestic actors.

Movement of workers between foreign and domestic firms and corporate spin-offs originating from foreign MNEs can further propagate knowledge spillovers from foreign to domestic firms. The low-carbon transition creates many new jobs related to low-carbon technologies (IRENA-ILO, 2021[24]). Foreign MNEs play an important role as employers in developing skills related to these new technologies and in creating a capable low-carbon workforce (Chapter 3). As such, labour mobility is a key conduit for the diffusion of these skills and low-carbon operating procedures more broadly to domestic companies. Labour mobility also allows new foreign entrants to seek out talent and hire the skilled workers needed to run their businesses, and can therefore contribute to additional low-carbon FDI attraction.

5.2.3. Socio-economic determinants of FDI's carbon impacts

The level of socio-economic development determines a country's production specialisation, industrial structure, positioning in global value chains, and the sophistication of its infrastructure and technology. Some theories conjecture an inverted-U relationship between output growth and the level of emissions (known as the 'Environmental Kuznets Curve'), expected to increase as a country develops and the economy grows, but begin to decrease as rising incomes pass a turning point and create demands for tougher environmental regulation, bringing forth cleaner techniques of production (Grossman and Kruger, 1991[13]). According to these theories, differences in comparative advantage of advanced and developing countries result in differing FDI profiles, with developing countries attracting relatively more polluting investments in heavy manufacturing and extraction activities, and advanced economies attracting less polluting investments in services and high-tech manufacturing. Though exceptions exist, empirical studies are consistent with this hypothesis, as they find evidence of positive FDI effects on emissions more frequently in low- and middle-income countries than in high-income countries (Hoffman et al., 2005[25]; Pao and Tsai, 2010[26]; Behera and Dash, 2017[27]).

The OECD FDI Qualities Indicators also suggest that differences in the carbon intensity of FDI can be explained in part by differences in comparative advantages. According to the indicators, only resource-rich countries, where fossil fuels constitute a large share of GDP, tend to attract carbon-intensive FDI (Figure 5.5). This is likely because extraction and energy transformation offer lucrative investment opportunities for large multinationals with the requisite capacity for these heavily capital- and energy-intensive activities.

Figure 5.5. FDI and CO_2 emissions

Is greenfield FDI concentrated in cleaner activities? (yes if value > 0; no if value < 0)

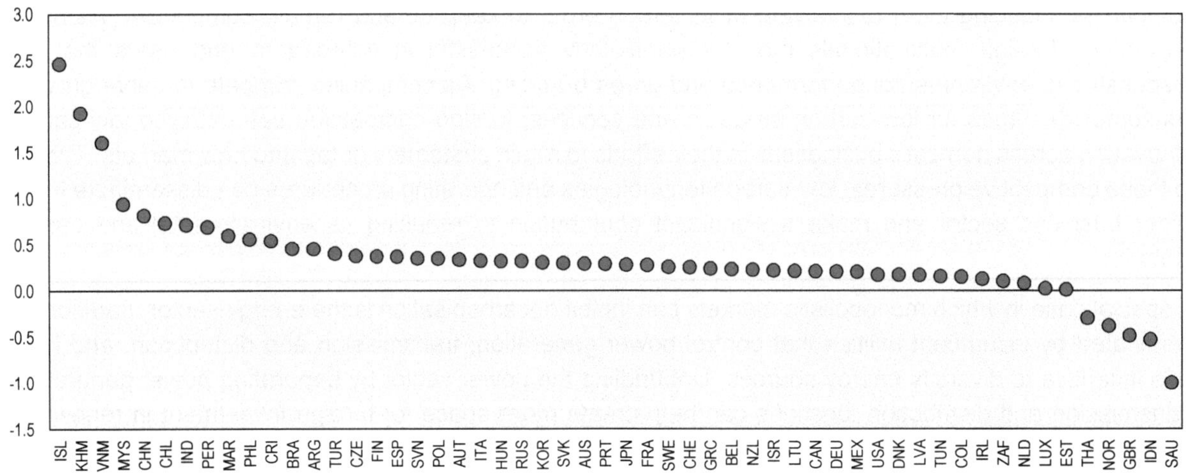

Note: See OECD (2019[10]) for explanatory details.
Source: Update of OECD (2019[10]), *FDI Qualities Indicators: Measuring the sustainable development impacts of investment*, www.oecd.org/fr/investissement/fdi-qualities-indicators.htm.

Locational pull factors specific to low-carbon investments are related to the characteristics of FDI discussed above, and in particular to investor motives. Countries with underdeveloped electricity grids outside of urban centres offer viable untapped markets for producers of small-scale low-carbon electricity alternatives, compared to those with more extensive and dependable grids. Consumers that are aware of and responsive to green credentials such as carbon labels provide attractive markets for producers of low-carbon consumer goods. Countries that enjoy an abundancy of wind, sun or tidal bays are the most profitable destinations for investments in wind turbines, solar plants, and tidal generators. Industry and technology clusters appeal to producers of low-carbon equipment seeking to gain from agglomeration effects, and other strategic assets such as skills or technologies similarly attract investors seeking to acquire knowledge and technical capabilities (UN, n.d.[28]; Hanni et al., 2011[29]).

5.3. Policies that influence FDI impacts on carbon emissions

The host country's policy framework influences its business environment, including the FDI entering the country and its carbon implications (Figure 5.2, blue box). A policy framework for low-carbon investment is in many respects comparable to an enabling environment that is conducive to investment in general. Policies conducive to FDI, however, will not automatically result in a substantial increase in low-carbon FDI. A policy framework for investment is thus a necessary but insufficient condition for low-carbon investment. Policy makers will also need to improve specific enabling conditions for low-carbon investment by developing policies and regulations that systematically internalise the cost carbon emissions, and facilitate low-carbon FDI and its knowledge and technology spillovers (OECD, 2015[30]).

This Policy Toolkit aims to provide a comprehensive policy framework for countries to maximise positive impacts of FDI on carbon footprint while mitigating adverse effects, in line with the OECD Guidelines for Multinational Enterprises. It builds on Chapter 12 on "Investment framework for green growth" of the OECD Policy Framework for Investment, and on the OECD Policy Guidance for Investment in Clean Energy Infrastructure, and complements these instruments by offering a comprehensive mapping of policies and institutional settings that influence FDI's carbon impacts across selected advanced and developing countries (see Chapter 1). The Toolkit is structured around four broad principles and the policy instruments that support these principles (Table 5.1). Annex Table 5.A.2 provides the core questions of the Policy Toolkit for governments to self-assess policies that influences the impacts of FDI on decarbonisation.

Table 5.1. Overview of FDI Qualities Policy Toolkit for reducing FDI impact on carbon emissions

Principle 1: Provide strategic direction and promote policy co-ordination and coherence on investment and climate action	Governance	National strategies and plans
		Oversight and co-ordination bodies
		Public consultation, data, M&E
Principle 2: Ensure that domestic and international investment regulations and standards reinforce climate objectives	International agreements & standards	International agreements on climate change
		International agreements on RBC
		Environmental provisions BITs & RTAs
	Domestic regulations	Legal framework for investment
		Environmental standards & requirements
		Regulatory incentives
Principles 3: Stimulate investment and build technical capabilities related to low-carbon technologies, services and infrastructure	Financial support	Carbon pricing instruments
		Subsidies and tax relief for green investments
		Public procurement of green investments
	Technical Support	Business & supplier development services
		Green technology parks
		Training and skills development services
Principle 4: Address information failures and administrative barriers to level the playing field for low-carbon investors	Information & facilitation services	Green investment promotion & facilitation
		Public awareness campaigns
		Corporate environmental disclosure

5.3.1. Provide strategic direction and promote policy coherence on investment and climate

Ensure coherence across climate, sectoral and investment strategies and plans

Strong government commitment to combat climate change and to support low-carbon growth, underpinned by a coherent policy framework and clear decarbonisation targets, provides investors with encouraging signals regarding the government's climate ambitions. Setting a clear, long-term transition trajectory that is linked to the national vision or goals for growth and development is critically important to build capacity for investors to understand transition risks, and to attracting foreign investment that contributes to the country's climate agenda (Box 5.2). Given the cross-cutting nature of climate change, a strategic framework for addressing climate change should include a comprehensive and coherent multi-sector approach, integrating environmental targets and ambitions into sector strategies and plans. For instance, incorporating climate considerations in national infrastructure development plans and priorities can help avoid locking-in environmentally unsustainable infrastructure for decades. This may require the establishment of new connections between national sectoral planning processes in order to avoid repackaging existing sectoral plans into a climate strategy.

Box 5.2. The EU Green Deal's integrated framework for the climate transition

The European Green Deal sets out a detailed vision to make Europe the first climate-neutral continent by 2050, safeguard biodiversity, establish a circular economy and eliminate pollution, while boosting the competitiveness of European industry and ensuring a just transition for affected regions and workers. Under the EU Green Deal, the European Commission pledged to raise the GHG emissions reduction targets to 55% by 2030, compared to the previous target of 40%. To implement the increased ambition, on 14 July 2021 the Commission presented the 'Fit for 55' package, which contains legislative proposals to revise the entire EU 2030 climate and energy framework, including the legislation on effort sharing, land use and forestry, renewable energy, energy efficiency, emission standards for new cars and vans, and the Energy Taxation Directive. The Commission proposes to strengthen the emissions trading system, extend it to the maritime sector, and reduce over time the free allowances allocated to airlines. A proposed new emissions trading system for road transport and buildings should start in 2025, complemented by a new social climate fund with a financial envelope of EUR 72.2 billion to address its social impacts. New legislation is proposed on clean maritime and aviation fuels. To ensure fair pricing of GHG emissions associated with imported goods, the Commission proposes a new carbon border adjustment mechanism.

By offering a holistic and integrated approach to mainstream decarbonisation across a multi-sector regulatory framework, the Green Deal provides investors with a clear long-term trajectory for Europe's climate transition. This long-term commitment and direction reduces uncertainty about regulation and taxation to advance the transition, and allows investors to better understand the transition risks associated with their operations going forward, and to take steps to mitigate these risks.

Source: https://www.europarl.europa.eu/legislative-train/theme-a-european-green-deal/package-fit-for-55

The investment promotion strategy must also reflect national climate objectives across priority sectors in alignment with the multi-sector strategic framework for addressing climate change. Concretely, it should translate national level emissions targets to science-based targets for the private sector in order to drive responsible climate action by business. In this regard, it is important that the investment promotion strategy and its main features are developed in co-ordination with other key ministries, including for instance the ministry of environment and the ministry of energy. The investment promotion strategy should be very clear and specific about targets, tools to reach the set targets, and performance indicators to measure progress. It should provide clear indications on its implementation, including how staff should be organised internally, what the main activities are that it should focus on, what the key performance indicators to measure outputs and outcomes are, and what procedures are in place to collaborate effectively with other relevant public agencies and stakeholders (e.g. the private sector). Clearly delineating the role of private investors, both domestic and foreign, in achieving climate objectives can help adequately tailor investment promotion efforts to target investors that help further these objectives. The government should consult with the private sector and other local stakeholders in the design and implementation of strategies and plans that are relevant for low-carbon investment, and regularly evaluate their effectiveness.

Ensure inter-ministerial and inter-agency co-ordination and alignment

As is the case for other policy areas covered by the Policy Toolkit, a complex system of institutions design and implement investment, climate and sectoral strategies, and it is important for co-ordination mechanisms to be in place to ensure their coherence and consistency, and to achieve desired outcomes related to FDI and carbon emissions. Overlapping and sometimes conflicting rules, procedures and regulations across ministries and levels of government, including between the central and provincial levels can create administrative burdens on investors (OECD, 2015[30]). Although co-ordination is a fundamental and longstanding problem for public administrations, there is still no standardised method for approaching co-ordination issues, and much of the success or failure of attempts to co-ordinate appear to depend upon context. Overall, co-ordination approaches and instruments should be matched to circumstances and policy areas. Instruments of co-ordination can be based on regulation, incentives, norms and information sharing. They can be top-down and rely upon the authority of a lead actor or bottom-up and emergent (Peters, 2018[31]). Common approaches for co-ordination are summarised in Box 5.3.

Box 5.3. Examples of inter-agency co-ordination approaches and instruments

National strategies and action plans typically involve wide consultation and deliberation, and provide diagnostic overviews of the strengths, weaknesses, opportunities, and threats associated with their stated objectives. If properly designed, national strategies and plans can set a shared vision of the goals pursued across climate and investment policy domains, and how one can contribute to the other. Costa Rica's National Decarbonisation Plan, for instance, explicitly states that the priorities related to FDI attraction for decarbonisation will be addressed in co-operation with the Ministry of Trade and Commerce (COMEX), the investment promotion agency (CINDE) and the export promotion agency (PROCOMER).

Dedicated agencies or ministries assume the leadership of the national policy agenda in some policy domains (e.g. environment, energy, investment) and often responsibility of co-ordination. At the same time, inter-agency joint programming can draw together a number of interested agencies and facilitate co-ordination and other aspects of governance as agencies share agenda and action.

The *Centre of government* (e.g. the President's or Prime Minister's Office) can bridge political interests and bureaucratic boundaries. *High-level policy councils* can also deal with aspects of policy co-ordination although they have variable roles and composition across countries. In Jordan, for instance, the higher steering committee for green growth, responsible for the overall strategic framework for green growth, reports directly to the prime minister, who also sits in the high-level investment council, responsible for the country's investment strategy, ensuring that the strategic directions of the two are aligned.

Informal channels of communication between officials or job circulation (of civil servants, but also experts and stakeholders) can play a role and suggest a relatively well-developed culture of inter-agency trust and communication. Such arrangements tend to work best where there already exists a relatively well-developed culture of inter-agency trust and communication.

Source: OECD (2022[36]), FDI Qualities mapping: A survey of policies and institutions that can strengthen sustainable investment.

Design and implement effective environmental assessment processes and ensure stakeholder involvement and consultation

Environmental assessment processes, including Strategic Environmental Assessment (SEA) and Environmental Impact Assessment (EIA), are structured analytical and participatory approaches for obtaining and evaluating environmental information prior to its use in decision-making. This information consists of assessments of how the environment will be affected if certain alternative actions are implemented and advise on how best to manage environmental implications if one alternative is selected and implemented. SEA focuses on strategic and policy actions such as new or amended laws, policies, programmes and plans. EIA focuses on proposed investment projects such as highways, power stations, water resource projects and large-scale industrial facilities, which are sometimes linked to the implementation of a policy or plan (e.g. extended highway network may be an outcome of a new transport policy). Environmental assessment systems are fundamental to ensure that international investments contribute to sustainable development, and in particular to climate and environmental goals. As an integral part of the policy programme and plan life-cycle, SEAs guarantee that the policies, regulations and standards that influence the attraction and environmental performance of investments are aligned with national climate objectives. In Senegal, for instance, to ensure the success of the new energy policy, the government has set up a monitoring and evaluation system for major energy projects through an inter-ministerial committee chaired by the Prime Minister. EIA systems, additionally support investors in minimising environmental risks associated with their investment projects.

Strong political will is important for the effectiveness of EIA systems in mitigating potential adverse environmental impacts of FDI. When the EIA authority is under financial pressure or politically inferior to other government institutions that support the investment project, EIAs may be used to rationalise predetermined outcomes, rather than to provide independent and rigorous analysis, upon which the approval is based. In such cases underestimation of the role and impact of EIA can negatively influence the impact of foreign investments on the host country's environment (Dung, 2019[32]). Strengthening the implementation of EIA systems is essential for their effectiveness in greening FDI and reducing its carbon impacts. In some countries investment proponents face major delays in the review and approval of EIAs due to lack of human and financial resources. Another factor exacerbating delays may be the lack of quality of EIA documents submitted to the authority, as a result of lack of capacity in the environmental assessment industry. Relevant authorities at national and subnational levels may also lack the capacity to monitor and audit implementation of investments to ensure compliance with EIA results (OECD, 2020[33]). Building capacity at national and subnational levels to review EIAs and reduce delays in this process, and improving the transparency and information systems supporting EIAs can significantly improve the environmental impacts of foreign investments.

Public consultation is a vital component of successful EIA/SEA systems and specific EIA/SEA studies. Timely and well-planned public consultation programmes will contribute to the successful design, implementation, operation and management of proposal actions. Stakeholder engagement also enhances the effectiveness of the EIA/SEA process. Stakeholders, including foreign multinationals, provide a valuable source of information on key impacts, potential mitigation measures and the identification and selection of alternatives. Their consultation further ensures the EIA/SEA process is open, transparent, and robust, and also that individual EIAs/SEAs are founded on justifiable and defensible analyses.

Collect data to monitor the impact of FDI on carbon emissions

Measuring and tracking the impact of FDI on carbon emissions, and its potential contribution to decarbonisation can help identify appropriate policy responses. The first section of this chapter presents a framework for understanding FDI impacts on emissions, and factors that may influence these impacts. The collection and production of timely and internationally comparable date on FDI by sector, is important for monitoring its contribution to decarbonisation. Supplementing this with firm-level surveys that capture different aspects of their environmental practices can provide policy makers with a valuable tool for self-assessment of FDI impacts on carbon emissions, and green growth more generally. Annex Table 5.A.1 provides a set of core questions and indicators that can guide policy makers in this self-assessment.

5.3.2. Adhere to international agreements and standards that reinforce climate objectives

Ratify major international agreements promoting climate action

Carbon emissions have global effects, regardless of where they were released, meaning that the impact of one country's climate policies is dependent on the climate policies of other countries. Given the short-term economic costs of climate policies, the ambition of domestic policies depends on the perceived economic impacts those policies may create, as well as the perceived risks of carbon leakage that may render domestic climate action vain. Policy makers, as well as industry and the general public, seek reassurance of commensurate action from their trade partners, through treaties or other forms of international agreement, whether bilaterally or multilaterally (OECD, 2015[23]). The international agreements that directly or indirectly influence carbon emissions and the economic activities that generate them include multilateral environmental agreements (MEAs) negotiated at the global level, under the auspices of the UN. These MEAs span several environmental fields, including GHG emissions reductions, cross-border air pollution, soil and desertification, and environmental governance (Table 5.2).

The UNFCCC is the central forum for global negotiations on climate change and for international co-ordination of climate policies, and plays a crucial role in advancing national climate policies. In December 2015, 196 states negotiated a landmark climate change agreement at the 21st Conference of the Parties (COP21) of the UNFCCC in Paris. The resulting Paris Agreement aims to limit climate change to 1.5°C global mean temperature change, and expects progressively more ambitious climate mitigation commitments from all parties over the coming decades. As of January 2021, 190 members of the UNFCCC are parties to the agreement, and 187 states and the EU, representing about 79% of global greenhouse gas emissions, have ratified or acceded to the Agreement (UNFCCC, 2015[2]). The central mechanism of the Paris Agreement is a 'pledge-and-review' process. Every five years the parties submit increasingly ambitious nationally determined contributions (NDCs) that lay out mitigation plans, and may include ones related to adaptation. Parties are left to establish their own national policy framework to achieve the commitments outlined in such NDCs, but are required to report emissions, with progress reviewed by an independent review system. The Paris Agreement is instrumental in providing political space for policy makers to strengthen climate action domestically. Fulfilling the Paris Agreement will require substantial new domestic climate policies in each state party to the treaty, including pollution controls that also result in GHG mitigation, land use regulations, clean infrastructure investment targets, or policies aimed at fostering low-carbon innovations.

Technology transfer is a crucial element of the new international climate regime. Developing countries, led by India, advocated for strong technology transfer provisions, and in particular the increased availability of free intellectual property for the purpose of faster diffusion of clean technologies. The Paris Agreement also creates scope for further development of a regime for technology transfer: it establishes as norms the 'strengthening of co-operative action' and 'promoting and enhancing access,' and builds on the 'Technology Mechanism' established under its predecessor treaty, the 2010 Kyoto Protocol. While little detail is provided as to how these norms should be pursued in practice, international trade and investment are likely to play a pivotal role in fostering the needed technology transfer.

Table 5.2. Summary of MEAs that influence GHG emissions

Year	Title	Theme	Objective	Parties
1979	Geneva Convention on Long-Range Transboundary Air Pollution (CLRTAP)	Air pollution	To protect human health and the environment against air pollution and to limit and, as far as possible, gradually reduce and prevent air pollution including long-range transboundary air pollution.	51
1991	Espoo Convention on EIA	Governance	To prevent, reduce and control significant adverse transboundary environmental impact from proposed activities	44
1992	Framework Convention on Climate Change (UNFCCC)	Climate change	To achieve stabilisation of greenhouse gas concentrations in the atmosphere at a level that prevents dangerous anthropogenic interference with the climate system.	197
1994	Convention to Combat Desertification (UNCCD)	Soil	To combat desertification and mitigate the effects of drought, particularly in Africa, with a view to contributing to the achievement of sustainable development in affected areas.	196
1994	International Tropical Timber Agreement (ITTA)	Nature and biodiversity	To promote and apply comparable and appropriate guidelines and criteria for the management, conservation and sustainable development of timber-producing forests.	74
1997	Kyoto Protocol	Climate change	To ensure that greenhouse gas emission do not exceed the assigned amounts, with a view to reducing overall emissions of such gases by at least 5% below 1990 levels in the commitment period 2008 to 2012.	192
1998	Aarhus Convention on Access to Information	Governance	To guarantee the rights of access to information, public participation in decision-making, and access to justice in environmental matters	47
2015	Paris Agreement	Climate change	The Paris Agreement builds upon the UNFCCC Kyoto Protocol and commits all to undertake ambitious efforts to combat climate change and adapt to its effects, with enhanced support to assist developing countries to do so.	192

Adhere to international agreements on RBC and promote environmental due diligence

Home country governments can also influence the impacts of outward FDI on global emissions by implementing international agreements on responsible business conduct (RBC), and encouraging environmental due diligence across supply chains. The OECD's Guidelines for Multinational Enterprises (OECD Guidelines) recommends that businesses take due account of the need to protect the environment, including improving environmental performance in their own operations and supply chain and addressing any adverse environmental impacts of their own operations and their supply chains, within the framework of laws, regulations and administrative practices in the countries in which they operate, and in consideration of relevant international agreements, principles, objectives, and standards. In particular, Chapter 6 of the Guidelines on "Environment" addresses aspects such as environmental management systems, continual improvement of corporate environmental performance, training of workers on environmental matters, and raising environmental awareness. Adherence to the Guidelines and efforts to facilitate corporate compliance with the Guidelines is therefore instrumental in minimising any adverse environmental impacts associated with FDI, and increasing its contribution to climate and environmental objectives.

The OECD Due Diligence Guidance for Responsible Business Conduct provides practical support to enterprises on the implementation of the OECD Guidelines for Multinational Enterprises, by providing plain language explanations of its due diligence recommendations and associated provisions (OECD, 2018[34]). Implementing these recommendations helps enterprises avoid and address adverse impacts related to workers, human rights, the environment, bribery, consumers and corporate governance that may be associated with their operations, supply chains and other business relationships. Further tailored guidance for businesses on addressing climate risks in sector supply chains is included in the OECD Due Diligence Guidance for Responsible Supply Chains in the Garment and Footwear Sector (OECD Garment Guidance), which has a risk module dedicated to GHG emissions, and the OECD-FAO Guidance for Responsible Agricultural Supply Chains. These guidance advocates a risk-based approach to addressing

GHG emissions in a company's supply chain, using leverage with suppliers to encourage suppliers to reduce emissions and to support suppliers directly in implementing measures to reduce GHG emissions.

Growing demands to hold corporations accountable for their climate impacts are leading some courthouses to draw heavily on international instruments like the OECD Guidelines award legal victories to citizens, by ordering multinational giants to cut GHG emissions of their operations and those of their supply chains independently of their home and host country regulations (Box 5.4). Such rulings raise questions on the need for mandatory due diligence legislation that defines the obligations of companies to prevent environmental damage, and enables public regulators and judges to enforce such legislation.

Box 5.4. The Shell climate ruling

Basing its verdict on the United Nations Guiding Principles on Business and Human Rights (UNGPs) and OECD Guidelines for Multinational Enterprises (OECD Guidelines), in May 2021, a Dutch court ruled that Royal Dutch Shell (Shell) must reduce its CO_2 emissions by 45% by 2030 (compared to 2019), regardless of the policies of the Dutch Government. The ruling asserts that Shell's total CO_2 emission levels, from its own operations and from those of its supply chain and end users, present a breach of the company's legal obligation to prevent climate change, explicitly linking climate change to human rights. It also emphasises the responsibility Shell headquarters has over the entire Shell group, thereby acknowledging the parent companies' responsibility for subsidiaries. The ruling makes clear that the severity of the impact of climate change on human rights justifies the economic sacrifices Shell will be required to make. This historic ruling is the first to impose a clear and measurable emissions reduction target on a company and its value chain, making clear that preventing climate change harm is an essential element of responsible business conduct as defined by the UNGPs and the OECD Guidelines.

Source: https://www.business-humanrights.org/en/blog/the-shell-climate-verdict-a-major-win-for-mandatory-due-diligence-and-corporate-accountability/

Ensure that investment and trade agreements reinforce domestic environmental laws and allow for sufficient domestic climate policy space

Trade and investment agreements can promote and facilitate trade and investment in environmental goods and services. However, depending on the way in which they address or fail to address environmental concerns, these treaties may in some cases be perceived to conflict with climate objectives and with the measures taken by governments to implement the Paris Agreement.

WTO rules may prevent governments from regulating traded goods on the basis of the climate impacts of their production (OECD, 2020[9]). Governments may seek to protect low-carbon industries as a means of achieving long-term decarbonisation targets, and these trade protections may run contrary to free trade principles. Investment treaty rules and interpretations of them can allow investors to claim damages and lost profits in investor-state arbitration from governments that take measures to decarbonise their economies (Financial Times, 2022[35]). Governments with both an interest in seeing robust climate action and a deep involvement in investment and trade negotiations are in an important position to ensure alignment and mutual reinforcement across climate, trade and investment regimes.

Comprehensive free trade agreements (FTAs) seek to reconcile trade, investment and environmental policy objectives and often address issues related to the environment in a dedicated chapter. Some existing environment chapters include obligations such as effective enforcement of environmental laws, domestic procedural protections, or promotion of public participation in environmental matters. In addition, FTAs increasingly seek to promote international co-operation on a variety of policy objectives, including climate action. References to specific climate objectives, such as the removal of tariff and non-tariff trade barriers related to climate-friendly goods and services, or the reduction of fossil fuel subsidies, are sometimes included in hortatory provisions about shared government goals and imperatives (e.g. EU-Singapore FTA 2018, Art. 7.1 and 12.11). In other cases, FTA treaty parties commit to specific measures of co-operation, such as international responses to climate change; exchanging expertise on environmental regulations and their implementation; sharing investor records of compliance with the home state environmental laws; or establishing a committee to supervise the enforcement of environment and trade matters covered in the agreement (USMCA 2018, Art. 24.26).

In international investment agreements (IIAs) – defined as standalone investment treaties (e.g. BITs) and the investment provisions included in regional FTAs – the nature, design, context and interpretation of treaty provisions used for claims and dispute settlement arrangements are of key importance for impact on environmental and climate action. For example, investment protection obligations, if not carefully drafted and interpreted, may come into conflict with several principles and performance standards included in multilateral environmental agreements (e.g. precautionary principle, polluter pays principle). Measures to safeguard the implementation of multilateral environmental agreements (MEAs) can therefore include clarifications of hierarchy in the event of a conflict to the advantage of the environmental agreements.

Poorly drafted investment agreements or broad arbitral interpretations that remain unaddressed may limit the ability of governments to restrict new fossil fuel investment projects, or increase the perceived costs of phasing them out. Investment agreements can be adjusted to preserve policy space to regulate on environmental matters. The scope of absolute protections and government action with regard to their interpretation are key factors affecting policy space for non-discriminatory regulation. A number of recent treaties limit protection to discrimination or to direct expropriation and discrimination. Other recent treaties provide for state-state dispute settlement (SSDS) rather than investor-state dispute settlement (ISDS) for investment protection claims.

Express language addressing the environment is also increasingly used in investment agreements to seek to avoid conflicts with climate objectives, although concrete impact in preserving policy space has been difficult to demonstrate. A growing number of IIAs include clauses in the body of the treaty that seek to reserve the host state's right to regulate environmental matters. The scope of the environmental concern that the clauses describe varies in specificity. In some cases, provisions limit treaty coverage, and potential recourse to international arbitration, to investments made in accordance with applicable laws, including environmental law. A recent treaty carves out non-discriminatory and legitimate environmental measures from the scope of ISDS and provides governments with the power to jointly apply the clause (China-Australia FTA, 2015, Section B). The fear of a race to the bottom in the competition to attract foreign investment has motivated the inclusion of clauses in IIAs that discourage or prohibit the lowering of environmental standards for the purpose of investment attraction. Such clauses have appeared in IIAs since 1990 but have only recently been subject of a few claims.

Trade and investment agreements can also help to reinforce domestic laws and regulations related to the climate and strengthen environmental governance. For example, some agreements require the parties to ratify and effectively implement their obligations under an MEA. For instance, in the recently signed agreement between the EU and UK, each signatory commits to effectively implementing the UNFCCC and the Paris Agreement (EU-UK Trade and Co-operation Agreement 2020, Art. 8.5). A similar proposal has been made by the EU in relation to the modernisation of the Energy Charter Treaty.

Recent IIAs have begun to seek to influence business conduct, generally through hortatory provisions. More demanding provisions in a few treaties may require business to comply with environmental assessment and screening processes; maintain an environmental management system; observe RBC standards related to the environment; or conduct an environmental impact assessment (e.g. Morocco-Nigeria BIT 2016, Arts. 14; 18, 24).

Going forward, investment and trade agreements should form part of wider policy efforts to create incentives for investments that help transition to low-carbon energy infrastructure, reform the current reliance on fossil fuels or correct regulations that weaken the business case for investment and innovation in low-carbon infrastructure. Efforts to understand the impact of investment treaties on the environment and climate action are therefore vital. These effects are under consideration in ongoing OECD work on the future of investment treaties, which will focus in particular on climate change. Results from this work will be reflected in future iterations of this Policy Toolkit.

Table 5.3. Illustration of how FTAs and IIAs explicitly refer to environmental protection

Policy objective	Type of reference	Example
Encourage international co-operation	General promotion of progress in environmental protection and co-operation	EU-Singapore FTA (2018), Arts. 7.1, 12.11 (Trade and Sustainable Development)
	Commitment to co-operate on environmental matters	USMCA (2018), Art. 24.25 (Environment)
Reinforce domestic law	Explicit safeguards or enhancements of international environmental agreements	CARIFORUM-EU FTA (2008), Art. 72
	Non-lowering of environmental standards for the purpose of attracting investment	Japan – Jordan BIT (2018), Art. 20
Preserve domestic policy space	Explicit affirmation of environmental regulatory power of host state	Korea – Uzbekistan (2019), Art. 17
	Carve-out clauses for environmental measures with respect to treaty provisions	China – Australia FTA 2015, Art. 9.8
	Exclusion of non-discriminatory environmental measures from ISDS	China – Australia FTA 2015, section B
Influence investor conduct	Investor obligations related to environmental protection	Morocco – Nigeria BIT (2016), Arts. 14(1), (3); 18(1), (4),24(1)

Note: This table contains selected examples of FTA and IIA provisions, based on the OECD (2022[36]) FDI Qualities Mapping. The impact of these references is uncertain and is likely to depend on factors like treaty design, context and interpretation.

5.3.3. Ensure that domestic regulations reinforce climate objectives

Ensure transparency, openness and non-discrimination

A fair, transparent, clear and predictable regulatory framework for investment is a critical determinant of investment decisions and their contribution to decarbonisation (OECD, 2015[30]). Transparency and predictability matter even more when considering returns on investments with long time horizons, to ensure planning certainty and clear expectations on investment and climate policies and actions. Strong government commitments at both the international and national level are necessary to catalyse low-carbon green investment. With clear, long-term and ambitious signals and emission goals, nationally and internationally, investors and markets will have a better view on where to invest (OECD, 2015[23]). While these signals are important for all business, they are crucial for giving the confidence to multinational investors with the requisite capacity and skills to invest in risky new technologies that are highly capital- and R&D-intensive.

The non-discrimination principle provides that investors are treated equally, irrespective of their ownership. Discriminatory restrictions on the establishment and operations of foreign investors can deter FDI in general, and diminish its low-carbon impacts. While manufacturing industries have undergone significant FDI liberalisation worldwide, over the last three decades, some sectors that present significant opportunities for decarbonisation efforts remain partly off-limits to foreign investors in many countries – notably, transport, electricity generation and distribution, and construction. Many services, typically associated with lower carbon emissions and in some cases crucial for energy-saving technologies (e.g. digital services), are also more frequently restricted to foreign participation (Gaukrodger and Gordon,

2012[37]). Restrictions on FDI in these sectors are likely to result in sub-optimal flows of investment, limit the transfer of know-how and hamper the deployment of low-carbon technologies.

Discriminatory measures can also be used to actively target low-carbon investments, enhance their spillover potential, or deter carbon intensive-investments. Technology transfer obligations could support low-carbon spillovers to domestic firms. However, trade-distorting discriminatory measures, such as local content requirements (LCRs) and subsidies, even if targeting low-carbon products, can hinder international investment across the value chains by raising the cost of inputs for downstream activities. Particularly in small developing countries with low domestic demand and relatively poor supporting infrastructure, policies of this type could increase the costs of domestically purchased environmental goods (OECD, 2015[30]).

The opportunities presented by international investment can sometimes bring risks, including for security interests of host countries. Since 2016, governments are taking these risks increasingly seriously and most OECD countries now have screening mechanisms allowing them to intervene in a much broader section of the economy if international investment may threaten their essential security interests (OECD, 2020[38]). Investment screening could conceivably affect the energy transition and low-carbon innovation in several ways: energy infrastructure (e.g. energy storage) is itself considered "critical infrastructure" in many countries (EU, 2019[39]); advanced technologies (e.g. semiconductors) are likewise typically included under investment review mechanisms, with knock-on effects on energy-related technologies (e.g. solar panels, smart grids). Finally, foreign-funded research and international R&D co-operation, which may be needed or accelerate the energy transition, have come under scrutiny for their national security implications as well, and governments may heighten their attention to such arrangements. Policymakers need to balance the benefits of international investment and international co-operation with the potential implications for essential security interests and seek to mitigate and manage the associated risks. While scrutiny of investment in sensitive sectors is necessary and legitimate, governments should ensure that such screening remains closely tailored to risk and that it is guided by the principles of transparency, predictability, proportionality, and accountability as described in the OECD Guidelines for Recipient Country Investment Policies relating to National Security (OECD, 2009[40]).

Strengthen competition and property rights

Competition rules are designed to promote and protect effective competition in markets, encouraging firms to invest efficiently and to innovate and adopt more energy-efficient technologies. Such competitive pressure is a powerful incentive to use scarce resources efficiently and complements climate policies and regulations aimed at internalising the environmental costs of carbon emissions. By helping to achieve efficient and competitive market outcomes, competition policy hence contributes in itself to the effectiveness of climate policies. These pressures not only influence the foreign investor's operations and direct carbon impacts, but also push local businesses to imitate or improve foreign low-carbon technologies in order to remain competitive.

Competition policy may be especially important for supporting decarbonisation of the power sector, which is traditionally characterised by vertically integrated monopolies. Unbundling the power sector by separating power generation, transmission and distribution functions can help create more space for foreign investment. Moreover, by opening competition in power generation, unbundling provides more space for clean energy technologies to enter the market and can therefore stimulate changes in the national energy mix. The decentralised nature and the smaller generation capacity of clean energy projects compared to their fossil fuel counterparts, makes independent power production well-suited for mainstreaming clean energy technologies. In the areas of transmission and distribution, increased competition can also render the national energy network more flexible, increasing its capacity to accommodate both on- and off-grid renewable energy (OECD, 2015[41]). Even where structural separation has been implemented, dominant incumbent enterprises may deter independent renewable power producers from entering a market through tender procedures (Ang, Röttgers and Burli, 2017[11]). Therefore, countries in which regulators adequately address anticompetitive practices by incumbent utilities, including state-owned enterprises (SOEs), are likely to be more attractive destinations for multinationals seeking investment opportunities in renewable power. In general, policy makers need to ensure that producers of low-carbon electricity benefit from non-discriminatory access to the grid, as uncertain grid access increases project risk; investment in the grid is open to private investment, including foreign investment (potentially through joint ventures); private developers benefit from non-discriminatory access to finance, e.g. from state-owned banks; tenders for public procurement are carefully designed with clear and transparent bid evaluation and selection criteria (OECD, 2015[23]).

Intellectual property rights (IPRs) create strong incentives for innovation as they ensure that investors earn a fair return on their technological innovations. IPRs can be used to generate revenues from licences, encourage synergistic partnerships, or create a market advantage and be the basis for productive activities, and are especially important for the development of low-carbon technologies, which are both research- and capital-intensive (IRENA, 2013[22]). At the same time IPRs can be perceived as an obstacle to the transfer of low-carbon technologies from developed and emerging economies to developing countries. Defining an IPR regime conducive to low-carbon innovation is particularly challenging as it needs to strike a balance between providing a secure environment for investment in innovation, while ensuring that small investors can afford valuable technologies. The importance and impact of IPRs on the transfer of technology are likely to be context specific. In remote areas of low-income countries, the need to expand energy access requires the rapid deployment of well-known renewable energy technologies, for which IPR protection might be less critical. In some African markets very few low-carbon technologies are protected under IP regimes (Haščič, Silva and Johnstone, 2012[42]). By contrast, a strengthening of the IPR regime is likely to play a positive role in emerging economies, responsible for a third of global patenting in clean energy technologies, and representing most of the projected growth in energy demand in the coming decades. With two-thirds of the patenting in clean energy technology being submitted by foreign companies, consolidating the IPR regime could give more incentives to foreign developers to transfer technologies to these emerging markets (OECD, 2015[41]).

The ability to enforce contracts and minimise transaction costs associated with litigation plays an important role in investment decisions in general, but may be crucial for largescale low-carbon infrastructure projects, which typically require a set of complex and interlinked contractual arrangements. The potential costs of litigation are magnified by the many risks associated with low-carbon infrastructure projects (e.g. completion risk, technology risk, revenue risk, supply risk, weather risk, etc.), and may disproportionately affect smaller investors (OECD, 2015[41]). Securing land use rights is similarly vital for large-scale utility projects, which so far have dominated renewable energy investment in developing countries. Most renewable energy plants demand more surface per megawatt installed than their fossil-fuel counterparts, and will require the company leading the project to engage with more than one landowner. Therefore, although not strictly related to low-carbon investments, inadequate property registration systems can increase the transaction costs associated such projects, particularly in the area of clean energy investments. At the same time, governments need to ensure that land concessions do not undermine the subsistence of vulnerable members of the population, which may depend on plots of land that offer the critical natural renewable resources. Prior mapping of natural resources and stakeholder consultations can help minimise these risks.

Set environmental standards that are aligned with national climate objectives

Environmental performance standards, such as emissions standards, restrict the emissions or energy use of vehicles, power plants, buildings, appliances and industrial processes. For instance, fuel economy standards apply to the fuel efficiency of new road vehicles, and blending mandates apply to the use of biofuels in transport. Building standards apply to the thermal insulation of new buildings or to the retrofitting of old ones. Emissions standards of power plants regulate the carbon intensity of their electricity mix. Efficiency standards for consumer appliances remove certain products from the markets. Given that performance standards require, the uptake of more efficient technologies, but do not make their use more expensive, not all energy-efficiency improvements result in net energy savings (OECD, 2019[43]). Counter to the pollution haven hypothesis, there is little and often conflicting empirical evidence that investors locational decisions are driven by differences in stringency of environmental standards and regulations. Indeed adopting regulations and standards that reinforce climate goals can help level the playing field for foreign investments in low-carbon technologies, services and infrastructure. Countries should indeed regularly assess whether their technology and performance standards are in line with long-term climate goals, as strong vested interested may result in targets set at the most feasible level rather than the optimal level necessary to meet objective (OECD, 2015[23]).

Environmental screening and approvals regulation refers to all government environmental regulation that companies need to comply with before they can gain environmental approval for a new, or expanded, investment project. This includes legislation and policy in the areas of environmental impact assessment (EIA) and environmental licensing and permitting, typically applied to investments with potentially significant environmental impacts. These regulations can help mitigate any adverse effects of FDI on emissions, and the environment more broadly, although there is some disagreement on how these regulations affect the attractiveness of a country to foreign investors. The environmental approvals process for proposed investments is considered by some industry representatives and academics to be burdensome because it is perceived as causing delays and increased uncertainty, and therefore likely to discourage FDI. At the same time, empirical evidence on international mining companies in Canada and Australia suggests that investors tend to see EIA as a catalyst for integrating environmental design into the early planning of an investment project, thereby alleviating the need to spend money on overcoming environmental problems once a poorly designed project has been commissioned (Annandale and Taplin, 2003[44]).

5.3.4. Stimulate investment and building technical capabilities related to green technologies, services and infrastructure

Ensure that price signals reflect environmental costs of emissions

Carbon pricing is a core climate policy instrument that provides a technology-neutral case for low-carbon investment and consumption. Carbon pricing raises the cost of carbon-intensive assets and behaviours and effectively encourages the required shift of production and consumption decisions towards low- and zero-carbon options. Carbon pricing can internalise the climate costs of carbon emissions. Not reflecting the full costs that carbon emissions impose on society results in extensive consumption of carbon-intensive goods, such as fuels or final products, as well as investment in production processes that risk becoming stranded in a net-zero carbon economy. Policies that keep the price of carbon artificially low, such as direct transfers and preferential tax treatment granted to the consumption, extraction and production of fossil fuels run counter to effective carbon pricing, and should be gradually phased out.

While carbon pricing policies do not specifically target FDI, they are a necessary first step to send the socially optimal price signals to all investors, including foreign ones, and raise the returns on low-carbon relative to high-carbon investments. Moreover, carbon pricing is pro-competitive as it prepares companies for strong performance in a low-carbon economy (OECD, 2018[45]). At the same time, carbon pricing policies are, by design, intended to reduce the competitiveness of carbon-intensive industries, and ultimately downsize these industries. While many new jobs are created, this can result in job destruction as some jobs cease to exist, and workers may struggle to find alternative employment opportunities (Chapter 3). Appropriate measures to mitigate these adverse social effects, such as direct compensation or retraining of workers, are necessary to ensure a just transition, as set out by the ILO Guidelines for a Just Transition (ILO, 2015[46]).

Taxes on energy use (notably fuel excise taxes and explicit carbon taxes) increase the final price of the taxed energy products, encouraging businesses and consumers to use less energy and, if appropriately designed, to switch to cleaner energy sources.[2] Taxes that are designed based on the carbon content of the fuel, irrespective of whether the resulting carbon price is uniform across fuels and uses, provide abatement incentives in support of decarbonisation objectives. Recent evidence shows that countries are not deploying energy and carbon taxes to their full potential. Across 44 OECD and G20 countries accounting for over 80% of carbon emissions from energy use, taxes on polluting sources of energy are not set anywhere near the levels needed to reduce the risks and impacts of climate change and air pollution. While all countries tax road fuel, 85% of energy-related CO2 emissions take place outside the road sector, where taxes only cover 18% of emissions, leaving a tax of zero for the remaining 82% (OECD, 2019[43]).

Some countries implement emissions trading (or cap-and-trade) systems to price carbon emissions in addition or instead of carbon and fuel taxes. The price of tradable emission permits represents the opportunity cost of emitting an extra unit of carbon regardless of the method to allocate pollution permits. Authorised bodies set a cap on GHG emissions and allocate or auction a limited number of tradable permits that allow a discharge of a specific quantity of a specific pollutant (e.g. CO_2) over a set time period. Emitters are required to hold permits in amount equal to their emissions, but can increase their emissions by buying permits from others willing to sell them. Carbon pricing through taxes or emissions trading provides incentives for emissions abatement where it can be done at least cost, but setting the cap too high results in a low carbon price that provides little incentive to invest in carbon abatement.

Domestic climate policies, such as carbon pricing, can reduce the competitiveness of locally established firms (both foreign and domestic) as they raise costs of carbon-intensive production. In theory, this can discourage new FDI in carbon-intensive operations in some countries or push existing investors to relocate carbon-intensive operations to countries with less stringent climate policies (i.e. the 'Pollution Haven' hypothesis). Indeed, there are growing concerns that cross-country differences in climate policy stringency can lead to changes in countries' comparative advantages, trade flows, and the geographic distribution of production. For a global pollutant like CO_2, this implies that the abatement efforts of one country are offset by a rise in emissions in other countries (i.e. carbon leakage), both undermining the efficacy of domestic climate policies and diminishing domestic competiveness.

Foreign multinationals may be particularly susceptible to relocating emissions-intensive activities to other countries given their networks of affiliates spread across the world. A recent study on the role of the European Union's Emissions Trading System (EU ETS) as a possible driver of outward FDI by Italian manufacturing firms in the automotive industry suggests that the EU ETS had a weak effect on the number of new subsidiaries abroad, while it had a larger impact on production taking place in foreign subsidiaries, especially in trade-intensive sectors (Borghesi, Franco and Marin, 2020[47]). As countries consider more ambitious climate policies in order to curb GHG emissions, securing buy-in by domestic consumers and producers will require carbon leakage and competitiveness effects to be addressed (OECD, 2020[9]).

A border carbon adjustment (BCA) is a "measure applied to traded products that seeks to make their prices in destination markets reflect the costs they would have incurred had they been regulated under the destination market's greenhouse gas emission regime" (Cosbey et al., 2012[48]). BCA regimes have long been discussed, but only recently started gaining traction in the EU and US as a potential instrument to address carbon leakage and competitiveness issues. A number of design and implementation challenges associated with such regimes that will need to be overcome include compatibility with WTO rules, scope of coverage, carbon embodiment measurement issues, and use of revenues (OECD, 2020[9]). Potential conflicts between climate, trade and investment objectives must be taken into consideration in designing a suitable policy mix to promote low-carbon FDI.

Ensure that financial support is transparent and subjective to regular reviews

Private investors do not internalise the positive spillovers of low-carbon investments and are likely to under-invest in related technologies and skills compared to socially optimal levels. Targeted financial and technical support by the government is therefore warranted, but must be, transparent time-limited and subject to regular review. Studies have shown that the variations in the cost-effectiveness of these technology support policies depend on the country context rather than on the specific tool used. In general, government support should decrease over time as the renewable energy sector matures (Box 5.6). In certain countries foreign investors need to limit their equity in clean energy projects to certain thresholds in order to benefit from financial support, which may limit the potential for FDI to contribute to decarbonising the energy sector. Minimum investment size thresholds for securing financial support can also discourage investment by smaller foreign and domestic enterprises, despite their high innovation potential (OECD, 2015[41]). In some cases countries provide investment incentives to both green and non-green substitutes, limiting their overall effectiveness in reducing environmental impacts of FDI (Box 5.5).

Investment tax incentives are widely used to promote FDI and to influence its characteristics and impacts. Incentive programmes can target low-carbon investments by increasing related after-tax profits, reducing costs associated with certain expenses or exempting recipients from indirect taxes. Different instruments present advantages and disadvantages related to their fiscal and administrative costs, and their effectiveness in promoting the desired investment. Profit-based incentives are often used to promote the development of strategic sectors. For instance, Rwanda offers a 50% corporate income tax (CIT) reduction on investments in renewable energy. The main drawback of these incentives is that they are very costly in terms of forgone public revenues, and that by reducing (or eliminating) the CIT rate on any amount of profit earned by the investor, they benefit investments that would have materialised anyway. Cost-based incentives that target low-carbon investments are instead linked to specific expenses and lower the cost of related inputs. For instance, Mauritius and South Africa offer accelerated depreciation allowances on machinery used to generate renewable energy. By lowering the cost of capital they are expected to facilitate investment that would otherwise not be made and have the potential to mobilise more investment per dollar of forgone tax revenue (Clark and Skrok, 2019). A downside of targeted cost-based incentives is that they require greater tax administration capacities and are associated with higher compliance costs in terms of qualifying and reporting requirements.

Exemptions from indirect taxes paid by businesses, such as value added tax (VAT) on machinery and equipment, land tax, property tax, and customs duties on imported and exported goods, allow investors to avoid contact with tax and customs administration, lowering their cost of paying taxes. In the case of renewables, these fiscal measures often reward installation of capacity rather than production, which does not encourage investors to locate clean electricity generation in the most optimal geographical locations (according to resource availability and grid location). A notable exception is the US renewable electricity production tax credit, which benefits production rather than capacity.

Box 5.5. Green and non-green investment incentives in Thailand

Thailand's Board of Investment (BOI) provides investment incentives for green activities including a three-year corporate income tax holiday if they invest in renewable energy. Another incentive to green business behaviour offers tax deductions on expenses towards biodegradable plastics in a bid to reduce plastic pollution (OECD, 2021[49]). At the same time, investment incentives are also offered to 'non-green' activities in similar targeted sectors, including non-renewable energy generated from fossil fuels or waste, and standard plastic products and packaging. Providing similar incentives to both green and non-green substitutes reduces the ultimate effectiveness of efforts to promote green investment. In fact, significantly more investment applications were received for non-biodegradable plastics, and the value of investments in non-renewable energy benefitting from these investments is also significant. According to the recent *OECD Investment Policy Review of Thailand*, the country would benefit from classifying green and non-green activities in targeted sectors using emerging taxonomies, and scaling down or phasing out investment incentives for non-green activities.

Figure 5.6. Applications for investment incentives submitted to BOI in 2018

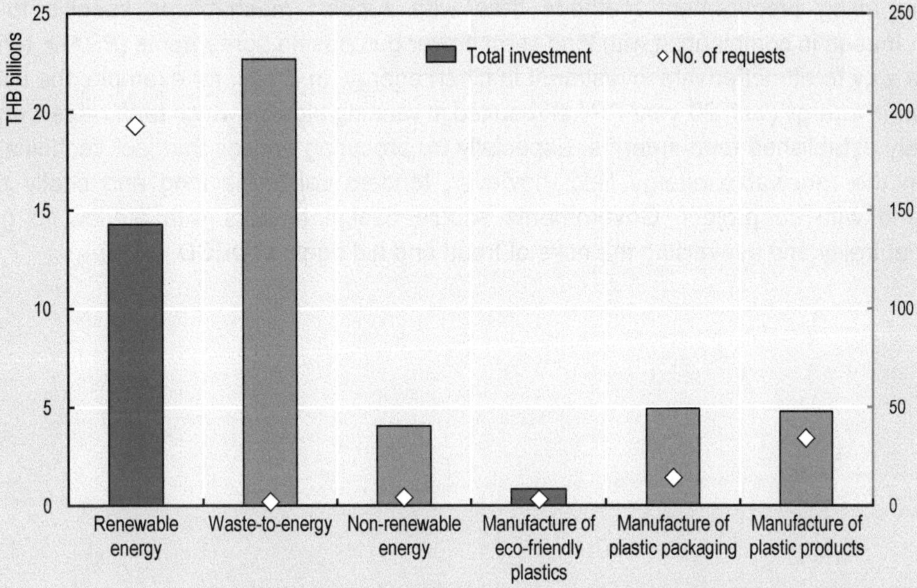

Source: OECD (2021[49]), *OECD Investment Policy Reviews: Thailand*, https://doi.org/10.1787/c4eeee1c-en.

Feed-in tariffs (FiTs) are a type of incentive designed specifically to accelerate investment in renewable energy technologies by offering long-term contracts to renewable energy producers. They reduce the risk of renewable energy investments by guaranteeing a predetermined price (or revenue) for the electricity generated for a predefined period of time. Payments can be provided at a fixed 'tariff' level set independently of the wholesale electricity price, or as a 'premium' payment above the wholesale electricity price. They are typically combined with guaranteed access to the grid for renewable generators. Studies have found evidence that feed-in-tariffs are a powerful tool for attracting FDI in renewables, both in advanced and developing countries (Wall et al., 2019[50]; Kathuria, 2015[51]; Zhang, 2013[52]). At the same time, feed-in-tariffs come with some important drawbacks. The tariff needs to be accurately calculated, and clarity needs to be given to investors as to when and on what basis the tariff is susceptible to change (e.g. to adapt to changes in input costs, achievement of targets, etc.). Setting the right tariff is a complex exercise, with the rapidly decreasing cost of the technologies, and particularly in young markets where government capacity in the design of FiTs may be low and there may be asymmetry of information between regulator and companies. To overcome such informational asymmetries, countries in Europe have moved toward auctioning renewable capacity to determine the price of the FiT.

Tradable renewable energy certificates (also known as renewable energy credits or green tags) can also be used to support clean energy investments. They consist of a market-based mechanism involving the exchange of certificates derived from electricity generation from renewable energy sources. They are usually combined with renewable portfolio standards that require electric utilities to source a fixed share or quantity of electricity from renewable sources, either by installing an equivalent amount of renewable electricity generation capacity, or by purchasing green certificates. Tradability enhances the cost-effectiveness of renewable power generation, although high administrative costs may reduce the cost-effectiveness of implementation. Investors may additionally require capacity building before engaging in such markets.

Public procurement is a useful tool to decarbonise infrastructure investment. Beyond bringing existing low-carbon solutions to market today, it can create 'lead' markets where government demand is significant (e.g. transport, construction), and can spur innovation without engaging new spending (OECD, 2016[53]). Partly as a result of their experience with fossil-fuel technologies, developing countries tend to have greater experience in using procurement methods than with support mechanisms specific to low-carbon technologies. If used in combination with long-term power purchasing agreements (PPAs), tenders can be an alternative way to attract private investment in clean energy. In Brazil, for example, the use of reverse auctions for wind energy (with 20-year PPAs) resulted in winning bids for which tariff rates were 42% lower than previously established feed-in-tariffs. Especially for procuring entities that lack technical capacity or experience in the renewable energy field, however, tenders can be a long and costly process and sometimes end with no project. Governments should design tenders with a view to guaranteeing competitive neutrality and minimising the risks of fraud and bid rigging (OECD, 2015[41]).

Box 5.6. Financial support for renewables decreases as technologies mature

The extent and type of financial support provided to expand renewable energy generation capacity varies across countries, often as a function of the extent of penetration of renewable energy technologies. Climate leaders like Sweden and Costa Rica, which rely overwhelmingly on renewable energy, tend to offer little or no government support for renewable energy generation in the form of tax incentives, grants or subsidies (aside from subsidies for micro-production by households and non-energy enterprises). Sweden rather combines strong carbon pricing with market-based support measures, like tradable electricity certificates. Costa Rica focuses on developing domestic supply chains to produce renewable energy equipment locally.

Countries that still depend heavily on fossil fuels but where renewable capacity is rising rapidly, like Thailand, Morocco and Jordan, tend to offer a mix of investment incentives on renewable energy equipment, fixed feed-in-tariffs for renewable electricity fed into the grid, and public tenders for new installations of renewable energy infrastructure. Studies provide some evidence that price-based support schemes such as FiTs and premiums are more positively correlated with investors' ability to raise private finance than quota-based schemes, and therefore may be more appropriate for countries at an earlier stage of the energy transition (Cárdenas-Rodríguez, Haščič and Johnstone, 2014[54]).

Countries with still limited renewable energy capacity like Tunisia and Uzbekistan primarily employ a combination of public tenders, corporate tax holidays and import duties exemptions on machinery and equipment.

Table 5.4. Summary of financial support for renewables

Country	Tax incentives	Feed-in-tariffs	Public procurement	Tradable certificates
Canada	Accelerated depreciation of RE machinery and equipment			
Costa Rica	VAT exemption on imported machinery and equipment			
Jordan	Customs and VAT exemption on machinery and equipment	Wind, solar PV, thermal, biomass and biogas	Direct Proposal Submission, Build Own Operate scheme	
Morocco		Wind power (EnergiPro Programme)	ONE IMs tender process	
Rwanda	CIT reduction (50%) and VAT exemption (machinery)	Small hydro power	Tenders for solar plants	
Senegal	Deductions on installations, VAT and customs exemptions	Solar PV	Tenders for suppliers of solar mini-grids	
Sweden	Energy tax exemption for self-produced RE			Tradable Electricity Certificate
Thailand	CIT holiday, customs exemption (machinery)	Distributed solar systems		
Tunisia	Exemptions on CIT (4 years) customs and VAT (machinery)		Build Own Operate scheme	
Uzbekistan	Exemptions on CIT (5 years), property and land tax (10 years)		Several tenders for RE installations	

Source: OECD (2022[36]), FDI Qualities mapping: A survey of policies and institutions that can strengthen sustainable investment.

Build domestic low-carbon knowledge and capable low-carbon workforces

Technical support is a useful tool for reducing the emissions intensity of investments, building capabilities related to low-carbon technologies, and promoting low-carbon innovation and spillovers. These initiatives are important for attracting foreign investors that seek skills related to green technologies and local business partners in green supply chains. By developing low-carbon capabilities of domestic firms and workforces these programmes are crucial for the transfer of knowledge and technology from foreign to domestic firms. Countries use a variety of programmes to develop domestic know-how and support low-carbon innovation (Box 5.7). In many cases governments finance these programmes but outsource their delivery to specialists.

Business support initiatives are typically designed to help investors reduce their energy use, waste, or emissions levels. They include seminars, events, and specialised technical assistance (e.g. support for energy audits). In Morocco, the audit results of an energy efficiency training programme for large corporations showed that 5% of the 8 000 companies audited accounted for 70% of industrial energy consumption, suggesting that there may be opportunities to achieve large energy savings by targeting a relatively small number of investors. While these initiatives tend to target local businesses, and often SMEs, rather than foreign investors, they can help create a pool of low-carbon champions that attract MNEs concerned with the carbon footprint of their supply chains. By increasing the opportunities for local linkages, these initiatives can be an important driver of FDI spillovers that advance decarbonisation of domestic industry.

Training programmes that target workers can similarly help encourage FDI spillovers by creating pools of qualified workers with the skills necessary to operate low-carbon technologies, and by increasing the potential for labour mobility between foreign and domestic firms. These programmes include specialised training, learning-by-doing, apprenticeships and secondments, and in-depth professional certification programmes (see Chapter 3). Other programmes offer community-level capacity building (e.g. energy literacy) to influence consumption behaviours, and reduce the demand for energy- or emissions-intensive products and services. These initiatives can help create new markets for foreign investors seeking to expand their low-carbon investments.

Beyond mitigating adverse environmental effects of business, technical support can be used to foster innovation and commercialisation of new climate-friendly technologies (see Chapter 2). Technology parks, incubators and accelerators can be tailored to support businesses in finding innovative solutions to reducing GHG emissions, and create low-carbon innovation hubs that attract talent and investors. Eco-friendly by design, and often located close to universities and research centres to promote the exchange of knowledge, these parks can help facilitate synergies and partnerships between foreign investors, local business and research institutions, and support local industries in acquiring knowledge and know-how. By upgrading the capabilities and innovation potential of domestic industry, green technology parks and incubation facilities can heighten competitive pressures and encourage FDI spillovers that arise from imitation of foreign technologies and operating procedures.

Box 5.7. Examples of technical support for developing low-carbon capabilities

Countries tend to offer a mix of technical support initiatives directed at businesses and workers. Many countries support businesses in reducing GHG emissions, by providing technical assistance for improving energy efficiency (Sweden, Morocco, Jordan, and Uzbekistan), reducing waste (Tunisia), and developing electrifying industry (Costa Rica). More advanced programmes can support entrepreneurs in developing breakthrough technologies and solutions to reduce GHG emissions (Canada).

Training and skills development initiatives are also increasingly tailored to green technologies. In Costa Rica, in order to boost green jobs, the National Apprentice Institute has incorporated environmental courses into its training catalogue, including subjects like GHG emissions control. Jordan offers vocational training on renewable energy and energy efficiency, and an in-depth professional certification programme for energy managers tailored to the Arab region. Training programmes in Canada target rural communities, encouraging regional collaboration and knowledge-exchange, and seek to reduce their reliance on diesel products. Since 2016, the Swedish Energy Agency in co-operation with other actors has been responsible for a set of capacity building programmes in the area of building for low energy consumption. The programmes target different construction stakeholders, such as architects, engineers, clients, technicians, installers, and site managers.

Countries at more advanced stages of the low-carbon transition sometimes seek investors with high innovation potential, and support them in developing innovative solutions to address climate change across sectors. Incubators and technology parks in Canada (Net Zero Accelerator), Costa Rica (Green Tech Incubator) and Morocco (Green Energy Park) serve as platforms for researching, developing, testing, and rolling out low-carbon technologies and processes.

Figure 5.7. Summary of types of technical support offered

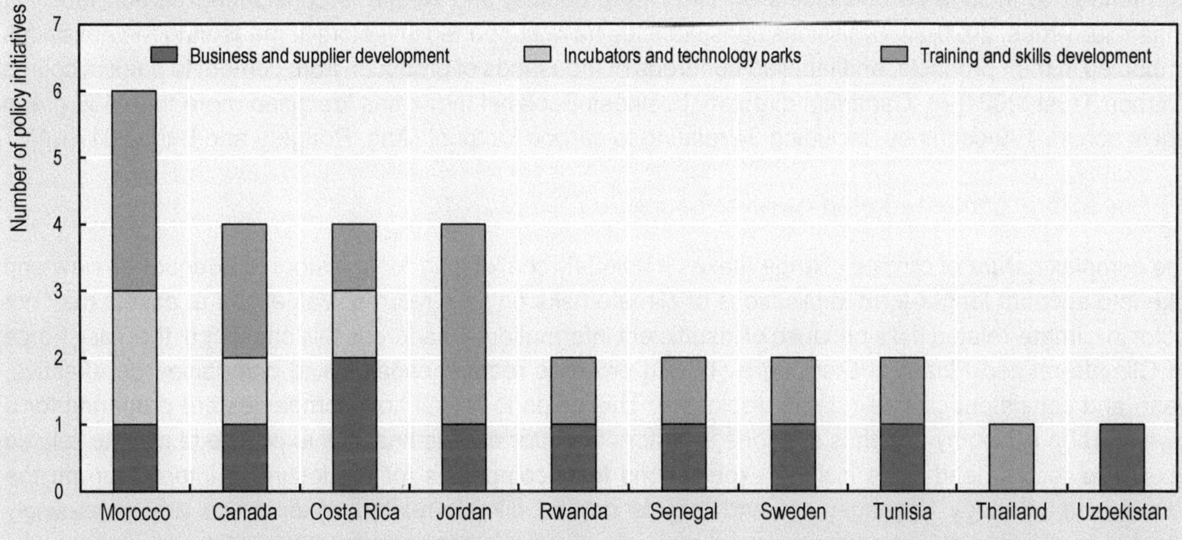

Source: OECD (2022[36]), FDI Qualities mapping: A survey of policies and institutions that can strengthen sustainable investment.

5.3.5. Address information failures and administrative barriers that deter low-carbon investments

Raise public awareness on carbon performance

Insufficient, inaccurate or costly information on the carbon performance of different technologies, products or services leads to sub-optimal decisions by consumers and investors, and generally results in under-investment in low-carbon technologies. For instance, lack of awareness on the energy performance of household appliances leads to an inability of consumers to interpret the impact of energy prices on the operational costs of one product relative to another, meaning that price signals do not influence purchasing behaviour as expected and carbon pricing instruments may be ineffective.

Concerns about access to information on the carbon footprint of consumption and investment choices have led many governments to introduce measures to raise public awareness and understanding of carbon performance, including platforms for dialogue and information sharing, information campaigns, and product labelling schemes. For instance, many governments have long ago introduced mandatory energy labelling schemes for appliances, which have been key in helping consumers choose more energy-efficient products. According to the Eurobarometer on energy, in 2019, the EU energy label was recognised by 93% of consumers and considered by 79% when buying energy-efficient products. The energy label has also encouraged manufacturers to seek more energy-efficient technologies and stimulated innovation, in an effort to see their energy-labelled products in the highest available category when compared to competitors. For example, roughly two-thirds of refrigerators and washing machines sold in 2006 were labelled as class A, compared to over 90% in 2017 (Ang, Röttgers and Burli, 2017[11]).

While there are still no regulatory requirements on carbon labelling, some investor-driven initiatives are emerging to cater to customers that are responsive to climate credentials. The meat substitute, Quorn, started including carbon labels on its most popular products in 2020; Popular oat milk brand, Oatly, began using the labels in 2019; Unilever, one of the world's largest consumer goods companies, recently stated its intention to include carbon labels on all of its products; and Nestlé is considering carbon labelling (Financial Times, 2020[55]). Emissions consultancies have supported investors in measuring the emissions embodied in their products, and labelled hundreds of thousands of products, from cement to bank accounts (Carbon Trust, 2021[56]). Canadian directory business Ecolabel Index has identified more than 455 green labels across 199 countries, including 34 relating to carbon footprint (Ang, Röttgers and Burli, 2017[11]).

Encourage climate-related risk disclosure

The complex nature of climate change makes it uniquely challenging for investors to adequately view and take into account longer-term implications of climate risks on their returns. Valuations of assets may not factor in climate-related risks because of insufficient information. To address this challenge, the Task Force on Climate-related Financial Disclosure (TCFD) provides recommendations to companies on effective, clear, and consistent climate-related disclosure. This helps to reveal how companies are preparing for a lower-carbon economy and thus supports investors to better assess financial exposure to climate-related risks. The recommendations include expectations from companies for disclosure of information on the governance, strategy, management and targets around climate-related risks, which are increasingly adopted by the largest carbon emitters and supported by the public sector (TCFD, 2021[57]).

Better corporate disclosure of climate-related risks will also help aligning the environmental pillar of ESG investment ratings with a low-carbon transition. Inconsistencies in the construction of ESG ratings across providers, the multitude of different metrics, and insufficient quality of forward looking metrics prevent agencies from supplying consistent and comparable information on transition risks and opportunities across firms and jurisdictions. Notably, rating providers appear to place less weight on negative environmental impacts while placing greater weight on the disclosure of climate-related corporate policies and targets, with limited assessment as to the quality or impact of such strategies. Such limitations could mislead investors with an aim to align portfolios with the low-carbon transition. Greater transparency and precision of climate-related corporate risks along the TCFD recommendations, for example, would facilitate investments into lower carbon assets (OECD, 2021[58]).

Beyond non-binding recommendations, environmental regulations on reporting requirements are increasingly being used to address the cross-border environmental footprint of multinationals. The EU Taxonomy Regulation, which entered into law in 2020, for instance, places a reporting obligation on certain companies to disclose how much of their global investment is aligned with environmentally sustainable activities (Box 5.8). Starting from 2022, large investors (with over 500 employees) with operations in the EU must disclose which proportion of their turnover, capital expenditure and operating expenditure is associated with environmentally sustainable economic activities. Non-financial investors can use the EU Taxonomy to plan their climate and environmental transition and raise finance for this transition, while financial companies can use the EU Taxonomy to design credible green financial products. Going forward, implementation of the Regulation is likely to have significant influence on the carbon implications of inward and outward FDI of companies operating in the EU. The emergence of new taxonomies in other countries and regions can result in inconsistent definitions of what is environmentally sustainable and create additional uncertainty and costs for multinational investors.

Box 5.8. The EU Taxonomy Regulation

The EU Taxonomy is a regulatory classification system that helps investors and companies define which economic activities are environmentally sustainable. To qualify as environmentally sustainable, the activity must substantially contribute to at least one of six environmental objectives (i.e. Climate Change Mitigation, Climate Change Adaptation, Sustainable Use and Protection of Water and Marine Resources, Transition to a Circular Economy, Pollution Prevention and Control, and the Protection and Restoration of Biodiversity and Ecosystems), while at the same time not significantly harming any of these objectives and meeting minimum social safeguards.

The Regulation is a transparency tool that will introduce mandatory disclosure obligations on some companies and investors, requiring them to disclose their share of Taxonomy-aligned activities. Reporting under the Taxonomy will be a mandatory requirement for three key users: (1) financial market participants and issuers offering financial products within the EU; (2) large companies (with over 500 employees) who are already required to provide a non-financial statement under the EU Non-Financial Reporting Directive (NFRD); and (3) EU and Member States when setting public measures, standards or labels for green financial products or green bonds.

The EU Taxonomy is not a mandatory list of economic activities for investors to invest in. Nor does it set mandatory requirements on environmental performance for companies or for financial products. Companies are free to choose what to invest in. Companies with products and services that are not sustainable will have to state that their investments do not consider the regulation. However, the mandatory disclosure of the proportion of Taxonomy-aligned activities will allow for the comparison of companies and investment portfolios, and can guide market participants in their investment decisions.

Source: https://ec.europa.eu/info/business-economy-euro/banking-and-finance/sustainable-finance/eu-taxonomy-sustainable-activities_en

Promote and facilitate low-carbon investments and their spillovers

Investment promotion agencies (IPAs) are key players in bridging information gaps that may otherwise hinder the realisation of foreign investments, and their potential sustainable development impacts. Their primary role is to create awareness of existing investment opportunities, attract investors, and facilitate their establishment and expansion in the economy, including by linking them to potential local partners.

Most IPAs prioritise certain types of investments over others, by selecting priority sectors, countries or investment projects, and allocating resources accordingly (Box 5.9). The prioritisation approaches and tools adopted by IPAs are intended to influence the kind of investment that is attracted into the local economy and, increasingly, their sustainable development impacts, and should reflect the national investment promotion strategy and any climate considerations embedded in the strategy. Since few economies can offer an attractive environment for all low-carbon technologies and all segments of their value chains, IPAs should review and identify specific economic activities where they see a potential to develop low-carbon activities or growth poles. On this basis they can design investment promotion packages combining a variety of tools that range from intelligence gathering (e.g. market studies) and sector-specific events (inward and outward missions) to pro-active investor engagement (one-to-one meetings, email/ phone campaigns, enquiry handling).

IPAs are also responsible for investment facilitation and retention. Facilitation services can help reduce administrative barriers to low-carbon investments. While imperative for curbing environmental impacts of FDI, the multitude of permits and licenses for air emissions, water abstraction, wastewater discharges, waste generation, storage and disposal, and other environmental impacts, can create significant hurdles for foreign investors and discourage investment rather than help improve their environmental performance. As the first point of contact of foreign investors, IPAs can support them in acquiring the necessary permits and clearances, including from environmental authorities, by guiding them through the required procedures facilitating access to relevant government bodies. Having a single window portal for all administrative procedures can help reduce transaction costs for investors, as long as it does not create additional duplication and complexity in the company establishment process. As a general rule, one-stop shops should not be mandatory entry points for investors, as allowing businesses to opt for alternative routes to open a business if they so wish is an incentive for one-stop shops to remain efficient. Additionally, they should be equipped with a Customer Relationship Management (CRM) system, including indicators for monitoring performance, and customers should be invited to fill in satisfaction surveys and forms. It is also important that the decisions to grant or refuse a business licence are transparent and made publicly available, with a right of appeal for those investors who have seen their licence rejected.

Investment aftercare services are an important channel for the propagation of FDI spillovers through the interactions of foreign MNEs with domestic firms and workers. In the context of improving FDI impacts on carbon emissions, aftercare services can help foreign investors overcome information barriers associated with identifying low-carbon business partners, suppliers and distributors, and help them reduce emissions along their supply chains. When IPAs engage in matchmaking, they should look for complementarities with local firms. Even if these firms do not have a low-carbon profile, they may possess skills and technologies that could be used for low-carbon projects. Examples include skills and technologies in the field of electronic components, computer software, and various biological processes that could be used in the production of biofuels.

As discussed throughout the chapter, a range of targeted policies are necessary in order transition to low-carbon economies and to attract low-carbon foreign investment, including those that create a market for low-carbon products and services by addressing market failures, administrative barriers and information asymmetries, and those that build low-carbon capabilities across workers and firms through financial and technical support In order to ensure that such issues are given due consideration by governments and that they are in a position to proactively market the country as a low-carbon investment destination, IPAs need to pay particular attention to their advocacy function. IPAs can be more up to date on the latest trends in foreign investment flows and serve as the primary interface between TNCs and government. Their role in making policy makers aware of regulatory needs to promote low-carbon investment are thus be crucial.

Box 5.9. IPA prioritisation and tracking of contribution to climate-related SDG

According to the OECD Survey on Prioritisation and Monitoring and Evaluation of IPAs, close to 40% of OECD IPAs prioritise investments that help mitigate climate change (SDG 13); 60% prioritise investments that support the energy transition (SDG 7); and 70% prioritise investments that contribute to resilient infrastructure, sustainable industry and low-carbon innovation (SDG 9). In contrast, between 23% and 30% of IPAs track their investment attraction efforts along transition-related indicators (e.g. number of new renewable energy projects). Virtually no IPAs monitor the impact of the investments attracted against climate-related indicators (e.g. GHG emissions). This suggests that IPAs in the OECD tend to allocate considerable resources to investment attraction activities that can support decarbonisation objectives and tailor their activities accordingly, but continue to struggle to measure and monitor their contribution to these climate objectives. Potential approaches to overcome these challenges may include translating climate goals (e.g. based on the SDGs) to specific key performance indicators (KPIs) and complementing these measures with official sources of data to evaluate targets (Sztajerowska and Volpe Martincus, 2022[59]).

Figure 5.8. IPA prioritisation and tracking of contribution to climate-related SDG

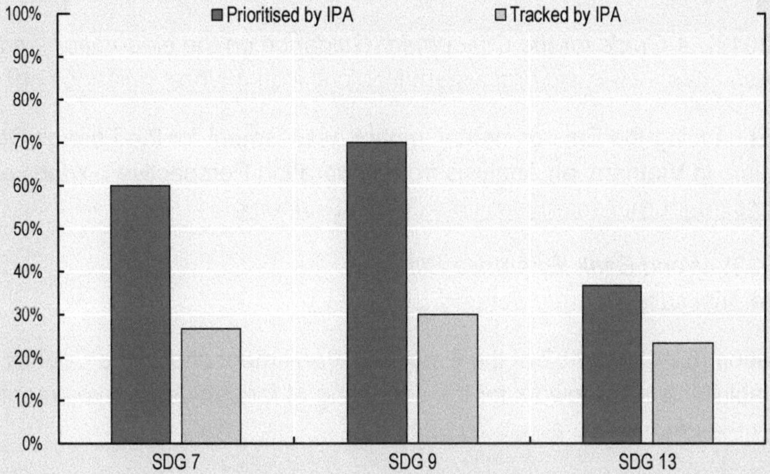

Source: OECD survey on IPA monitoring and evaluation and prioritisation, 2021

References

Ang, G., D. Röttgers and P. Burli (2017), “The empirics of enabling investment and innovation in renewable energy”, *OECD Environment Working Papers*, No. 123, OECD Publishing, Paris, https://doi.org/10.1787/67d221b8-en. [11]

Annandale, D. and R. Taplin (2003), “Is Environmental Impact Assessment Regulation a ‘Burden’ to Private Firms?”, *Environmental Impact Assessment Review*, Vol. 23/3, pp. 383-397, https://doi.org/10.1016/S0195-9255(03)00002-7. [44]

Behera, S. and D. Dash (2017), “The effect of urbanization, energy consumption, and foreign direct investment on the carbon dioxide emission in the SSEA (South and Southeast Asian) region”, *Renewable and Sustainable Energy Reviews*, Vol. 70, pp. 96-106, https://doi.org/10.1016/j.rser.2016.11.201. [27]

BloombergNEF (2022), *Energy Transition Investment Trends 2022*, https://about.bnef.com/energy-transition-investment/. [19]

Borghesi, S., C. Franco and G. Marin (2020), *Outward Foreign Direct Investment Patterns of Italian Firms in the European Union’s Emissions Trading Scheme*, https://doi.org/10.1111/sjoe.12323. [47]

Carbon Trust (2021), *Product carbon footprint label*, https://www.carbontrust.com/what-we-do/assurance-and-certification/product-carbon-footprint-label. [56]

Cárdenas-Rodríguez, M., I. Haščič and N. Johnstone (2014), “Inducing Private Finance for Renewable Energy Projects: Evidence from Micro-Data”, *OECD Environment Working Papers* 67, https://doi.org/10.1787/19970900. [54]

Copeland, B. and M. Taylor (1994), “North-South trade and the environment”, *The Quarterly Journal of Economics*, Vol. 109, pp. 755-787, https://doi.org/10.2307/2118421. [14]

Cosbey, A. et al. (2012), *A Guide for the Concerned: Guidance on the elaboration and implementation of*, https://www.iisd.org/system/files/publications/bca_guidance.pdf. [48]

Dung, T. (2019), “Enhancing the Environmental Impact Assessment for the Foreign Direct Investment Regime in Vietnam: an Analysis from Integration Perspective”, *Yuridika*, Vol. 34/3, pp. 527-547, https://e-journal.unair.ac.id/index.php/YDK/index. [32]

EBRD-EIB-WB (2022), *World Bank Enterprise Surveys*, https://www.enterprisesurveys.org/en/enterprisesurveys. [20]

EU (2019), “Regulation (EU) 2019/452 of the European Parliament and of the Council of 19 March 2019 establishing a framework for the screening of foreign direct investments into the Union”, https://eur-lex.europa.eu/eli/reg/2019/452/oj. [39]

Financial Times (2022), *FDI Markets: the in-depth crossborder investment monitor from the Financial Times*, https://www.fdimarkets.com/. [18]

Financial Times (2022), *Governments should not foot the bill for stranded assets*, https://on.ft.com/3sZoeOr. [35]

Financial Times (2020), *Could carbon labelling soon become routine?*, https://www.ft.com/content/45dbe119-391b-41e5-8b6a-c6b5a082d062. [55]

Gaukrodger, D. and K. Gordon (2012), “Investor-State Dispute Settlement: A Scoping Paper for the Investment Policy Community”, *OECD Working Papers on International Investment*, No. 2012/3, OECD Publishing, Paris, https://doi.org/10.1787/5k46b1r85j6f-en. [37]

Gordon, K. and J. Pohl (2011), “Environmental Concerns in International Investment Agreements: A Survey”, *OECD Working Papers on International Investment*, No. 2011/1, OECD Publishing, Paris, https://doi.org/10.1787/5kg9mq7scrjh-en. [60]

Grossman, G. and A. Kruger (1991), “Environmental Impacts of a North American Free Trade Agreement”, *Working Paper Series No. 3914*, https://doi.org/10.3386/w3914. [13]

Hanni, M. et al. (2011), “Foreign direct investment in renewable energy: Trends, drivers and determinants”, *Transnational Corporations*, https://doi.org/10.18356/673b9e6f-en. [29]

Haščič, I., J. Silva and N. Johnstone (2012), “Climate Mitigation and Adaptation in Africa: Evidence from Patent Data”, *OECD Environment Working Papers* 50. [42]

Hoffman, R. et al. (2005), “FDI and pollution: a Granger causality test using panel data”, *Journal of International Development*, Vol. 3/311-317, p. 17, https://doi.org/10.1002/jid.1196. [25]

ILO (2015), *Guidelines for a just transition towards environmentally sustainable economies and societies for all*, https://www.ilo.org/wcmsp5/groups/public/@ed_emp/@emp_ent/documents/publication/wcms_432859.pdf. [46]

IPCC (2018), *Global Warming of 1.5°C above Pre-industrial Levels and Related Global Greenhouse Gas Emission Pathways, in the Context of Strengthening the Global Response to the Threat of Climate Change, Sustainable Development, and Efforts to Eradicate Poverty.* [3]

IRENA (2013), *Intellectual Property Rights: The Role of Patents in Renewable Energy Technology Innovation*, https://www.irena.org/-/media/Files/IRENA/Agency/Publication/2013/Intellectual_Property_Rights.pdf. [22]

IRENA-ILO (2021), *Renewable Energy and Jobs – Annual Review 2021*, International Renewable Energy Agency, International Labour Organization, Abu Dhabi, Geneva., https://www.irena.org/publications/2021/Oct/Renewable-Energy-and-Jobs-Annual-Review-2021. [24]

Kathuria, V. (2015), *Does Feed-in-Tariff Explain Foreign Investment in Wind Energy Sector in India?*, Springer, https://doi.org/10.1007/978-981-10-0083-6_9. [51]

McKinsey (2020), *Plugging in: What electrification can do for industry*, https://www.mckinsey.com/industries/electric-power-and-natural-gas/our-insights/plugging-in-what-electrification-can-do-for-industry. [17]

McKinsey-GFA (2020), *Fashion on Climate*, https://www.globalfashionagenda.com/publications-and-policy/fashion-on-climate/. [21]

OECD (2022), *FDI Qualities mapping: A survey of policies and institutions that can strengthen sustainable investment.* [36]

OECD (2021), *ESG Investing and Climate Transition: Market Practices, Issues and Policy Considerations*, https://www.oecd.org/finance/ESG-investing-and-climate-transition-market-practices-issues-and-policy-considerations.pdf. [58]

OECD (2021), *OECD Investment Policy Reviews: Thailand*, OECD Publishing, Paris, https://doi.org/10.1787/c4eeee1c-en. [49]

OECD (2020), *Acquisition- and ownership-related policies to safeguard essential security interests*, http://www.oecd.org/Investment/OECD-Acquisition-ownership-policies-security-May2020.pdf. [38]

OECD (2020), *Climate Policy Leadership in an Interconnected World: What Role for Border Carbon Adjustments?*, OECD Publishing, Paris, https://doi.org/10.1787/8008e7f4-en. [9]

OECD (2020), "COVID-19 and the low-carbon transition: Impacts and possible policy responses", *OECD Policy Responses to Coronavirus (COVID-19)*, http://www.oecd.org/coronavirus/policy-responses/covid-19-and-the-low-carbon-transition-impacts-and-possible-policy-responses-749738fc/. [7]

OECD (2020), "Green budgeting and tax policy tools to support a green recovery", *OECD Policy Responses to Coronavirus (COVID-19)*, http://www.oecd.org/coronavirus/policy-responses/green-budgeting-and-tax-policy-tools-to-support-a-green-recovery-bd02ea23/#abstract-d1e25. [6]

OECD (2020), *Green Infrastructure in the Decade for Delivery: Assessing Institutional Investment*, OECD Publishihng, Paris, https://doi.org/10.1787/f51f9256-en. [5]

OECD (2020), *OECD Investment Policy Reviews: Myanmar 2020*, OECD Investment Policy Reviews, OECD Publishing, Paris, https://doi.org/10.1787/d7984f44-en. [33]

OECD (2019), *FDI Qualities Indicators: Measuring the sustainable development impacts of investment*, http://www.oecd.org/fr/investissement/fdi-qualities-indicators.htm. [10]

OECD (2019), *Taxing Energy Use 2019: Using Taxes for Climate Action*, OECD Publishing, Paris, https://doi.org/10.1787/058ca239-en. [43]

OECD (2018), *Effective Carbon Rates 2018: Pricing Carbon Emissions Through Taxes and Emissions Trading*, OECD Publishing, Paris, https://doi.org/10.1787/9789264305304-en. [45]

OECD (2018), *OECD Due Diligence Guidance for Responsible Business Conduct*, https://www.oecd.org/investment/due-diligence-guidance-for-responsible-business-conduct.htm. [34]

OECD (2017), *Investing in Climate, Investing in Growth*, OECD Publishing, Paris, https://doi.org/10.1787/9789264273528-en. [4]

OECD (2016), "The Role of Public Procurement in Low-Carbon Innovation", *Background paper for the 33rd Round Table on Sustainable Development*. [53]

OECD (2015), *Aligning Policies for a Low-carbon Economy*, OECD Publishing, Paris, https://doi.org/10.1787/9789264233294-en. [23]

OECD (2015), *Policy Framework for Investment, 2015 Edition*, OECD Publishing, Paris, https://doi.org/10.1787/9789264208667-en. [30]

OECD (2015), *Policy Guidance for Investment in Clean Energy Infrastructure: Expanding Access to Clean Energy for Green Growth and Development*, OECD Publishing, Paris, https://doi.org/10.1787/9789264212664-en. [41]

OECD (2009), "OECD Guidelines for Recipient Country Investment Policies relating to National Security", *Recommendation adopted by the OECD Council*, https://www.oecd.org/daf/inv/investment-policy/43384486.pdf. [40]

Pao, H. and C. Tsai (2010), “Multivariate Granger causality between CO2 emissions, energy consumption, FDI and GDP: evidence from a panel of BRIC countries”, *Energy*, Vol. 36/1, pp. 685-693, https://doi.org/10.1016/j.energy.2010.09.041. [26]

Pazienza, P. (2015), “The relationship between CO2 and Foreign Direct Investment in the agriculture and fishing sector of OECD countries: Evidence and policy considerations”, *Intellectual Economics*, Vol. 9, pp. 55-66, https://doi.org/10.1016/j.intele.2015.08.001. [16]

Peters, G. (2018), “The challenge of policy coordination”, *Policy Design and Practice*, Vol. 1/1, pp. 1-11, https://doi.org/10.1080/25741292.2018.1437946. [31]

Porter, M. and C. van der Linde (1995), “Green and Competitive: Ending the Stalemate”, *Harvard Business Review*, Vol. 73/5, pp. 120-134, https://hbr.org/1995/09/green-and-competitive-ending-the-stalemate. [15]

Sztajerowska, M. and C. Volpe Martincus (2022), *ogether or apart: Investment Promotion Agencies' prioritisation and monitoring and evaluation for sustainable investment promotion across the OECD countries*, https://www.oecd.org/daf/inv/investment-policy/Investment-Insights-Investment-Promotion-Prioritisation-OECD.pdf. [59]

TCFD (2021), *Task Force on Clmiate-realated Financial Disclosures*, https://assets.bbhub.io/company/sites/60/2020/10/TCFD_Booklet_FNL_Digital_March-2020.pdf. [57]

UN (n.d.), *Transnational Corporations*, United Nations, New York, https://doi.org/10.18356/d3e73f33-en. [28]

UNFCCC (2015), *Paris Agreement*, https://unfccc.int/sites/default/files/english_paris_agreement.pdf. [2]

United Nations (2015), *Transforming our world: the 2030 Agenda for Sustainable Development*, https://www.un.org/ga/search/view_doc.asp?symbol=A/RES/70/1&Lang=E. [8]

Wall, R. et al. (2019), “Which policy instruments attract foreign direct investments in renewable energy?”, *Climate Policy*, Vol. 19/1, pp. 59-72, https://doi.org/10.1080/14693062.2018.1467826. [50]

WEF (2020), *The Global Risks Report 2020*, World Economic Forum, Geneva, http://www3.weforum.org/docs/WEF_Global_Risk_Report_2020.pdf. [1]

WRI/WBCSD (2004), *The Greenhouse Gas Protocol*, https://ghgprotocol.org/sites/default/files/standards/ghg-protocol-revised.pdf. [12]

Zhang, F. (2013), “How Fit are Feed-in Tariff Policies? Evidence from the European Wind Market”, *Policy Research Working Paper* 6376, https://openknowledge.worldbank.org/handle/10986/13185. [52]

Annex 5.A. Assessing the impacts of FDI on carbon emissions

Annex Table 5.A.1. Core questions to assess the impact of FDI on carbon emissions

Dimension	Questions	Potential data sources
Carbon performance	How does the country perform in terms of carbon and other GHG emissions? What sectors are driving these emissions?	Carbon emissions by sector (IEA)
	How does the country perform in terms of energy efficiency (e.g. power generation, end-use fuel, end-use electricity, transmission losses)?	Energy intensity by sector (IEA)
	How does the country perform in terms of fuel switch technologies (e.g. renewables, electric vehicles, hydrogen fuel)?	Renewable energy, energy storage, EVs, hydrogen tech (IEA, OECD)
	How does the country perform in terms of end-of-pipe solutions (e.g. carbon capture and storage for power generation and industry)?	Capture, storage, sequestration or disposal of GHGs (OECD)
	How much does the country invest in R&D related to low-carbon technologies?	Public R&D budget for low-carbon technology (IEA)
Economic structure and comparative advantage	Is economic activity concentrated in carbon- or energy-intensive sectors?	Value added by sector (OECD, UN)
	Is the country endowed with fossil fuels? Is it endowed with renewable natural resources?	Oil and coal rents as a share of GDP (WB), Global RE Atlas (IRENA)
	Does the country export fossil fuels? Does it export electricity? Does it export high-tech goods?	Export data by sector (WITS
	To what extent does the country participate in green global value chains? (see EU taxonomy) Where is it position along these value chains?	Foreign value added share of gross exports (OECD TiVA)
FDI transmission channels	How polluting are the sectors that account for most of the country's FDI? How much FDI do renewables/ fossil fuels attract?	FDI inflows by sector (OECD, UNCTAD, Financial Times)
	How green are foreign firms relative to domestic peers (e.g. strategy and management, energy use and monitoring, environmental impacts)	Green economy indicators by firm ownership (WBES)
	To what extent do firms monitor emissions along their supply chains? How does this vary by firm ownership?	Green economy indicators by firm ownership (WBES)
	How does the extent of supply chain linkages between foreign and domestic firms vary across sectors with differing carbon emissions?	Share of local sourcing of foreign firms (WBES)

Annex Table 5.A.2. Assessing policies that influence the impact of FDI on carbon emissions

Dimension	Instrument	Questions
Governance	National strategies and plans	Has the government adopted a cross-sectoral national climate strategy? Does it outline targets for GHG reductions, renewable energy and energy efficiency? Does it clarify expectations on private sector contribution to these targets/
	Oversight and co-ordination bodies	Are there high-level cross-ministerial co-ordination mechanisms in the policy areas of investment promotion, environmental regulation and energy policy?
	Public consultation	Have relevant institutions set up mechanisms to consult with the foreign investors to receive feedback on the relevance of their policy programmes?
	Data, monitoring & evaluation	Do relevant institutions monitor and evaluate the impact of FDI on carbon emissions, including knowledge spillovers to domestic firms? What environmental impact assessment and strategic environmental assessment requirements are in place and are they adequately enforced?
International agreements & standards	International agreements on climate change	What are the country's international commitments in terms of GHG emission reduction targets under the UNFCCC?
	International agreements on RBC	Has the country adhered to the OECD Guidelines for Multinational Enterprises? What measures are in place to promote the OECD Due Diligence Guidance for Responsible Business Conduct
	Environmental provisions of BITs and RTAs	Do international investment agreements to which the country is a party, take into account environmental issues? If so, which ones and how?
	Legal framework for	Are there any exceptions to national treatment in sectors with large emissions reduction potential

Dimension	Instrument	Questions
Domestic regulation	investment	(e.g. energy, transport)? Are technologies critical for the transition subject to review mechanisms? Do all investors (SOEs, domestic, foreign) compete on a level playing field in energy markets? Are any anticompetitive practices addressed? What steps is the government taking to protect intellectual property rights and facilitate patenting for low-carbon technologies? What steps is the government taking to ensure that contracts between clean energy providers and their partners are enforced?
	Environmental standards & requirements	Are existing performance and technology standards aligned with the country's emission reduction objectives? Are investors with potentially significant emissions impacts subject to EIAs and environmental permits? How effective is the implementation of EIA systems?
	Regulatory incentives	Are any regulatory concessions available to foreign investors for specific low-carbon technologies, or for the transfer or low-carbon knowledge to domestic firms?
Financial & technical support	Carbon pricing instruments	Has the government taken measures to remove inefficient fossil-fuel subsidies? Has the government put in place pricing mechanisms, such as carbon taxes or emissions trading systems?
	Subsidies and tax relief	Are incentives (e.g. subsidies, tax exemptions, feed-in tariffs) in place to stimulate investment in low-carbon technologies? Are incentives time-limited and subject to regular review?
	Public procurement	Do public procurement policies include environmental and green growth considerations such as resource efficiency, pollution abatement and climate resilience?
	Business & supplier development services	What initiatives are in place to support companies in reducing energy use, waste, or emissions? What initiatives to develop supplier capabilities related to low-carbon technologies?
	Green technology parks	Are initiatives and facilities in place to support low-carbon innovation (e.g. green tech parks, incubators)? Have efforts been made to reduce the carbon footprint of other economic zones?
	Training and skills development services	What measures are in place to promote skills development and prepare the labour force in areas relevant to low-carbon investment
Information & facilitation services	Green investment promotion, facilitation and aftercare?	Do investment promotion agencies tailor their activities to promote low-carbon investments? Are procedures for obtaining investment and environmental permits consistent and streamlined? Does the government maintain a local supplier database with information related to carbon performance? Is it easily accessible and regularly updated? Are business matchmaking services available?
	Public awareness campaigns	How is the government consulting with civil society groups and encouraging public awareness of and engagement with low-carbon objectives?
	Corporate environmental disclosure	What corporate disclosure mechanisms exist (e.g. carbon labelling, fuel economy)? Are the mandatory or voluntary? What measures are taken to ensure that end-users are aware of and understand these reporting mechanisms?

Notes

[1] Climate change adaptation will also become increasingly relevant in the discussion on understanding and improving the contribution of FDI to achieving the SDGs in face of the climate crisis, but is not addressed in this Policy Toolkit. Other environmental challenges (e.g. biodiversity loss) that may be affected by FDI are also beyond the scope of this Policy Toolkit.

[2] Electricity excise taxes are also taxes on energy use but may run counter to carbon pricing if they do not take into account how electricity is generated.

Printed by Libri Plureos GmbH in Hamburg,
Germany

9 789264 724532